500

Greatest Gambles & Gamblers

Graham Sharpe

RACING POST

DEDICATION

To Mike Raper and John Kay, neither of whom is averse to the
odd little wager, without whose encouragement, enthusiasm and support
my career would have been a very much tougher – and almost certainly
much shorter – journey.

Paperback edition published in Great Britain in 2009 by
Racing Post Books
Raceform Ltd, High Street, Compton, Newbury, Berkshire, RG20 6NL

First published in hardback by Highdown in 2008

1 3 5 7 9 10 8 6 4 2

A catalogue record for this book is available from the British Library.

ISBN 978-1-905156-66-5

Designed by Fiona Pike

Printed in the UK by CPI William Clowes Ltd Beccles NR34 7TL

www.racingpost.com/shop

INTRODUCTION

You can blame – or thank – me for being able to bet on so many weird and wonderful things today. When I began working for William Hill back in the early 1970s there was very little 'novelty' betting going on. Horses, dogs, major sports, yes. Anything a little out of the ordinary was frowned upon.

When I began to work in the company's publicity department my journalist background began to kick in when I noticed that the company received many letters and phone calls asking for unusual bets. These were usually ignored or politely rejected. No-one had the time to devote to doing anything about them. Besides which, pricing them up when we had only three full time odds compilers on the books wasn't a practical proposition.

However, I believed that it may be worth devoting some resources to these bet requests, as I thought they might strike a chord with the media – and also bring us in a few bob in the process.

Before I joined we had – almost inadvertently – taken a few bets on the chances of man walking on the moon. When it happened it proved to be very expensive for the company and the word went out that we shouldn't be risking hefty payouts on such matters – however unlikely they seemed to come to fruition.

Over at Ladbrokes, their pr guru, Ron Pollard, had been thinking along the same lines as me and had begun to take bets on the likelihood of alien life being proved to exist. The seeds were sown, and between us we began to prompt our respective companies to become a little more adventurous.

When I launched a book on 'Who Shot J.R.?' when the TV soap opera 'Dallas' was at its extraordinary height of popularity, the burning question of who had attempted to murder its main character, J.R. Ewing, became the centre of a media frenzy. Our odds proved irresistible to punters and press alike. They attracted worldwide attention.

The principle was proved – strange bets meant media coverage – and the ability to attract a previously untapped section of the betting market to our doors.

Over the years I worked hard to drive this kind of betting into the mainstream. Today it is possible to bet on virtually any subject in the public domain – and many that aren't.

Hence, I have been able to quote odds about anything and everything, from promising young sportsmen and women growing up to achieve great success – as the father of England goalkeeper Chris Kirkland found to his profit; he collected £10,000 when his son won his first cap – to the incredible Jon Matthews and the £5,000 he won by backing himself to fight off a life-threatening disease.

Others have joined the punting pilgrimage along the way, and very few wannabe wagers are now unachieveable.

Mind you, to some extent, what I and others have done is really to take us back to the past, to the days when great gambles and great gamblers were in their prime. The days of the 18th and 19th centuries when the offspring of wealthy aristocrats sat around gambling vast amounts against each other. When historic estates could be put at risk on the turn of a card or the run of one man's horse against another. Today's equivalent might well be Cheltenham Gold Cup winner, Harry Findlay.

I have tried to catalogue the strangest and greatest of gambles and gamblers in this volume, casting my net across the centuries and continents and shining a light into some of the dark, gloomy corners of betting history which have rarely been illuminated.

I wouldn't call myself a major gambler by any means, although I do enjoy a bet, but I think I have an archive of gambling material and personal experience which few can match and if you have ever had a small flutter or a huge punt you will find plenty to interest and intrigue you in these pages.

And if , after reading them, you believe that you would like to make an unusual bet yourself, then feel free to contact me at gsharpe@williamhill.co.uk to tell me all about it and invite me to offer you some odds.

The stranger the subject, the better.

Graham Sharpe

1. RAMMED FOR £77 MILLION

Flamboyant, long-haired, super-punter Terry Ramsden was a wheeler dealer on foreign financial markets, who owned many horses including Mr Snugfit, placed in the Grand National, and who lost £57 million in a three-year betting spree up to 1987.

His losses were revealed in court documents filed in Los Angeles in 1992 when the Serious Fraud Office was endeavouring to extradite Ramsden to London to face fraud charges. Ramsden's overall losses for the 1980s were estimated at £77 million by Customs and Excise.

Ramsden, once rated the 57th richest man in Britain, bet so big that I remember when we at William Hill were taking him on during the 80s, his bets were recorded and treated entirely separately from any other wagers – if they had been included in the run-of-the-mill business they would have totally unbalanced every book we ever made.

We knew that while Terry – 'I'm a stockbroker from Enfield, I've got long hair and I like a bet' – was betting hugely with us, he was also doing so with almost every other bookie he could find.

Before the bubble burst, 'Rammo the Rottweiler', as he was once dubbed, saw his Katies, for whom he paid half a million pounds, win the 1984 Irish 1,000 Guineas and then beat Pebbles in the Coronation Stakes, winning him bets worth a reported £1m. 'It wasn't one million. It was two million,' he told the *Racing Post*'s David Ashforth in November 1999, adding that his 'biggest single losing bet' was £1m on Below Zero.

His chaser, Mr Snugfit, became the medium of probably the greatest ever individual betting plunge, on the 1986 Grand National. I remember personally taking a call from Terry, about a bet of £50,000 each-way on the horse, which went off as 13-2 favourite.

With three to jump Phil Tuck, wearing the blue and white hooped Ramsden colours, finally got the horse to put its best foot forward and they made up a terrific amount of late ground to finish fourth, albeit 22 lengths behind, but nonetheless ensuring the each-way bets were profitable.

In the same year, Ramsden would have 'won several million' if his 16-1 chance Brunico had not been touched off by half a length by a 40-1 shot in the Triumph Hurdle.

He did win at least a million, though, when Motivator won the Coral Golden Hurdle at 15-2. 'The truth of that is that I had half a million quid each-way. Anything else you hear is bullshit,' he told guardian.co.uk .If so, he must have won the best part of £5m. On August 23, 1986, Terry placed a £10,000 win treble on Lack A Style, who won at 16-1 at Newmarket, giving him £170,000 running on to his next selection, Cry For The Clown at Windsor – who won at 4-1, leaving him with £850,000 on Miss Milveagh, a 9-1 chance, also at Windsor.

Victory would net him £8.5m, and the horse was ahead late in the race – only for 20-1 outsider Remain Free to catch Miss Milveagh and beat her into second.

The extravagant lifestyle ended in tears in 1987 when Ramsden was jailed for fraud with his company, Glen International, which dealt in the Japanese stock market, collapsing with debts of £100 million.

He was warned off racing by the Jockey Club in 1988 when he failed to keep up repayments to Ladbrokes on a reported £2m debt. Ramsden became prisoner number 95899 in prison in Los Angeles during 1991 when he spent six months inside.

He was back in Britain in February 1992, when he was declared bankrupt and given a two-year suspended sentence 'after pleading guilty to recklessly inducing fresh investment in his company,' reported guardian.co.uk.

The full extent of Ramsden's gambling was only revealed when, in 1992, court documents were filed in Los Angeles when the Serious Fraud Office was endeavouring to extradite him to London to face fraud charges.

They purported to show that he had lost £57m through betting in just the three years up to 1987. His overall losses for the 1980s were estimated at £20m more than that by Customs & Excise.

After serving ten months of a 21-month sentence for matters related to his bankruptcy, he was released in 1999.

Racing writer Raymond Smith dubbed him 'the heaviest gambler of all time', estimating his losses at more than £100m, and the *Racing Post* agreed, calling him 'the biggest punter in the history of the turf'. Ramsden disappeared from the scene, but returned in December 2003 when his two-year-old Jake The Snake was a 12-1 winner at Lingfield – and he claimed to have made the bookies suffer,

By the end of 2004, with a new business venture under way, he showed himself to be a little wiser as well as a little older when he told journalist Emma Cook: 'The more horses you bet on, the bigger chance you've got of being beaten.

'You just can't win 'em all.'

2. THE BREAST BET EVER

Brian Zembic won a $100,000 bet by having breast implants – and leaving them in place for a year. Originally from Winnipeg, Canada, Zembic was, in the late 1990s, a gambler operating in the twilight world of the casinos and card tables of Las Vegas.

Zembic's bizarre bet-busting gamble was first reported by writer Michael Konik in 1999, who first met him when the Canadian won a $14,000 wager by the simple expedient of spending a month living in a bathroom.

Zembic felt that his chances of winning the bet were compromised when the owner of the bathroom, with whom the bet was struck, began 'sending people over to take a dump'.

After 12 days the bet was called off, with Zembic settling for $7,000 winnings.

Konik then learned that Zembic had already been 'walking around for a year with a nice pair of womanly breasts', one of which he permitted Konik to squeeze – 'it feels pretty good, almost natural'.

Zembic revealed that while playing backgammon in New York in the winter of 1996 with a wealthy gambler known as 'JoBo' the pair had begun discussing women with breast implants.

'Tell you what, pal,' declared JoBo, throwing down an irresistible gauntlet – or bra – 'I'll give you a hundred thousand if you get tits.'

Terms were drawn up – he must keep the implants for a year. The bet was struck.

Zembic spent $4,000 paying a plastic surgeon to operate on him in Manhattan.

'I couldn't get out of bed for two weeks,' said Zembic. When he showed him the evidence that he had won the bet, JoBo – later reportedly revealed to be professional backgammon player Mike Svobodny, felt physically sick. 'I didn't think he would do it, he said. 'It made me sick that I lost the $100,000. I offered him $60,000 and he could take them out. He said no.'

Zembic not only completed the year – he left the implants where they were.

3. HARRY UP?

Denman's sensational Cheltenham Gold Cup triumph in 2008 established Harry Findlay's name with the general public as being synonymous with mega-punting.

'Around £600,000, he told Matt Dickinson of *The Times*, when asked how much he won on his own horse, adding, 'I see life as a casino. Money is chips to play life with.'

A year or so earlier, Harry had dominated the relatively new pool bet called the Race-O in early May 2007. The former greyhound owner/trainer-turned-serious punter and owner managed to win on consecutive days, collecting a cheque for £2,040,791 as a result. He did comment, modestly, 'There was a bit of pressure because I'd say we were about £350,000 down beforehand.'

This was in a season in which he had already claimed winnings of almost £1m when his mum's horse, Desert Quest, won at Cheltenham. He had funded the purchase of the horse by betting on a tennis match. 'I laid out £400,000 to win about £300,000. When Andre Agassi went a break up in the third set I had another lump (£100,000 in fact) on Roger Federer. If he'd lost, I wouldn't have been in the comfort zone to buy a horse.'

Not content with such a spectacular run of coups, 45-year-old Findlay – admittedly a big syndicate player in the pool bets – popped up on May 12 as a winner of the Scoop6, taking a share of the record win pool of £1,646,865 when he held five of the 11 winning tickets. Mind you, he had laid out £180,000 to do it. He boosted his own winnings to £1.3m when landing the Scoop6 bonus pool the following week.

In March 2007 Findlay claimed he had won 'just under a million' when Denman burst into the public consciousness with a devastating victory at 6-5 in Cheltenham's Royal & SunAlliance Chase – regaining the substantial amounts he confessed to having lost on cricket bets.

Findlay did not find it easy establishing himself as one of the biggest and most successful high-rolling punters of his day – 'In trying to get by on gambling without a job I was almost considered a rogue. I was potless a million times, and homeless, too, after my mum threw me out. I've lost everything including my freedom, my self-respect and that of my friends and family. I've frightened myself badly.'

Findlay also confessed that in less successful days he had pawned all the jewellery belonging to his wife. 'Kay and I have been together for 18 years and she's never moaned, including when we've sold the house, the car and, many years ago, pawned all the jewellery. That's been a massive help,' he said.

Kay soon found out what Harry was like when they began going out: 'The second time we went away he'd won £30,000 at the dogs and we went to Scotland to have it on a horse. The horse fell and it was all gone. I was on £52 a week.'

Kay revealed how close Findlay came to going under, in an interview with the *Racing Post*'s Peter Thomas in March 2008. 'To be honest, we were pretty much bankrupt going into the World Cup in 1998. I remember having to go to Brighton to take the deeds to the house down to the solicitor,' she said.

However, despite Kay recalling that 'the team we'd bet against scored – Harry was drinking a can of Coke and he threw it against the wall', Findlay's football betting came to the rescue in that tournament.

It isn't only horses and dogs that Harry has punted on – he admitted to losing a seven-figure sum not unadjacent to £2,600,000 when the hotly fancied All Blacks failed to win the 2007 Rugby Union World Cup. Mind you, he had won much of that on Roger Federer at that year's Wimbledon. Findlay's partner in Denman, Paul Barber, a Somerset dairy farmer, does not gamble.

4. OUT OF THIS WORLD BET

David Threlfall, a 26-year-old bachelor at the time, bet £10 at odds of 1,000-1 in 1964 that man would walk on the moon before 1971. He won £10,000 in July 1969 thanks to astronaut Neil Armstrong.

The actual terms of the bet were that 'a human being will set foot on the moon, or any other planet, star or heavenly body of comparable distance from the Earth before January 1, 1971.'

Threlfall was handed his winning cheque on a special Man on the Moon TV programme at the time, and commented: 'I've no idea why I did it. It just came to me one day. I think I've had my share now – I don't think I will put any money on people getting to Mars.'

Threlfall's winnings went towards buying a sports car in which, tragically, he died.

I arrived at William Hill a few years after that bet had been paid out – and could never find anyone willing to own up to being the one who quoted the 1,000-1 odds. I did, though, once meet a Professor Archie Roy on a TV programme when he told me that he had won a considerable amount on the same bet, having toured US labs where they were taking the space race very seriously indeed and working towards landing a man on the moon before the end of the 1960s – he was astonished at the odds on offer and helped himself.

Since those days we have taken a fairly substantial chunk of the cash we lost back from different punters who remain convinced that the moon landing never happened and who happily take odds of 500-1 that the US government will admit that it faked the whole thing. Yeah, and the moon's made of green cheese, I suppose . . .

5. DOTTY PAGET

Imagine being able to bet on horseraces that have already been run. And being permitted by your bookie to stake bets worth thousands of pounds.

Few gamblers have ever been permitted that privilege. Almost certainly, only one high-rolling gambler has been. And DEFINITELY only one female, high-rolling punter has been. She was without doubt the heaviest backer of her time; definitely the most eccentric and without doubt the most charismatic female ever to grace the Sport of Kings with her presence.

Born in 1905, Dorothy Paget was a wealthy heiress – so wealthy that she would travel to the races in one luxury motor car, with another one driving behind so that in the event of a breakdown she could swap vehicles.

When she wasn't out racing – often to watch her five-time Cheltenham Gold Cup winner, Golden Miller – she would turn night into day at her mysterious mansion in Chalfont St Giles, Buckinghamshire where, due to her pronounced dislike of the male half of the human race, she employed an almost entirely female staff. She often slept all day, as she liked to stay up for most of the night.

When she did so, her bookmaker, the late, eponymous William Hill, was reportedly quite happy to accept massive bets from her, even though the races were already over, because Ms Paget's honesty and integrity were unimpeachable.

That, and the fact that she bet enormous sums of money – and lost more often than she won.

Her gambling equalled and almost eclipsed her huge commitment to the turf (she owned countless horses), and her behaviour became more and more eccentric to the outside world.

She would rise at twilight and retire at dawn at her mysterious, female-dominated 'Hermits Wood' home where troupes of secretaries, housekeepers and chefs worked round the clock at such tasks as transcribing and making up to seven copies of all her phone calls, and phoning in her bets.

She would pad around during the night-time, clad in her favourite 'woolly teddy-bear dressing gown', phoning her trainers at all hours to demand details of her expensive four-legged assets.

One source described her as 'betting like a Chinaman, eating like Henry VIII, and living at night, like Winston Churchill'.

She would risk ten thousand pounds a time on her 'banco' bets –confident tips from her trainers – and twenty thousand on the less frequent 'double banco' selections.

Ms Paget also had an unusual method of occasionally varying her betting stakes – if someone rang her on the morning of a race she would discover their phone number, then stake that number in pounds on her runner.

Otherwise, she would usually stick to backing her selection to make her a profit of £20,000. This caused a sensation once when she took it into her head to back a horse who went off at 1-8 odds – meaning she had to risk £160,000 to make her twenty grand.

When the odds about this horse shortened dramatically, her bookmaker called one of her secretaries to check whether DP still wanted to place the bet with such an unprecedented sum at stake.

Anxious not to be seen to be backing down, she told her secretary that 'I consider his question a piece of gross impertinence'.

The bet stayed on, the horse won – and a very relieved DP promptly handed out congratulatory fivers to everyone she could find! It had been her biggest ever wager.

She didn't always back winners, by any means, though. Once, her trainer Fred Darling told her confidently that her horse Colonel Payne was an absolute certainty for a race at Ascot. She started off with a bet of £10,000 and kept backing the horse, turning up at the course to see the race.

Colonel Payne finished nearer last than first and Ms Paget strode to the unsaddling area to quiz jockey Gordon Richards, asking him grimly 'Where's Mr Darling?'

'I wouldn't be quite sure, Miss Paget,' replied the 26-times champion jockey. 'But I've a pretty shrewd idea he's on top of the stand cutting his throat.'

Setbacks such as Colonel Payne occasionally caused Paget to decide to tone things down a bit. After a run of losers she once told one of her staff – 'We must economise. From tomorrow we will do without grapefruit for breakfast.'

Veteran racing journalist Geoffrey Hamlyn, who was on the racing circuit at the same time as Paget, declared in 1994 that she 'lost more money on the British turf than any man or woman before or since'. He reported one bookmaker, Jack Woolf from Birmingham, as having won £85,000 from her in a single day in the late 1940s.

Paget's driving style would not have been out of place on a Grand Prix circuit. She regarded 80mph as a perfectly reasonable cruising speed.

Finding herself in an unfamiliar area on the way to Manchester races, in a broken down car, she immediately endeavoured to commandeer a local butcher's Baby Austin, offering the astonished fellow £200. When this was rejected, on the understandable grounds that the chap had arranged to take his mother out for a drive, she upped the ante to £300, plus a trip to the races.

When he accepted, he was paid at once from the £5,000 wad of cash routinely carried by her secretary, Miss Clarke, for just such eventualities. That's why she began to travel with a reserve vehicle backing her up.

On January 30, 1960, by which time she was rarely seen on a racecourse, Miss Paget's horse Fortescue won a race at Naas in Ireland. It was to be the last winner she would have.

She drank only Malvern water and tea, except for an occasional snifter of brandy or weak buck's fizz, but smoked up to 100 Turkish cigarettes a day through a holder, and died tragically early, on February 9,1960.

In an obituary, leading racing writer Richard Onslow wrote: 'She was outrageous, impossibly anti-social and madly unpredictable, but she did more for jump racing in the decade before the war than any other person.'

6. KERRY ON GAMBLING

Bruce McHugh, an Aussie bookie, was able to retire in the late 1980s at the age of just 44, reportedly due entirely to the lack of success enjoyed by his main punter, the tycoon and mega gambler Kerry Packer.

'He'd made a few million by then, perhaps £10 million and he didn't want to lose it all on one race,' said a Packer confidant. The 6ft 6in Aussie was literally a larger than life – and death, for that matter – character, who actually died twice – first on October 7, 1990 when he was pronounced clinically dead following a cardiac arrest on a polo field. After being resuscitated he said, 'I've seen the other side, and let me tell you, there's nothing there.'

The second time he died was on Boxing Day 2005, at the age of 68, and he hasn't yet been brought back.

Packer's love of a wager was legendary. 'Like many Australians, I like to bet,' he said. An understatement. In April 1985 he bet – and won – an even A$1m on Golden Vogue at Eagle Farm racecourse. At the time he was disguising his identity by the nom-de-wager of 'Mr Millions', but few were fooled. Bookie Bill McHugh – father of Bruce - had earlier taken two losing bets from Packer's agents – of A$1.5m and A$1.1m.

Mind you, he was worth an estimated £3bn at the time.

He gambled worldwide. In London his casino of choice was Crockfords where, it was said, he would frequently bet the maximum permitted stake of £250,000 per hand of blackjack – on all seven hands dealt to the table.

In September 1999 he lost between £7.5m and £11m in a three-week losing streak there – 'the biggest loss in British gambling history,' according to US reporter James Bone.

In August 2000 it was reported that he had lost '£13.6m during a three-day baccarat binge in Vegas'. That amount, it was said, brought his gambling losses to £27.4m in the previous ten months.

But he didn't always lose. A £13m win at the MGM Grand in Vegas got him banned, it was said. And in 1990 he apparently won £5m from the Clermont – oh, and at Christmas 1996 he took the Vegas Hilton for £13.25m.

'Packer has made it known he would like to play even higher at baccarat – to raise the stakes to $1m per hand,' revealed writer David Spanier.

Packer was a classy gambler, too. When actor George Hamilton was £125,000 light but holding an excellent blackjack hand, Packer handed over the cash. Hamilton duly won and offered back the loan, plus interest, but Packer only took the £125,000.

Once, while playing, and losing £2m he asked for a meal. The casino flunkey asked, 'Lobster or caviar, perhaps?'

He requested – and received – a boiled egg with raw onion.

He once tipped a casino cigarette girl £50,000 and on another occasion asked a fellow, elderly female gambler how much she owed on her mortgage – giving her in chips the £23,000 figure she told him.

And once, after a losing session of £6m at the Vegas Hilton, he handed croupiers £166,000.

On the horses he cleaned up to the tune of £2.8m on the 1997 Melbourne Cup as he forced the price of Might And Power down from 9-2 to 5-2.

'I've never seen anything like it in 20 years,' gasped bookie Michael Eskander, who lost half a million Aussie dollars himself. 'I reckon he's destroyed at least seven bookmakers today.'

The gambling gene must have been inherited – his grandfather was said to have found a ten-shilling note in a Tasmanian street and staked it all on a horse, who won, and with the profits he bought a boat ticket to the mainland, where he launched a media empire. Former Packer pal and fellow owner-gambler Robert Sangster once told a fine Packer punting yarn about a day when they were both at the races in Sydney: 'I was about A$140,000 up when Kerry Packer came up to me and said 'Are you going to back your horse? Because it's a f****** certainty'. I said, 'I know it's a f****** certainty'. He said 'Well, you get on first, then I'll follow you'. I said 'Fine'. So I put the whole A$140,000 on, even money.

'Kerry then went and put about $8 million on. The horse won by eight lengths.'

7. DARREN'S MAGNIFICENT HALF-MILLION

'How much do you think you've won?' I asked Darren Yates. 'I don't know, but it must be into five figures,' replied the man from Morecambe who had staked £59 on Frankie Dettori's seven mounts at Ascot that afternoon of September 28, 1996, when every one of them won, at SP accumulative odds of over 25,000-1.

'Close enough – try £550,000,' I told him. As Darren had set off that morning to place his usual bet en route to a football match he was playing in that afternoon, his long-suffering wife Annaley, aware that their business was struggling a little, had told him, 'And don't waste any more money on that Dettori – we just can't afford it.'

Fortunately, he ignored her advice and became the biggest winner of all on a day when Frankie removed up to an astonishing £50m from the coffers of Britain's bookies on a day unique in racing history.

Mary Bolton also backed all seven winners – and should have won £900,000, after her husband John gave her a bet to place as part of their anniversary celebrations. She broke through Ladbrokes' payout limit, though, and received their maximum £500,000. She was philosophical about being deprived of an extra £400,000 and mollified when Frankie himself handed over her cheque.

8. 'IF ONLY I'D STUCK TO THE ORIGINAL PLAN'

Bookie Gary Wiltshire was one of the worst affected by 'Frankie day'. An off-course bookie who had worked hard to afford his £500,000 house in Buckinghamshire, he woke up intending to spend his working day at Worcester racecourse.

However, before setting off he'd taken another look at the Ascot card – 'I thought,' he told me ruefully, 'that it looked a hard one for punters'.

It was. And when Fujiyama Crest won the seventh race for Frankie, the loquacious Wiltshire was almost struck dumb – 'My clerk Peter Houghton was absolutely stunned. He just stood there, gripping the book and staring into space. I had to punch him quite hard to bring him back.'

Wiltshire was facing a loss of £800,000. 'The mountainous Mr Wiltshire looked like he had received a direct hit from a torpedo,' recalled racing writer Jamie Reid.

Normally, Wiltshire would dine out at his favourite Italian restaurant after a big race meeting. That evening all he could face was fish and chips.

That night he pulled himself together enough to turn up at Milton Keynes dog track to take bets. 'The first bet I took was a pound. I was thinking it was going to be a long way back,' he said.

When BBC TV's correspondent, Julian Wilson, asked Wiltshire the next day what would happen if Frankie were to repeat the feat, he told him, 'I'll be in that river over there.'

Wiltshire did eventually bounce back and is now a familiar face on course for Totesport bookmakers and on TV commentating on dog racing.

Wiltshire reflected on his own most memorable winners in 2008, recalling that he backed shock 1990 Cheltenham Gold Cup winner Norton's Coin at 200-1 and that a horse he bred himself, Mi Odds, was considered a certainty at Hereford on his hurdles debut.

The horse was backed from 6-1 to 9-4 and won. 'That win paid for many a holiday – or to put it another way, I wouldn't be the size I am today if it hadn't won and I wouldn't have to go to WeightWatchers every week.'

9. ROYAL COMMAND

The Queen Mum placed a bet from the cockpit of Concorde while travelling over the Irish Sea on a day trip to celebrate her 85th birthday.

Everyone's favourite royal was born on August 4, 1900, and loved racing and having a flutter – yet her 'advisers' would often go to ludicrous lengths to try to deny the latter aspect of her life, for reasons peculiar to the hypocritical British attitude to such matters.

In 1986, I was told by her personal press officer Major A Griffin that 'the Queen Mother does not bet' and that 'to the best of my knowledge never has done' – note the get-out clause in that statement!

Today newspaper reported in April 1989 that the Queen Mother had ordered a satellite dish for her Clarence House home 'so she can follow her runners on racecourses throughout the realm via the latest high-tech system, SIS – Satellite Information Services. The gambling great-grandmother has until now made do with the Extel Tannoy system,' it revealed.

The paper also quoted a recent guest of Her Majesty as saying that the Queen Mother had disappeared during tea for a few minutes. 'The sound of racing commentators gave the game away and when she returned, Her Majesty had that special glow of a winner.'

She once summed up her own feelings about the turf when she said: 'It's one of the real sports that is left to us – a bit of danger and a bit of excitement, and the horses, which are the best thing in the world.'

Her first winner running in her own name came on November 24, 1950 when Manicou, trained by Peter Cazalet and ridden by Tony Grantham, won over fences at Kempton in the Wimbledon Handicap Chase, returning 5-4.

In 1956 her Devon Loch, partnered by thriller-writer-to-be Dick Francis, collapsed inexplicably on the run-in with the Grand National at his mercy. She did not return to Aintree for 35 years, when she opened the new £3m Queen Mother Stand.

Her Laffy (see also story 70) did give her a National win, claiming the Ulster version at Downpatrick in 1962. On December 9, 1961, Laffy, evens; Double Star, 4-1 and The Rip, 8-13, had all won to give the Queen Mother a Lingfield treble.

Bali Hal' won at Sandown on May 16, 1959 to give the Queen Mother her first winner on the Flat. It was ridden by Willie Snaith and trained by Cecil Boyd-Rochfort.

By 1964 she was celebrating her 100th winner over jumps as Bobby Beasley rode the Jack Donoghue-trained Gay Record to victory at Folkestone on October 20.

Her 200th winner over jumps came on December 3, 1969 when Master Daniel won at Worcester for jockey Richard Dennard and trainer Cazalet.

Sunyboy, trained by Fulke Walwyn and ridden by Bill Smith, was the Queen Mother's 300th winner over jumps, at Ascot in the Fernbank Hurdle on February 18, 1976. In 1984, her Special Cargo won the Whitbread Gold Cup in what many consider to be the greatest steeplechase ever run. Second in the Sandown feature was Lettoch, just a short head down, and third, a further short head behind, was Diamond Edge, on which royal jockey Bill Smith was riding his last race, having opted for that mount in preference to Special Cargo.

The *Racing Post* revealed in November 1989 – not on April 1 – that Special Cargo, a gelding, had got a mare pregnant. He had been turned out with the mare, On The Hill, and the speculation was that Special Cargo was actually a 'rig' – a horse in which one testicle has not descended.

She became such an institution at the Cheltenham Festival, where the Queen Mother Champion Chase is still run, that in her latter years she was driven around the course in a buggy painted in her racing colours, which were: blue; buff stripes; blue sleeves; black cap; gold tassel.

10. HAIR-RAISING STORY OF £100,000 COUP

'A green light flashed. And the most daringly successful swindle in greyhound racing, or possibly in any other form of sport, reaped its unjust reward,' revealed Tom Stenner of the victory on the mild winter's evening of December 8, 1945 at White City of the near-white greyhound, Bald Truth.

It was the last race of the evening, worth a tenner to the winner, and 16,000 racegoers could barely believe what they had just seen – and even less that track officials would permit the result to stand officially.

War-time Director of the Army Sports Board, former England rugby cap and President of the English Rugby Union, Colonel B C 'Jock' Hartley, was the innocent owner of Bald Truth, who lined up in trap four. All the runners were trained at the Greyhound Racing Association's kennels at Northaw, near Potters Bar.

Shortly before the off-time two runners had been withdrawn and Bald Truth added in as a substitute runner, leaving a field of five – Kilmacoe Lad in one; Fly Bessie in two; Victory Speech out of three; Jimmy Chicken in five; trap six was vacant.

Hartley, enjoying a meal at the track that night, told Stenner, publicity director for the GRA, that Bald Truth was not fancied and that he would be placing a £2 each-way bet on the dog on the tote 'just for luck'.

However, there seemed to be no little support for Bald Truth and his price with the course bookies had plummeted from 33-1 to 5-1 as the traps opened.

Stenner takes up the tale. 'The starting bell clanged and the most extraordinary race I have ever witnessed commenced. Fly Bessie showed in front with Jimmy Chicken running wide and Bald Truth in a reasonable, if not good, position. Following the dash to the first bend of this 525-yard event Fly Bessie appeared to wobble and swerve. My first thought was that she must have lamed herself.

'But then everything happened. Every runner, with the exception of the conspicuous white dog Bald Truth, appeared to stumble and stagger round the track. I could hardly believe that it was actually happening. As Bald Truth raced past the post, fifteen lengths ahead of any rival, I glimpsed the blank astonishment on his owner's face and heard the angry shouts of heated onlookers.

'Seconds seemed minutes and minutes hours as officials deliberated and discussed whether to void the event and declare 'No Race'. They were, I imagined, awaiting the veterinary surgeon's report, but then that too hasty hand reached out and the green light flashed.'

Stenner went on to explain that 'a gang of crooks had discovered the effect of chloretone, a derivative of alcohol, on greyhounds. The drug did not take effect until the dogs were warmed up, when the heat and stress of racing set the dope coursing through their veins.'

Bald Truth had been the only dog not 'got at' in this way. It transpired that a gang member had infiltrated the White City kennels before the race and fed the dogs pieces of fish treated with chloretone – all apart from Bald Truth. 'Agents piled on money with bookmakers and totalisator at the track and at SP offices throughout the country. Chief Inspector Robert Fabian – Fabian of the Yard – and Detective-Inspector Dinley carried out extensive enquiries and the GRA offered a reward of £1,000 but the perpetrators were never brought to court.'

11. HUSBAND IN A MILLION

Geoff Sartin, 43, was looking for a bookie to take a bet from him that would make him a cool million. He wanted to wager that he could accurately predict the date on which his wife would die. Inevitably, in September 1996, he wrote, asking me to lay the bet. Even I was surprised. After a working life taking some of the oddest odds requests imaginable, this one was unique.

I wanted to know more. Why did this former coach driver from Shanklin on the Isle of Wight believe he knew the date on which his wife would expire?

He had found out when he had hypnotised her, he told me. Well, wouldn't that be one of the first questions anyone would ask the missus once they had her under the 'fluence?

The fatal date was 25 March 2007. Why did he want to bet on it? He wanted to make a lot of money – £1m, to be precise. What did his wife think of the idea?

She was fine about it, he said. 'I'm fully in agreement with the bet,' she later insisted. 'If I go first, then I want to ensure that Geoff and my children will be well cared for. The money will give me a good send-off. I want my coffin pulled through the streets by a black horse and carriage.'

Didn't he think that if I laid him the bet and his hunch proved to be correct the local constabulary might want to talk to him before his winnings could be sent to him?

He didn't seem to have considered that eventuality.

'People may say I'm morbid, but I'll need the money. Of course, I'd be delighted if the bet was a loser.'

After giving the matter more thought I decided that it really was in the worst possible taste and that I would have to decline the request.

Nonetheless, The Sun ran a prominent story on its famous Page Three about Mr Sartin's bet request, illustrated with a picture of him and his wife.

I forgot all about Mr Sartin until the date on which he had given for his wife's death loomed up and prompted my memory.

The Sun also noticed the approaching date and decided it would make an interesting follow-up story. It set about contacting Mr Sartin. It couldn't find him or his wife.

12. THE CHAMPION NATIONAL GAMBLE

Sometimes the outcome of a big race seems pre-ordained. The story surrounding one of the contenders is just so 'right' that surely the fates will collude to ensure that the expected result actually comes about.

It happened when Princess Anne married Captain Mark Phillips and Royal Mark won the Royal Wedding Chase at 11-10. It happened when Red Rum won his third National, and when Desert Orchid won the Gold Cup.

The 1981 Grand National was just such a race. It was perhaps the most emotional gamble of all, as the punting public got behind 'two old crocks' – the phrase jockey Bob Champion used to describe himself and his mount, Aldaniti.

For Champion had battled and beaten cancer – enduring six courses of chemotherapy to survive, having once been told 'you have only eight months to live', while Aldaniti had broken down in 1975 on his off-fore, after which he was beset by leg problems. He was off the course for 14 months before Champion partnered him as an 11-year-old to win the 1981 Whitbread Trial Handicap Chase at Ascot to set up a National bid that quickly captured the ever-sentimental public's imagination.

What turned out to be one of the hugest public gambles started somewhat inauspiciously as Aldaniti's realistic trainer, Josh Gifford, deliberately halved the bet owner Nick Embiricos wanted to stake on his horse.

He was away skiing and rang Gifford, asking him to put £500 each-way on for him at 66-1.

'Don't be silly, it's 66-1 that he'll get there, let alone win,' replied the handler, who went close to winning the great race himself on Honey End, runner-up in Foinavon's infamous 100-1 triumph.

'I forgave him for not putting on the whole lot,' Embiricos told me 'Shortly after collecting my winnings I received a letter from the bookmaker concerned, inviting me to bet with them more often!'

The bookie clearly wanted to win his £20,000-plus back.

'There must have been a huge amount of emotional money put on the horse on the day,' added Embiricos.

Indeed there was, as Bob Champion also confirmed to me – 'I'd never had the sort of response that occurred after winning the National on Aldaniti. I had thousands of letters, many of them telling me that people had had bets on us because of my illness and because of Aldaniti's comeback from injury.'

This partnership of patched-up horse and written-off jockey who had taken on and defeated the dread disease cancer, combined to spark off one of the heftiest public plunges of all time. It cost Britain's bookies millions, but they paid almost (mustn't get too carried away) happily, brushing away the odd tear of joy in the process – and partially placated by the fact that it had happened in the Grand National when they did, at least, have one or two losing bets in their satchels too.

One of the letters Bob received was from Geoff Moorhouse, the father of a young patient who had recovered from the same cancer – 'We always look out for your mounts and we even have a bet or two on you.'

Bob's nurse, Carol, went mad and had three quid on him – nurses don't earn much, after all   while an oap told Bob: 'My prayers, your hopes – and my wager – will be on you.'

Two bank managers wrote from Wootton Bassett and told Bob: ' Several members of our staff are richer than they were on Friday.'

'I knew I was the one people were backing, and I genuinely never thought we could be beaten – the only danger was the first fence, after that I never felt a moment's worry,' explained Bob, almost prophetically, as the pair lined up again for the National in 1982 – and fell at the first.

Sixteen and a half million watched the National on TV, betting an estimated £30 million on the outcome. Aldaniti went off at 10-1.

Part of the reason for the double-figure odds was that the horse who finished second and started as 8-1 favourite provided very nearly as good a human interest story as the winner – the horse was bred, owned, trained and ridden by 54-year-old grandfather John Thorne.

13. ONE OF THOSE DAYS

The Day family were one of the foremost racing families from the early 19th century, when in 1826 John Barham Day sent out Dervise and Problem to win the 2,000 and 1,000 Guineas respectively.

Although they were at the top of their profession, the members of the family were not averse to the odd wager. And if they could get an edge on the layers, so much the better.

John's sons, John junior and Billy, rode for their old man, who had acquired perhaps the most powerful turf administrator around, Lord George Bentinck, as an owner.

Well, he had until 1841 when Billy, 18 years old at the time, plotted a betting coup.

In order to land the coup, he wrote a letter to Lord George telling him to back a particular horse, which would be the proverbial 'good thing'.

He wrote another letter to one of his preferred bookmakers, informing him that he could lay the same horse for all he was worth.

Expecting the bookmaker to express his gratitude to the jockey in the traditional, financial manner, when he ensured that the horse lost, Day was a happy lad as he put the letters in their envelopes and dispatched them. Unfortunately for Billy he had put the wrong letter in each envelope – so Lord George was, to say the least, unhappy when he read the contents of the missive.

As a result he conducted a lengthy vendetta against the Days – starting by removing his horses from John Barham Day's yard.

14. FRANKLY, BARRY DID GIVE A DAMN!

Barry Hills is one of the most respected trainers in the business. His sons Michael and Richard became top-flight jockeys.

But his career owes much, if not everything, to the successful gamble he carried out when he backed a horse called Frankincense to win one of the most difficult handicaps of the season, the 1968 Lincoln, landing an absolute fortune in the process – 'He has never boasted about it but in today's money I suspect it was in the region of £150,000 – £200,000,' wrote racing journalist George Ennor in 1991.

Hills was working as travelling head lad for John Oxley in Newmarket when the way he saw the horse working on the gallops persuaded him to start backing him at 66-1, even though no horse had carried his allotted 9st 5lb to victory in the race in the whole of the 20th century.

Barry was not deterred, and kept on backing the four-year-old all the way until race day. At one point he became ante-post favourite, but on the day went off at 100-8.

Frankincense, under Greville Starkey, had 30 opponents to beat, and did so by half a length after hitting the front with a furlong to run.

'It wouldn't have been possible to buy South Bank without Frankincense – he paid for a large part of it,' said Hills of the Lambourn stable where he set up in his own right as a trainer in 1969.

15. THE FIRST POKER HAND

'Two or three people were drinking one day last week at the Angel Inn at Spalding in Lincolnshire,' reported the Leeds Intelligencer of June 1784, 'when one of the company, for a trifling bet, offered to carry a red-hot poker in his teeth as far as the obelisk in the market place, there and back again.

'The bet being agreed to, the man took the poker between his teeth and performed it.' So far, so good. But there's more. 'The consequence was, the poor man was so affected that his teeth dropt (sic) out, his mouth and throat were so scorched that he languished till the next day, and expired in great agonies.'

16. JON BEAT CANCER FOR FIVE GRAND

It was the most unlikely request for a bet I'd ever received. Jon Matthews, 57 years old, wanted to bet that he would live longer than his doctor believed possible, after he had been diagnosed with a form of lung cancer.

Matthews, from near Milton Keynes, told me in October 2007 that he was determined to survive until June 1, 2008 or, literally, die trying. If he reached that date he would have exceeded the 25 months that his doc had told him was the longest he had ever heard of any patient lasting once having been diagnosed with mesathelioma.

Jon was very persuasive, and told me that I would be doing him a big favour by laying the bet and giving him an incentive to keep going when, as he knew they would, times became hard for him.

Eventually I agreed to let him stake £100 at 50-1 that he would still be alive on his chosen date. On June 1, 2008 I visited a William Hill shop in Fenny Stratford, near Bletchley, and quietly, with only a live Sky News and BBC Look East camera for company, along with one or two reporters, the odd photographer (all snappers are odd), the Press Association news agency, and a phone-full of interested callers, handed Jon his five grand.

He looked healthier than the day I agreed the bet with him, but as he said, 'I have good days and bad days. Collecting £5,000 represents a good day.'

I was in two minds about whether to wish him well – as he also stood to win another £5,000 if he made it to June 1, 2009 and ten more if he could also breathe on June 1, 2010!

17. THAT'LL DO MIKELY

Newcastle FC owner and retail tycoon Mike Ashley, who loves to attend matches wearing his club's black and white shirt, hit the jackpot at a casino when he cleaned up by backing number 17 on the roulette wheel.

The Mail on Sunday reported in early May 2008 that Ashley won £1,284,000 after starting off with a £2,000 bet on the number at odds of 35-1.

Playing at the luxurious 50 London casino in Mayfair, the 45-year-old took just 15 minutes to land his coup, following up the initial win by staking £4,000 on four bets that the next number would be 17 or the numbers immediately alongside (14, 16, 18 or 20) – a £16,000 total stake at 17-1, which won him another £272,000.

He then placed four more bets on numbers also including 17, costing £32,000 and paying out at 8-1, to win £256,000.

A £6,000 bet on 16, 17 and 18 then landed a £66,000 win.

Two £12,000 bets paid out £120,000 when he bet on 13-18 and 16-21.

He then, said the MoS, gambled three £100,000 even-money bets on black, odd and 1-18. Further winnings of £300,000 resulted. Finally, £50,000 on each of two 2-1 shots – the middle column of numbers, and the middle dozen numbers 13-24 – led to a £200,000 profit. Then, said an eyewitness, Ashley looked at the croupier and said: 'That'll do me, thanks very much.'

Seventeen must be Ashley's lucky number – which makes one wonder why the player wearing it at the time he landed his great win, 'striker' Alan Smith, had managed 36 appearances that season, scoring no goals whatsoever. However, in August 2008, the *Mail on Sunday* carried another story about Ashley – claiming that 'he recently lost £5m playing roulette and blackjack in one all-night session'.

Still, how much difference the reported winnings or losses would make to Ashley's life was not clear. The *Sunday Times* Rich List had him ranked as the 54th wealthiest person in Great Britain.

18. BY HOOK OR CROOK

Out for a stroll during 1809, Georgian author Theodore Hook spotted a neat-looking house in Berners Street, near London's Oxford Street – and promptly offered to wager his companion £1 that within a week this would become the most famous house in the capital. The companion accepted the wager.

Hook won. First, he sent out 1,000 letters to tradesmen, ordering goods to be delivered to the address at exactly the same time – coal, potatoes, books, ices, jellies, prints etc, from suppliers all over the city.

Then Hook sat and watched as the chaos grew, and contacted more and more people to tell them what was happening. Within hours people were flocking to the scene. It had cost I look far more than he collected – but he won the bet.

19. SAY IT AIN'T SO, JOE!

Arnold Rothstein was a notorious gambler who was deeply implicated in one of sport's darkest episodes – the 'fixing' of the 1919 World Series of baseball in the USA.

However, that event is outside of the compass of this book, but Rothstein is in for what he achieved on July 4, 1921 in the last race of the afternoon at Aqueduct racetrack, a $1,172.94-to-the-winner, 13-runner event. It was run over five furlongs in 94 degree heat, and Rothstein single-handedly forced the price of the outsider, the two-year-old Sidereal, down from 30-1 to 5-1 in a bid to achieve his ambition of winning $1 million from a single bet.

He failed. To win $1m, that is. The horse won, under jockey Willie Kelsay, but Rothstein only cleared an $800,000 profit – 'more money than anyone in America ever before had won on a horse,' reported the racing editor of the *New York Daily Mirror,* Toney, ahem, Betts!

If Rothstein was rumoured to be a gangster, Al Capone most certainly was. But he, too, had a $1m ambition, reported Betts. 'An obsession,' he called it, 'to bet $1m on a horse. And he missed, too. He was able to get off only $980,000 in wire rooms throughout the country. The horse, an odds-on favourite, lost, but Capone pulled out on other horses the same day, for a small profit.'

20. BOOKIE FRED ALMOST PAID WITH HIS LIFE

Frederick Swindell(s) managed to overcome the implication of his name (some reports give him a final 's', others do not) and became one of the most respected layers of the mid 19th century – until his trusting nature almost cost him his life.

Swindell had become friendly with a surgeon named William Palmer, who was something of a plunger in the betting market and also rumoured to be a character of dubious moral values. Palmer had a 7-1 shot called Doubt running in the 1853 Wolverhampton Handicap. He had high hopes that it would win the race and wanted to stake £500 on it.

Despite racecourse rumours luridly suggesting that Palmer may have been associated with the fatal demise of two people to whom he had owed gambling debts, Palmer persuaded Swindell to travel to the races with him. Fred told fellow bookie George Hodgman of his trip.

'I shall be all right,' Swindell assured Hodgman. 'By the bye, Palmer says he has a good thing in Doubt for the handicap. I've put him £500 on at sevens, and I've got £250 on for myself.'

It would transpire that Palmer was exploiting the betting rule in force at the time that should a gambler expire before settling day, his betting debts would die with him.

Palmer and Swindell enjoyed a drink together in the evening before race day, Swindell knocking back so much brandy – which, it would later emerge, had been liberally laced with poisonous substances – that he became too ill to travel to the races on the next day.

Palmer was now in a position to ensure that he would profit if his horse won, but be no worse off if it didn't as he would just return to see Swindell and polish him off.

Running literally for Swindell's life, Doubt prevailed by half a length.

Palmer returned to Swindell, administered an antidote to the poison, convincing his victim that he was recovering from an upset stomach of some kind, and was duly rewarded with the profits from 'his' bet.

Swindell continued to pooh-pooh the rumours about Palmer until, in 1856, Palmer was tried – and convicted – of murdering another turf acquaintance, one John Parsons Cook. Palmer had also poisoned both his wife and brother after taking out hefty insurance policies on their lives. He was hanged.

21. GAMBLING GANG WARFARE

Darby Sabini was a gangster born in 1899 who, with his brothers Harry, Joseph, Fred and George and other disreputable types, ran a protection racket at racecourses during the 1920s and 30s, extorting cash from bookmakers.

Another gang leader, Arthur Harding, later confessed: 'The racecourse business was a profitable one. When a gang went to a racecourse like Brighton they could clear £4,000 or £5,000 easy. At Epsom on Derby day it could be £15,000 or £20,000.'

Sabini and his cohorts would use razors, guns and other unpleasant weapons.

Among their activities were driving legitimate bookmakers from their pitches and hiring them out to other bookies; selling them lists of runners, which cost under one penny to produce, for ten times as much; hiring them the stools on which they would stand; charging the bookmakers over the odds for 'services' such as chalk to write with on their boards and for sponges to wash the boards down with.

Complaints were often met by extreme violence; sometimes gang members would just stop punters from reaching the bookie, or they would wipe off the displayed odds before betting was finished.

One victimised bookie, Hymie Davis, enlisted Harding's gang to fight off the Sabinis at Kempton Park. Harding sent 60 men along, who were ambushed by the police. A pitched battle ensued.

Also involved in this racecourse warfare at the time were the 'Brummagem Boys' – yes, from Birmingham – led by a bookie called Billy Kimber, who had a lengthy feud with the Sabinis.

Kimber teamed up with a Leeds mob to take on the Sabinis at Epsom's Derby meeting, only for the two gangs inadvertently to set about each other by mistake.

Home Secretary of the day, Sir William Joynson-Hicks, vowed to crack down on the gangs. The battles came to a head at Lewes racecourse on June 8, 1936 when the Sabinis were involved in running fights with rival mobs. Sixteen men were arrested and sentences totalling over 53 years handed down.

Darby, who died in 1950, was the inspiration for the gangster character Colleoni in Graham Greene's famous novel, Brighton Rock.

Racecourse gangsterism flared up again briefly in the mid 1950s with characters such as Jack Spot, Billy Hill (no relation to William Hill, founder of the eponymous bookmaking empire), 'Mad' Frankie Fraser and the Kray twins involved.

22. NOT SUCH A QUICK BUCK

Will Buckley gambled his wedding presents away. The writer and broadcaster decided against putting his wedding list in a big store before his marriage to Grainne.

Instead, he placed it with me – and my company, William Hill.

No toasters, irons or fondue sets for the Buckleys – Will handed me a lengthy list of bets which he asked wedding guests to place on the happy couple's behalf.

Sadly, Will, who writes now for *The Observer*, has never been one of the world's great tipsters – and the couple ended up somewhat worse off than they might have been had they opted for a more traditional wedding list.

23. NOT SUCH A DICK, THEN

Richard Connolly, a pub landlord, celebrated his 23rd birthday on September 23, 1992 by visiting a casino on the Isle of Man, where, at 23 minutes past the 23rd hour of the day he bet £23 on number 23 – and won.

★ In May 2008, William Hill wrote out a cheque for £1,426,000 to a Sussex-based internet client who hit a winning streak online at williamhillcasino.com when his lucky number 23 came up trumps for him while playing roulette. Wishing to only be known as Jason H from Sussex, the 40-year-old local businessman, a regular player, hit a lucky run. Starting off with his usual bets, Jason built up his balance after a good run until his luck really kicked in. He wagered his entire balance around his lucky number and then watched in amazement as it came in for him, netting a cool six-figure amount. Not content to stop there, he followed the same tactics, seeing 23 drop again and again, boosting his payout to a total of £1,426,000! At this point, Jason H didn't believe his luck and called Hills to check that his computer wasn't playing up and confirm his win was real. It was. Mm, now then, my birthday is the 23rd!

24. ON THE EDGE

As if the last stories were not enough, in April 1995 Southend man Robert Edge celebrated his 24th birthday by staking £24 on number 24 at 24 minutes past the 24th hour in a local casino – he won £840.

25. SYSTEMATIC RIP OFF?

Classy TV illusionist Derren Brown performed a very useful task in exposing system scamsters in February 2008 when his Channel 4 show promised to reveal the perfect racing system that would guarantee to produce winners.

And it did. Except that everything wasn't quite as advertised, even though he had persuaded virtually every paper in the land – not least the Racing Post – to run preview pieces hinting very strongly that it would be.

Once the show began it very soon became obvious to anyone with even the briefest of experience with betting just what was going on.

The programme focused on a young lady called Khadesha who had been given four consecutive winning tips by Brown and had now begged, borrowed and blagged four grand to put on the next – and final – horse Brown was going to give her. She duly turned up at the racecourse and watched as Brown took her £4,000 and stuck it on the horse he named – which promptly finished a poor fourth.

Cue looks of panic and consternation as Khadesha realised that her money was lost, and that there was no perfect system.

Except that, for her, there was. Brown had not put her money on the beaten horse – he'd put it on the winner, and she was 13 grand to the good. Possibly.

Because he revealed the way he had actually constructed the perfect system. He had originally contacted some seven thousand people out of the blue, giving them a tip in a six-runner race. One-sixth of the people had been given each of the six runners in the race. Of course, more than 1,000 of them were on a winner. That 1,000 then received another tip. Once again one-sixth of them were winners. Same thing for the next race. Eventually, as the sixths divided down, Khadesha was the only one left who had been given only winners and was, of course, left believing that Brown had supernatural powers.

He didn't. He hasn't, although he is a supreme illusionist who makes tremendously entertaining TV shows, and spends a great deal of money doing so – everyone else in the programme who had put money on his losing selections had been given their cash back.

But he can't tip winners. What he can do, though – and did, on camera, during one of his shows, broadcast from Walthamstow greyhound track, was to persuade one of the tote staff to pay him winnings – on a losing ticket!

26. EYE SAY, EYE SAY, CHAMP MAKES SPECTACLE OF HIMSELF

Greg 'Fossilman' Raymer, a 40-year-old former attorney for drug company Pfizer, really eyeballed his opponents in the 2004 World Series of Poker in Las Vegas when he landed the title and a $5 million payout.

And he did so while wearing one of the most bizarre accessories ever assumed by a world champion in any discipline – apart, perhaps, from TV wrestling.

For Fossilman – the nickname is courtesy of his wife's hobby of, well, collecting fossils – eyed up his victory by wearing a pair of 3-D hologram lizard eye spectacles, in a fetching shade of yellow.

As you do.

Raymer, who gave up his job after his title triumph when he was asked to become a representative of an online poker site, explained how and when he came by his bizarre gimmick in an interview with *The Times* in March 2005: 'The first time I entered the world poker tournament was in 2002. I came about 80th. Just before, I'd taken Sophie and Cheryl (his daughter and wife respectively) to Disney World and bought these 3-D hologram lizard eyes. They were so funny I thought I'd put them on in the tournament.

'Things can get tense at the table, so it's good to lighten things up sometimes. But when I put these glasses on, the guy I was playing freaked out and ended up throwing his hand away.

'It made me think that there was more to them than I realised, so I wore them again. Several players demanded that the directors stop me wearing them, but they were overruled and I've worn them ever since.'

When he won the title he also told interviewers that he wore the special specs because he did not possess the ability to 'stare down' opponents.

This is not the only peculiarity associated with Raymer, who suffers from sleep apnoea, a condition in which the sufferer can temporarily stop breathing while slumbering. As a result 'I have a Cpap machine, which is an oxygen tank attached to a mask I wear over my nose'.

Raymer, who lives in Connecticut, pays close attention to his opponents when at the table. 'When you're sitting round a table a player's demeanour can be the crucial tell of how he is doing.' One of his techniques is to study a player's chest in an effort to gauge whether his heart rate is increasing through nerves thus making him breathe more quickly – a move that may not go down well with modest female players.

And now poker is in his family, with wife Cheryl deciding that if she can't beat the game she might as well join him in playing it. She has already chalked up a tournament victory – without the lizard eyes.

27. HILL OF A BET

Trainer Vincent O'Brien found himself alongside William Hill, founder of the bookmaking company of the same name, at a function in the autumn of 1966.

The pair chatted and Vincent asked whether William had yet opened his ante-post book for the 1968 Derby.

As the potential runners would be yearlings at that stage, Hill confessed that he hadn't, but asked O'Brien which horse he wanted to back.

The great trainer told Hill that there were three horses he was interested in – but only if 100-1 would be on offer.

O'Brien staked £100 on the first two colts he mentioned, but then sprung his trap by asking to back the third of them – an American-bred by Sir Gaylord out of Attica – for £500 each-way.

By now, others had begun listening to their conversation, and there were gasps when he asked for the 'monkey' each-way – probably the equivalent today of £10,000 or more.

Hill had not become known as the most fearless of layers for nothing, but even he must have experienced the smallest pang at the potential liability he was taking on board for his company.

Nevertheless, he displayed not the slightest outward reaction and accepted the bet with a handshake.

First time out, in July 1967, running over six furlongs at the Curragh, Sir Ivor, as the horse had been named, finished sixth of 13.

If Hill thought he was out of the woods, he thought again a month later as Sir Ivor reappeared and won over seven furlongs at the same venue – this time beating his conqueror from his debut race.

He cruised to victory in his final two-year-old start, in the National Stakes over seven furlongs.

By now, Hill was aware that O'Brien's bet had been struck on behalf of owner Raymond Guest – to whom Hill now offered a hedging bet that was courteously but emphatically turned down flat.

Sir Ivor was by now winter favourite for the Derby and odds-on for the 2,000 Guineas, which he came out to win, now becoming odds-on for the Derby.

Ridden by Lester Piggott, 4-6 favourite Sir Ivor won the Derby by a comfortable

31

length and a half. The bet had paid off to the tune of £62,500 – at least half a million pounds today. William Hill was shrewd enough to engineer at least that amount's worth of publicity out of what become one of, if not the, most famous of ante-post bets.

28. A MYSTERY EVEN DICK FRANCIS COULD NOT HAVE INVENTED

A successful coup, landing winnings of up to £500,000 with a horse rumoured to have been a ringer, followed within 48 hours by the death of the winning trainer – who shot himself.

These ingredients might be deemed just too extraordinary even for a Dick Francis novel, but they occurred on June 13, 1992 when Father Hayes, trained by Will Pearce, was backed pre-race in the morning, from 20-1 to 3-1, before winning by two and a half lengths at Sandown over an extended mile and three furlongs. He was partnered by David Nicholls, who punched the air in triumph as they passed the post.

The horse, who had run four times in the previous seven weeks, only once making the first four, was an American-bred who had previously been called Highland Johnny in 1990 – when trained by Dermot Browne, who would subsequently be warned off for ten years for selling information to a bookmaker.

By November 1991 the horse was renamed Dashing John – but four months later the four-year-old became Father Hayes.

Will Pearce, the 42-year-old trainer, who trained at Yorkshire's historic Hambleton House stables, had only been handling the horse, owned by his brother Rodney, for several weeks.

There is little doubt that the horse was the medium of a substantial gamble – with the trainer himself joining in – 'I don't bet heavily apart from the occasional two-year-old, but my owners do. This time was an exception,' he said after the race.

When the betting market had opened on course, by which time John McCririck had told Channel 4 viewers about the gamble, bookies had put the horse in at 7-2, pushed him out to 11-2, then brought him back to 4-1 joint-favourite.

Pearce explained the horse's previous poor form at Hereford (1m5f); Edinburgh (1m4f); Beverley (1m100yds); and Southwell (1m) – 'I had to get him qualified for handicaps and after the Southwell race, when he hated the track, the extra distance plus the mark he had been given made us fancy him a bit.'

The stewards questioned trainer and jockey about the horse's apparent improvement in form and were told he ran green at Edinburgh and was unsuited by the trips at Beverley and Southwell, and also did not like the surface at the latter.

After the race estimates of the amounts taken from bookies ranged from £50,000 to £500,000. Rumours that the horse was a ringer were probably sparked by his name changes.

On June 15, Pearce was found dead shortly after noon in a small wood close to his gallops with a 12-bore shotgun beside him. The coroner later recorded a verdict of suicide but could find no motive.

On June 16 the Jockey Club announced it was 'taking steps to establish that the correct horse was running in the name of Father Hayes'.

On June 24 the Jockey Club confirmed that it was satisfied that all was in order as far as the horse's identity was concerned.

29. GAMBLING ON THE PRESIDENT

Locked in battle to become the Democratic candidate for the 2008 US Presidential race, both Hillary Clinton and Barack Obama found themselves under fire for gambling-related reasons.

Hillary thought that advising people to 'place a little money on the filly for me' before the running of the 2008 Kentucky Derby would be non-controversial.

And it might have been, had her tip Eight Belles – the only filly in the race, who ran an excellent race to finish second – not broken both front ankles shortly after crossing the line. She had to be 'euthanised'.

Critics promptly attacked Hillary on the grounds both of encouraging gambling and being in favour of cruel sports.

Meanwhile, Obama was being criticised for being a poker player – a skill that in previous decades had been regarded as, if not an essential part of the presidential make-up, an indication of 'the right stuff' in the White House supremo.

He had answered that he was a 'pretty good poker player' when asked by a news agency to reveal a 'hidden talent', and confessed that along with fellow senator Terry Link, he had co-hosted a regular game – 'When it turned out that I could sit down and have a beer and go out for a round of golf or get a poker game going I probably confounded some expectations.' He certainly confounded those punters who backed Hillary Clinton to win the nomination as he won the right to take on John McCain for the highest office.

30. HADDOCK FISHES OUT BIGGEST WIN

Agnes Haddock became the most successful female betting shop customer ever when she collected a total of £688,620 for a £2 bet on the Scoop6, placed at her local Fred Done branch. 'I normally just go for names. I don't care if the horse is 66-1 or 100-1 and I don't study form,' she told reporters after landing the £410,332 jackpot in late January 2007. 'The names are always the first thing I look for, and if I fancy one, I'll go for it.'

The system worked for Agnes, a 50-year-old from Northwich in Cheshire, who had her own ironing business and told well-wishers she would celebrate by getting 'pissed'. She then went for the bonus winner, worth another £248,422, selecting Taranis in the Sandown Handicap Hurdle 'because I was born on the 13th and he was number 13'. The horse, partnered by Ruby Walsh, who jokingly asked for a percentage of her winnings for his efforts, duly obliged on February 3, 2007.

31. SEVEN-HUNDRED QUID WINNER? SLING HIM IN THE TOWER

Way back in the early days of horseracing, Master Michael Hudson, a gentleman of Lincolnshire, took full advantage of the fact that he owned 'an excellent Mare and so swift of foote, that at all races she did carry away the prize'.

Master Hudson turned up at a 1635 race meeting in London's Hyde Park 'for all the (Arch) Bishop of Canterburyes (sic) Gentlemen, without his Mare, leading those present to believe that he was ripe for the plucking'.

However, Hudson was fortunate that the new horse he had brought with him was 'a Nagge so full of speed as if he had bin of the Race of those who were begotten by the wind'. In trials he had plenty in hand of the famous Mare.

Unaware of this, the Archbishop's Gentlemen wagered heavily against Hudson, in fact, 'they would lay downe all the Moneys they have, or what they can borrow of their Friends' to back their equine representative.

The race took place, and Hudson's 'Nagge what with its owne swiftness and courage, and the art and helpe of his rider, doth make such hast that it doth out run the other almost halfe in halfe'.

As a result, recorded the London Post at the time, Hudson 'came from them a cleere gayner of at least seven hundred pounds'. Huge money for those times. The Gentlemen were not happy. They complained to their Archbishop, who hauled Hudson in front of them for an enquiry, but even after facing a Court of High Commission he could be found guilty of no offence and was grudgingly permitted to keep his winnings.

However, in 1647, Hudson was arrested and accused of having written to others 'on treasonable subjects against the Commonwealth, whereupon he was committed close prisoner to the Tower (of London) and no man should speake with him but in the presence of his Keeper'.

The Archbishop's Gentlemen evidently had very long memories.

Hudson somehow escaped to Lincolnshire but was there killed by 'rebels' in a somewhat unpleasant manner. He was thrown over the battlements at Woodcroft House in Northamptonshire. 19th century Newmarket historian J.P.Hore recorded that Hudson 'caught hold of a spout and hung there; but his hands being beat or cut off, he fell into the moat, much wounded'.

He struggled to dry land, where 'one Egborough knocked him on the head with the butt end of his musket. Which being done, one Walker, a chandler and grocer of Stanford, cut out his tongue and carried it about the country as a trophy'.

Be careful who you win money from in a bet.

32. PAGE THREE NATIONAL

It had to be a John McCririck scheme– but what a fantastic betting medium it would make, if hideously non-pc.

'What a great idea it would be to have a Page Three National,' suggested the be-whiskered one. 'We could have Page Three girls jumping over fences topless – and I could be one of the fences.'

33. YOU'RE NICKED

Nicholas Young was obsessed with the search for a perfect gambling system – and he spent nearly £11 million looking for it. However, most of it wasn't really his. And in May 1991, he was jailed for four years, after admitting to 11 deception charges.

The 45-year-old former public schoolboy and Cambridge graduate had been earning £34,500 per annum with a City accountancy firm, but he persuaded people to invest large amounts of money with him.

When the investors quizzed him about where their cash was, Young made an anagram of the word 'horse' and added three more letters – giving them the answer 'offshore'.

The court heard that in the five years before his arrest, Young staked bets totalling £10,922,000 on horses. He won back £8,729,000 in his quest for what he described as the 'holy grail' of a winning system – leaving him with losses of more than £2m.

Even after he had been arrested, Young was still trying to attract more cash for his scheme – he wrote to a potential investor from his cell, offering a copy of his latest betting system, which needed just 'a copy of the *Daily Mirror*, a copy of *The Times* and the odd million in cash'.

34. CORKING BET

Standing at a council election in Cork in 1985, independent candidate Bernard Murphy printed posters advising people to back him at 33-1 and then vote for him. He won and the local bookie lost £20,000.

35. BLOODY GOOD BET

An ingenious betting scam was pulled by a racehorse owner, which proved literally to be a bloody good coup.

Racing writer Jack Fairfax-Blakeborough recalled in his memoirs: 'In 1908 I remember a Malton owner running a horse at Thirsk in a race which looked a gift for him. He was made favourite, but the owner backed another horse – the ultimate winner.'

He had a jockey who was 'paid and did as he was told'.

His instructions were to get well away, make the running, and then pull up and dismount a couple of furlongs from home.

At the spot indicated, the horse pulled up, the jockey dismounted and the owner, who was standing conveniently nearby, rushed on to the course. Covered by the jockey, he produced a bottle, and with his handkerchief, smeared the horse's nostrils with the blood that he had that morning collected from a Malton slaughterhouse.

Together, jockey and owner led the horse back to the paddock with blood trickling from its nostrils, and the gory handkerchief much displayed. The crowd believed the horse to have suffered from a burst blood vessel.

The following week the same horse ran at another Yorkshire meeting, but almost no-one except the owner wanted to back the bloody beast. He duly won in style.

36. ROTHSCHILD'S REVENGE

One of the biggest plungers of the early 20th century, James Rothschild, MP, took up the turf early in his career – and entered wholeheartedly into the battle with the bookies.

He would bet thousands on a whim, not always on his own beasts, although he cleaned up spectacularly when his Bomba won the 1909 Ascot Gold Cup – before losing thousands on an Epsom selling plater.

So heavy were his losses during one losing streak that an acquaintance approached 'Jimmy's' uncle, Leo to warn him.

'And how much did you say he had lost?' asked that worthy, a member of the Jockey Club and owner of 1904 Derby winner St Amant.

Discovering it to be a six-figure sum, Uncle Leo declared: 'Oh, is that all? I thought you were going to tell me something serious.'

Jimmy won an estimated £250,000 on Brigand's 1919 Cambridgeshire triumph, but could be a sore loser.

When he plotted more than one losing coup on his horse Snow Leopard, he announced in the Racing Calendar that the animal's name had been changed – to Slow Leopard.

37. RETIRING REBEL

Cockney Rebel's 2,000 Guineas victory in 2007 encouraged his trainer, Geoff Huffer, to launch a new business – as a racing tipster.

'I personally made enough money from that bet to retire,' claimed the handler, whose tipping scheme was launched with letters telling potential subscribers 'This isn't a scam. It is 100% genuine.'

He also claimed responsibility for a 33-1 to 6-1 gamble on the February 2008 Wolverhampton winner Man Of Gwent, which landed an estimated £1m in bets.

A colourful character who allegedly played drums in The Troggs rock group at some stage of his career, Huffer declared in April 2008: 'I fully expect to make vast profits throughout this Flat season. The only thing I want to give people are certainties.'

In marked contrast to Huffer, fellow trainer Richard Hannon was outraged when he was linked with a website trading as richardhannon.co.uk, featuring a picture of the trainer, and offering tips at £1 per time.

Hannon raged in June 2008: 'I don't know who these people are but they've had no contact with me and genuine racing people should avoid them like the plague.'

38. MAKING A MONKEY OUT OF PUNTERS

A study by Dr Sarah Heilbronner of Duke University, North Carolina, claimed to show that chimpanzees like to gamble.

'When given the choice between a safe bet and a high-risk and high-stakes option, chimps will always choose the latter,' revealed the study, reported Dubai's *City Times* newspaper in March 2008.

Dr Heilbronner's team purported to prove that 'chimps evolved to take risks in the wild because their supplies of food are not secure'.

In 2005 another study, this time of macaque monkeys, at the same university, had also concluded that 'like people, they are willing to incur huge losses in the hope of an eventual win'.

39. HOW 'ARRY FIXED STEVE

Much-travelled footballer-turned-media pundit Steve Claridge has always enjoyed a flutter, but believes he was once hustled out of a certain winner by his then manager, Harry Redknapp.

Claridge was playing for Bournemouth in 1984 when Redknapp was boss. 'There was a record at the club for running round a circuit. I said I could beat it,' Claridge told *Times* journalist Tom Dart in May 2008.

'He [Harry] said, "No you can't". He bet me £100, and I knew I could do it. When we get to the day I've turned up and there are advertising boards on the inside lane.

'He says "Oh no, you can't move them", so I've got to go round the things. And he's got a pacemaker who did everything bar molest me.

'He was very gracious after the race. "You're just out. You got so close I'll let you off".'

There was a postscript: 'Twenty years later he owned up that he'd let the stopwatch run on five seconds. So I'd managed to do it.'

40. HERE'S THE NEWS – 40,000-1 WINNER

Few winners have ever started at 40,000-1 and, for sure, Monday's News, winner of the 1946 Greyhound Derby, was never quoted in public at those odds.

Even so, bookmaker Hector McDonald laid the dog's owner, Donald Stewart, £1,000 to 6d (2.5p) – effectively 40,000-1 – at the start of the competition.

41. ON YER BIKE, EVEL

He was best known as a fearless motorcycle stuntman, but Evel Knievel, who died in 2007, was not so successful as a gambler.

He revealed his propensity for a wager in October 1996 when he boasted to an interviewer, 'I'm the biggest gambler in town. I won $50,000 on golf and $100,000 in [American] football last year.'

When pressed by the interviewer he confessed that he had also 'lost $250,000 at blackjack'. And he also lost out on the ultimate wager he took out with the 37-year-old doctor treating him in 1998 for Hepatitis C – wagering $10,000 that he would outlive the medic.

He didn't.

Knievel – then known by his given name of Robert – won his first bet in the early 1960s, collecting ten bucks for driving his motorcycle 'up the backside of a parked VW Beetle, over the roof and back down the hood'.

But he was well and truly outdone when he took on world poker champion Amarillo Slim in a $100,000 golf match – in which the card ace used a carpenter's hammer against Evel's regular clubs and literally 'hammered' him. 'Evel loved risk so much that he was an easy mark for a gambler,' commented Slim.

Evel lost $10,000 to cabaret star Wayne Newton, betting that reclusive millionaire Howard Hughes was dead.

If Evel's biographer Steve Mandich is to be believed, he lost his wackiest bet. 'He claimed to have once wagered his finger against $18,000 on a single golf putt – and lost. Evel cut off his fingertip with a shovel, the only readily available tool, but later had it sewn back on.'

In April 2007, Evel announced he was giving up his bad ways, renouncing 'the gold, the gambling, the booze and the women' – well, it WAS April 1!

Still, Knievel may have been comforted by memories of a particular bet he struck in 1980, while touring Puerto Rico. He wagered $1,000 that he would sleep with eight different women in a 24-hour period – and collected.

He died, aged 69, in November 2007.

42. WHO WAS MYSTERY MEGA LOSER?

One high-rolling customer of Ladbrokes lost £159 million, revealed Howard Wright in the *Racing Post* in May 2008.

'Let's salute a man – and the Fly on the Wall [a Wright alter ego] believes it is a lone male – who almost single-handedly has thrust last year's levy yield to soaring new heights,' wrote Wright, adding: 'The most striking element in the unexpected increase was an additional contribution of £15.9m from Ladbrokes out of the money – £159m on this reckoning – they made from a single high-roller punter who probably wants to keep his light permanently hidden under a bushel on account of his spectacular propensity for backing losers.'

He calculated that the punter's total turnover, assuming that he managed to back at least an occasional winner, 'in the second half of the last financial year could have been as much as £300m'.

43. UNGODLEY TALENT?

John Godley rang the *Sunday Pictorial* newspaper in 1947, explaining to a disbelieving reporter that he had dreamed the names of two horses who would win that afternoon.

The 26-year-old said he'd done it before – when he was at Oxford University in 1946 he'd won £40 from his 'gift'.

A month later while at home in Ireland Godley dreamed that 'Tubermore' would win at Aintree – Tuberose was the closest sounding name, and won at 100-6.

On July 28, 1946 he dreamed that a horse called Monumentor had won at 5-4 – so backed Mentores for £4 who won at, er, 6-4.

There were no further sleep-induced tips until the night of Friday, June 13, 1947 when he dreamed he was at Lingfield watching jockey Edgar Britt win in the colours of owner the Gaekwar of Baroda, followed by a win for a hot favourite, The Bogey.

Translating the dream into runners Baroda Squadron and The Brogue, he staked a £5 double on them, deposited a written statement 'in the safe of an Oxford postmaster' and rang the Pictorial.

Reporter George McCarthy later confirmed all of these details after the horses both won – albeit at 11-10 and 1-9.

'I cannot undertake to dream outsiders only,' said Godley.

The Daily Mirror became interested in Godley and hired him for 25gns to contribute to a story, before offering him £1,100 per year to become their tipster-cum-racing correspondent.

Godley dreamed both winners and losers over the next 18 months, and wrote a book about his nocturnal exploits, published in 1950, in which he claimed, somewhat inventively, odds of 730,406,249-1 against his feats.

In 1958 Godley fell asleep in Monte Carlo, dreaming that What Man had won the Grand National. He staked £25 on Mr What, who won at 18-1.

Godley later became Lord Kilbracken, and served as a lieutenant-commander in the Fleet Air Arm.

He reported his experiences to the Psychical Research Society who, surprisingly realistically, decided 'that Mr Godley may, in his waking hours, subconsciously choose the winners he subsequently sees in his dreams'.

44. PICTURE THIS

Governor of California Leland Stanford was fascinated by racehorses – and by one of the burning issues of the day, whether when horses raced, at certain times, they had all four feet off the ground.

In 1872, irked that no-one had yet proved the point one way or the other, he staked a massive $25,000 bet that HE would come up with the proof.

Stanford's plan was to hire a photographer to produce the evidence.

He selected 45-year-old Englishman Eadweard Muybridge, who was based in San Francisco.

Given the slow shutter speeds of the day, Muybridge's early efforts proved ineffective.

His concentration on the task was somewhat interrupted when he was accused of murdering his wife's lover. A sensational trial in February 1875 somehow resulted in his acquittal.

After Muybridge had time out to recover from his ordeal, Stanford, whose opponents in the bet were claiming they had won the wager, urged Muybridge to get back to his equine investigations.

By 1880 technology had advanced to the point where Muybridge devised a system involving a battery of cameras catching the image of a moving horse.

Twenty-four cameras were used, each set off by a series of electrical connections as the horse passed by.

When the images were produced, there it was – photographic evidence of a horse with all four legs off the ground while galloping.

Stanford had won his $25,000 bet – which helped towards the $40,000 costs of finding the proof!

45. FIRST OF MANY

Widely acknowledged as one of the biggest punters on the scene, former bookie and wealthy racehorse owner J P McManus started as a modest gambler, confessing that his first ever bet was one shilling (5p) each-way on Orchardist in the 1962 Cesarewitch.

The horse won at 25-1 – but was disqualified and placed second.

46. WOULD YOU FALL FOR THAT?

In 1903 American punters were offered an intriguing variation on their bets on steeplechases.

A company called 'Steeplechase Insurance' took out an advertisement in the Thoroughbred Record in which they explained: 'The purpose of the Steeplechase Insurance Co, which is incorporated under the laws of the State of New York, is to insure amounts wagered on jumping races from loss occasioned by the horse falling during the race.

'If a man plays a horse for $100 against $2,000 and insures his $100 for, say $20, he has a chance of winning $2,000 less the $20 insurance if the horse stands up. On the other hand, he would lose only $20 if the horse falls.'

47. IS PALMER THE NEW BERNARD?

There hasn't been such a public confession of gambling disasters and triumphs and lifestyle revelations since the days when 'Jeffrey Bernard is unwell' was the phrase used whenever the writer of that name, whose life was eventually immortalised in a phenomenally successful stage-play by his friend Keith Waterhouse, was too under the weather to contribute his weekly *Spectator* column, Low Life.

But Steve Palmer's betting exploits, chronicled regularly in the *Racing Post*, are already threatening to rival those of the predecessor, of whom he may not even have heard.

Bernard, who died in 1997, coined plenty of gambling bon mots – 'one way to stop a runaway horse is to bet on him' and 'in most betting shops you will see three windows marked 'Bet Here' but only one with the legend 'Pay Out'.'

Bernard was hired to write a regular column for the *Sporting Life* on October 1, 1970. On October 1, 1971 he was fired, after an alcohol-fuelled year of excess and outrage, during which he upset many racing folk and wrote almost unfailingly about his punting disasters – 'I think I was the first person to write about things like losing in an official racing organ.'

One of the few winning bets he wrote about was his bet with a Brighton bookie at odds of 5-2 that the winner of Miss World would have a 36in chest!

On another occasion he recalled staying in an hotel and placing a hefty £100 bet on Muhammad Ali to beat Joe Frazier overnight before booking himself a 5.00 wake-up call, which duly came from the porter – 'Mr Bernard, it's 5o'clock and you've done your ton'!

In 1986 Bernard returned from a holiday in Portugal to discover a bill for £2,000 from the Inland Revenue waiting for him. In desperation he picked out four runners at an evening meeting at Pontefract and placed a yankee on them with his friend, bookie Victor Chandler. They all won, and he collected £2,535 to soften the tax blow.

He once ran a book in the Coach and Horses pub in Soho, which he made his base. His big mistake was offering the Customs & Excise men who came to investigate his illegal bet-taking a wager, whereupon he was arrested and subsequently fined £200 for the offence – despite, or perhaps because of, the appearance on his behalf by John McCririck.

When a harsh winter halted racing for a lengthy spell, Bernard organised cat racing for him and his pals to bet on – and he once famously wrote about a high-stakes game of Find The Lady played with a famous friend's newly born triplets – before mum found out and put a stop to proceedings! The friend was believed to be trainer Richard Hannon.

Palmer may be interested to learn that Bernard had a racehorse named after him, had 500 lovers and threw up in front of – some say actually on – the Queen Mother.

The *Racing Post* man fascinates readers with tales of bets they might wish they were bold enough to have themselves.

In May 2008 he staked a £400 double on Lewis Hamilton to win the Monaco Grand Prix and Phil Mickelson to win the Crown Plaza International golf tournament. Hamilton drove like a demon to land the first part of the bet, then Mickelson 'produced the shot of the season on the final hole to win by a single blow, sending £2,625 winging its way to my account. If I'd had access to Mickelson's gormless nodding head at that point, I may well have kissed every inch of it.'

Emboldened by this success he tackles another golf tournament – 'I had 200 eggs [pounds] on Geoff Ogilvy at 23; 100 eggs on Ernie Els at 44 and Anthony Kim at 32; 50 eggs on Camilo Villegas at 70 and Steve Marino at 160, as well as a 100 eggs each-way double on Kaymer and Ogilvy. When I found out Kim was a non-runner I was scrambling around for alternatives, but ended up just having another 50 eggs on Ogilvy. Discovered Villegas is a non-runner as well just before I went to bed, so my outlay on this week's golf is down to a mere 1,900 eggs. Pah, it's hardly worth the bother.'

Then Palmer reflects on Friday, May 30: 'Watch golf, worrying, fretting,agonising. This is definitely what God had in mind when he gave me the gift of life.'

48. HAT'S JUST RIDICULOUS

Ralph Nevill, chronicler of 18th and 19th century betting yarns, described a weird wager from the former period when 'Lord Cobham once foolishly bet Mr Nugent a guinea that he would spit in Lord Bristol's hat without the latter, who had a reputation for effeminacy, resenting it.

'Lord Bristol, being one day at Lady Cobham's talking to some ladies, he chanced to lean over a chair holding his hat behind him, into which Lord Cobham deliberately spat, at the same time asking Mr Nugent, who was present, for his guinea.'

Having been paid, Cobham then apologised profusely to Bristol who 'merely asked if his host had any further use for his hat and then resumed his conversation'.

Cobham was very pleased with himself and his winnings – until, next morning, he received a message 'demanding satisfaction' from Bristol via a duel.

Cobham was terrified and claimed the whole matter had been a foolish joke.

Bristol insisted on a public apology from both of the perpetrators, who were forced to appear in the Club room at White's, where they were humiliated as, 'amidst a crowd of members' they 'publicly expressed their regret'.

49. WHEELY ODD

Nevill also told of a novel form of roulette, introduced towards the end of the 19th century by a casino in France's St Germain.

'No wheel was employed, its place being supplied by a dial on which by an ingenious device, the winning number and colour appeared on a croupier firing a sort of rifle. The result was the same as at ordinary roulette – and just as in the old-fashioned form of the game, most people lost their money.'

50. BETTING ON THE BOOZE

Paul Carberry is a character among jockeys – some of his colleagues have been known to refer to him as 'mad', and any jockey who can excuse himself from missing a ride because 'I was head-butted by a deer' is not your conventional rider.

In common with all others of his profession, he is not permitted to bet, but it is unlikely that anyone would have taken issue with him over the one time he did so.

'I had a reputation a few years ago with drink and all that,' admitted Carberry in a March 2005 interview with writer Brian Fleming, explaining how at the 1999 wedding of Irish racing figure Paul Shanahan he found himself chatting to noted racehorse owner and gambler JP McManus, who tempted him with the offer of a unique wager. 'I met JP and we got talking about things in general. After catching up on bits and pieces, the subject of alcohol came up. He asked me did I think I could go off the booze for a while and, while I was thinking about what he said, seconds later he threw in – would I have a bet on it?'

Carberry thought quickly. 'I told him I would and a bet was struck that I would go off the drink for two years.'

Fleming wrote: 'Carberry won and the wager is reputed to have been a tidy five-figure sum.' Indeed it was, apparently – Alan Lee recalled the wager in *The Times* in March 2005, declaring that the stake was £50,000 and adding: 'When Carberry met the challenge, McManus not only paid up but offered to double the amount if he took the pledge for a further period.'

Carberry, commented Lee, 'declined the offer'.

But before any Jockey Club members get the idea that the jockey should be criticised for admitting to gambling, perhaps they should be aware of the story of one of their own, reported by magazine *The Field*, from the year 1830:

'At a meeting of the Jockey Club the question arose as to who could 'hold his liquor the best' and the Earl of Eglinton stated that he was prepared to back himself against all comers in that he could drink more champagne without inconvenience than anyone in the United Kingdom.

'A General Peel retorted that he would produce one whom he would introduce as 'The Novice' next day and that he would back his man for a pony (£25) to win. The match was bottle against bottle – that is to say, when one bottle was finished the other was required to empty his and each had to commence a new one.

'Lord Eglinton took the lead at a tremendous pace, hoping to choke off his antagonist before the first three bottles were consumed, at the same time chattering on merrily. Meanwhile The Novice, Sir David Baird, held his peace but stuck to his task without turning a hair, and it was seen that Lord Eglinton was evidently 'going' with difficulty. At last the latter rose from the table saying he 'could do no more'. The Novice then played five games of cards of which he won four.

'Next morning Lord Eglinton was walking up and down without his hat, which he said was 'too heavy to wear'. Sir David Baird was riding a hard-pulling cob and smoking a clay pipe.'

51. SUITS YOU, SIR

Mrs Alexandra Sergeyevna and a group of fellow textile workers clubbed together in 1993 to buy 100 lottery tickets at the cost of 50 roubles, reported Russian trade union newspaper *Trud*.

The first prize in the lottery was a 70,000 rouble Volga motor car, which, it was agreed, would be sold, with the profits split between them should their number come up.

Mrs S was duly allocated three of the lottery tickets – one of which she handed over to her husband, Ivan.

Somewhat inconveniently, Ivan proceeded to die of a heart attack shortly afterwards. He was buried, wearing his best suit – in the pocket of which, un-noticed at the time, was the lottery ticket.

No doubt you are a step ahead of me here – but stick around, because there is another twist.

Yes, Ivan's ticket turned out to be the winner.

Once Mrs S had searched the house, ripped up the floorboards etc, and invited her work colleagues around to see whether they could locate the ticket, she realised that it must have been buried with him.

So she applied to the authorities for permission to exhume Ivan's body.

After much wheeling and dealing, she received the relevant papers and the exhumation took place.

As the diggers opened up the grave, they and those present were astonished to find no coffin and, therefore, no body and no ticket.

It now transpired that the winning lottery ticket had been produced and handed over to the organisers, who had given the car to the 'owner' of the ticket.

Alexandra was not best pleased at this turn of events – in fact she was somewhat miffed and took her grievance to Moscow's finest, who decided then to interview the apparent winner of the car – probably figuring that he may also know the whereabouts of the missing corpse and coffin.

The man told them he had found the ticket in a suit that he had bought in a secondhand clothing store.

The police paid the recycling emporium a visit and soon discovered that there was a thriving underground – well, I suppose it would have to be underground – grave-robbing racket going on.

The robbers were selling the coffins back to the funeral parlours – one careful owner, guv! –and the bodies to the makers of animal feed.

Once the whole story had emerged, Alexandra was handed the keys to the car and her co-workers agreed that she should be allowed to keep it.

However, by now she was so distraught over the whole affair that she sold the car and handed the proceeds to a fund for the victims of the Chernobyl nuclear disaster.

52. GAME, WET AND MATCH TO CHARLIE

In 1888 Charles Bulpett, a 37-year-old friend of gambling historian Ralph Nevill, made a bet of £500 to his £200 that he would ride a mile (horseback); run a mile and walk a mile within 16 and a half minutes.

This he achieved with 23 seconds to spare – and despite 'suffering from a game leg'.

But Bulpett soon exceeded this feat. While dining at the Ship Inn, Greenwich, Bulpett wagered his £100 to a companion's £100 that he, Bulpett, would swim the Thames while wearing ordinary clothes.

The bet was struck, and next day Nevill was present to watch as Bulpett 'entered the water at The Ship dressed in a frock coat, top hat, with a cane in his hand'.

A boat with his friends in it followed his progress and he reached the opposite shore 'with the greatest ease, though he was carried a mile and a quarter down by the tide – and when he got there, he offered to lay the same bet that he would then and there swim back to the other shore'.

There were no takers.

53. ROBERT CON-NELL?

Bookies at the obscure Kalgoorlie track in Australia in 1975 found themselves inundated with bets for a horse running that afternoon in Melbourne.

Everyone seemed to want to back a horse called His Worship and they had to reduce the odds on offer significantly.

The horse won easily and bookies began to pay out – only for it to soon become public knowledge that the race description sent down to the course via a relay station in Perth had been held up before being transmitted, thus giving the perpetrators of the scam time to discover in advance of placing their bets the result of the race.

Renowned big punter Robert Connell was subsequently disqualified for two years for his role in the affair, which brought back memories of a £20,000 coup in December 1939 when radio links from Melbourne's Ascot track were cut to all except one local station, 3XY, which broadcast a code message telling plotters which horse they should back.

54. BATTLE OF HASTINGS

Born in London in 1842, Henry Rawdon-Hastings became the 4th Marquis of Hastings when he came of age in 1863, by which time he was already very keen on all aspects of the turf.

He could afford to be, having inherited a quarter of a million pounds and also being the recipient of an annual income of £20,000.

'The owning of horses and the betting upon them were both absorbing passions,' wrote a biographer.

He bet big – and often inadvisedly just accepted the first odds offered to him, with no thought given to whether they represented value for money. He would manage, though, to back his share of winners, leading one bookmaker – perhaps the Barry Dennis of his day – allegedly to tell him 'Heaven's been very kind to you, for you look a fool, and you aren't one.'

Ackworth won the Cambridgeshire for him in 1864, and he also married Lady Florence Paget that year.

However, Lady Florence had previously been engaged to Henry Chaplin, before eloping with Hastings.

Chaplin was also a racehorse owner – and there was naturally no love lost between the two gentlemen.

In 1865 Hastings attended the sales and bid £950 for a yearling, which was secured for £1,000 by – Chaplin.

The yearling was called Hermit and in 1867 he became a Derby contender. Chaplin backed the horse, but Hastings, once known as King of the Plungers, had become convinced that Hermit would not – and should not – win the Derby, so began to accept bets against the horse, from anyone and everyone who wanted to back it.

Inevitably, Hermit won. There had been no popular gamble on the horse among the public, and it started at 66-1.

But someone had backed the horse heavily – owner Chaplin had won a reported £140,000. His friend, Captain Machell, had won £60,000.

As for Hastings – he lost £100,000.

'Hermit broke my heart, but I didn't show it, did I?' he famously remarked.

It was true.

Hastings' fortunes had turned with a vengeance and he had to sell properties to cover his debts – his wife even wrote to Chaplin asking for financial assistance.

Hastings determined to put almost everything he had on Lady Elizabeth in the 1868 Derby. She started at 7-4 and finished well down the field.

Out again for the Oaks, Lady Elizabeth failed again.

Hastings was shattered. His debts were overwhelming. He resigned from the Jockey Club. His health suffered.

Appearing at Doncaster races he was on crutches and looking very unwell.

On November 10, 1868, aged 26, he died.

55. SOMEONE COCKED UP

Gambling writer David Newman told the story of an American businessman who never placed a bet in his life but won a $500 dollar wager when someone cocked things up, in 1935.

'The businessman was, and still is, very important. His annual business volume runs into millions.

'It seems he was in South America attending his first cockfight. Everybody around him was speaking in Spanish – of which he understood not a word.

'Bets, challenges, jokes, insults, greetings, cheers and jeers flew across the pit thick and fast and our wealthy tourist was having the time of his life. Finally, his eyes came to rest upon one particularly red-hot fan who appeared to be addressing a voluble flow of the baffling dialect directly at him. Our big man responded with a gracious wave and friendly smile. The South American waved and smiled back.

'A few minutes later, two gamecocks were brought into the pit and soon began to murder each other. This bored the rich visitor. He found no entertainment in a chicken fight.

'When the match ended, the South American with whom he had exchanged such pleasant smiles came to him, poured forth another flow of incomprehensible Spanish and dumped into his lap a size seven-and-a-half hatful of money.'

The businessman said: 'When I smiled and waved the South American thought I was accepting some kind of a bet. So, even though I have never been guilty of wagering a penny in my life, I walked away from that cockfight about a five hundred dollars winner.'

56. WORLD'S GREATEST GAMBLING SCAM?

Richard Marcus refers to himself as the 'World's number 1 Casino and Poker Cheating Expert' on his website in which he relates the tale of what he calls the 'World's Greatest Gambling Scam of all time' which he credits initially to Piers Morgan – which is presumably some sort of Freudian slip as he later corrects that to Piers Mason, which is also the name he uses for the perpetrator in his *World's Greatest Gambling Scams* book.

Marcus reveals the story of when con-man and card-sharp Mason took his girlfriend Isabel on board the Titanic's maiden voyage, with the express intention of winning money by gambling in whichever way presented itself to him.

Eventually he came up with a masterplan after discovering that two chess grandmasters were also on board – Messrs Borzov and Heilmann.

Mason convinced wealthy passengers that he believed his girlfriend was a good enough chess player to challenge both of these great players simultaneously and to draw with or beat either one of them.

What's more, Mason offered to put up a £40,000 stake to that effect.

In the end his challenge was accepted by sceptical fellow passengers, who offered to hand over £1,000,000 if Isabel could beat either, and £100,000 if she could draw with either.

The challenge captured the imagination of everyone on board and passengers flocked to watch the showdown. In the event, Isabel managed to draw with both of them – despite never having played a game of chess in her life.

She had done it because Mason had devised a strategy whereby she was playing simultaneously and actually repeating the move of each player in turn – against the other. Thus in effect Borzov was playing Heilmann and therefore if one of them won, the other would lose, giving Isabel the £1,000,000 victory, and if they drew, so would she, with both of them.

When the ship went down, so did Mason, Isabel and the two grandmasters. But before he drowned, Mason, clinging on to a liferaft, told the tale to a fellow passenger, who ultimately survived to recount the story. Wonderful stuff. If true, that is.

I made an exhaustive search of Titanic passenger lists and failed to discover details of anyone on board named Mason, Borzov or Heilmann.

57. NEW APPROACH IS A MISTAKEN DERBY WINNER

Trainer Jim Bolger claimed that he had left New Approach in the 2008 Derby by mistake.

On a number of occasions he made it quite plain that he had no intention of bringing the horse, who was runner-up to Henrythenavigator in both the English and Irish 2,000 Guineas, to Epsom for the Derby – and the horse's odds drifted to 209-1 on Betfair – at which price one punter snapped up a £25 wager.

In April he explained: 'I'm keener on the Irish Guineas and Derby than Epsom. I haven't won the Irish 2,000 Guineas. It's not possible to fit in that race, the Derby and the Irish Derby.'

On May 12 Bolger was adamant that: 'The only Derby I've spoken about for New Approach is the Irish Derby.'

On May 25 Bolger declared that although the horse was still entered: 'It was a mistake and that is all I have to say on the matter.'

Most bookies weren't even quoting the horse and ante-post punters had already made their selections, safe in the knowledge that they didn't have to include New Approach in their calculations – until, with just five days to go before the Blue Riband of the turf, Bolger suddenly announced that he was indeed going to run New Approach: 'I live in a changing world. My prediction was wrong.'

A Coral spokesman accused Bolger of treating ante-post punters with 'total contempt'.

Guardian betting expert Greg Wood commented: 'Ante post punters will feel that they have been treated like dirt.'

Claude Duval in *The Sun* pointed out that Bolger had previous 'form' – 'Last year we had a similar disgraceful sequence of events when his 2,000 Guineas favourite Teofilo drifted like the Kon-Tiki in the betting. On the day his odds went mad, Bolger did not answer his phone. He said later, "I fell asleep. But Teofilo is okay."

'A few days later he was scratched from the 2,000 Guineas and £3m in ante-post bets were sunk.'

James Willoughby, the *Racing Post*'s chief correspondent, recalled Finsceal Beo's appearance in ante-post lists for the 2007 Oaks – 'when her trainer had no intention of running – he was indignant that anyone should think it his duty to put hapless backers right'.

In the *Mirror*, racing editor John Curle was unhappy: 'Jim Bolger's late U turn over the colt's participation made a fool of me – and everyone else who placed an ante-post bet on the race.'

But on Saturday, June 7, New Approach, ridden by Kevin Manning, treated his 15 fellow Derby runners with almost total contempt, and won the Derby at odds of 5-1.

58. HANGING AROUND FOR LUCK

Writer Ralph Nevill had the chance to check out one of gambling's most macabre superstitions when a friend gave him a piece of rope from a hangman's noose, and suggested he tried out its ability to induce good fortune.

Nevill, who wrote *Light Come, Light Go* in 1909, said: 'A piece of rope which has been used by a hangman is a fetish reputed to be an almost certain passport to good luck.'

Handed 'a small hempen souvenir' by a friend, Nevill set off to the casino – 'From the very first, however, it was evident that the gruesome charm was not exercising its occult influence in a direction favourable to its new, and perhaps somewhat sceptical possessor.

'When runs were sought for, alternates appeared, and vice versa. Disaster followed disaster in an unbroken sequence, with the result that the little bit of rope was all that the player had in his pocket as he somewhat disconsolately strode out of the rooms, rather inclined to wish that the hempen relic had been utilised for its original purpose around the neck of its donor.'

59. BOOKIES WELL AND TRULY FOXED

There was a hefty gamble on Freddie The Fox to win the Mascot Grand National at Huntingdon racecourse in late September 2001.

And punters who had bet against the dungaree-wearing, hairy-suited runner, realised that they were on a loser from the start when it was revealed that within the Fox costume was an Olympic runner.

Despite the race having gathered a field of more than 100 mascots of all shapes and sizes, Freddie The Fox had hurtled down the track – with 24-year-old Matt Douglas, who represented GB at the Sydney Olympics, finishing sixth in the 400 metres hurdle final, leaving his rivals trailing and gasping for air.

The Foxy figure was the medium of a substantial gamble with bookies Sportingodds. com, whose spokesman Wally Pyrah claimed a 'four-figure payout'. He added: 'We have been done over and we are not particularly happy about it.' They opened up a dozen new accounts purely for bets on the event.

They were even less happy when Douglas handed his winner's trophy to runner-up Dazzler The Lion, mascot of Rushden & Diamonds FC, as it became clear he was not a 'proper' mascot and claimed he had only got involved to help raise cash for charity.

The event's sponsor, another bookmaker NetBetSports, actually withheld payment, also claiming four-figure liabilities on Freddie. Some bookies paid out on both Freddie and Dazzler.

There had been objections to Freddie, apparently appearing for the Countryside Appreciation Group, when rivals claimed he was breaching the rules by wearing spikes. Douglas claimed he knew nothing about any betting coup.

Since this outcome, mascot races have become relatively common and now seem to encompass deliberate foul play in running, deliberate attempts to disguise the identities of runners and all manner of skulduggery – while bookmakers are very reluctant to take anything other than the most modest of mascot wagers.

60. SADDEST BET EVER

I know of no more poignant bet than this one, struck on December 27, 1859 between two fellow officers of the 2nd Battalion (78th) Seaforth Highlanders, whose wager is recorded in that august army division's betting book:

'Captain Hunt bets Captain Bogle one bottle of champagne that neither he nor Capt Bogle will be killed in action this time twelvemonth.'

A note in the margin of the betting book records:

'Capt Hunt & Capt Bogle both killed.'

See story number 313 for further details of wagers entered into by members of this regiment.

61. HUNDRED-GRAND MISTAKE?

When Russia went a goal up early in the second half of their Euro 2008 quarter-final clash with Holland many people would have fancied an eventual 90-minute outcome to the game of a 1-1 draw.

That option would have been considered a single-figure odds option to most – 5-1, 7-1 maybe.

But on the betting exchange Betfair, one punter immediately offered odds of an incredible 1000-1 about the 1-1 draw.

He was promptly accommodated to the tune of £100. So, when Ruud van Nistelrooy equalised for the Dutch with four minutes remaining, the punter was £100,000 out of pocket as that was how the game stayed when the whistle blew – and was the score for betting purposes even though Russia went on to win 3-1 in extra-time.

The *Racing Post* commented: 'It looked an obvious rick from the Betfair layer, although just how it happened is open to speculation.'

Betfair's Tony Calvin would only say, 'One would assume this was done in error' and would not confirm whether the layer had made any efforts to lay off the liability he or she had inadvertently acquired.

62. WHEN DOWN WAS UP

The *Racing Post* and Channel 4's Alastair Down has been known to indulge in the odd tilt at the bookies – but says he has seldom enjoyed backing a winner as much as in the Derby in 1973, when he was still (he claims!) a schoolboy.

'I've been a punter since I was five,' Down recalled in an interview with Ian Carnaby in 1999, confessing that he and school pals had 'accounts in false names at local betting shops' before he was old enough to bet.

But he enjoyed one of the greatest touches of his life, thanks to his dad – 'Dad was a remarkable chatter-up of women – he never followed it up, but he was brilliant at the chat – and sat next to a niece of trainer Arthur Budgett's on a flight back from Chicago.

'Uncle Arthur says he's got one that'll win the Derby,' she said, in passing. We all thought this must be Projector, who ran in the Lingfield Derby Trial but disappointed. It was only afterwards that I realised it must be Morston, who ran away with a maiden at the same meeting.

'I told everyone – masters, pupils, EVERYONE – that it would win. But the history master was a miserable devil, and I remember we had to write this essay, how big were Anne Boleyn's nipples, or something like that, while the race was on.

'We turned the radio off when he came back in the room, but when we went downstairs all these people were jumping up and down. Morston had won at 25-1 and it was one of the touches of my life. It didn't involve that much money, but it's all relative isn't it?'

It wasn't winners all the way when Down was in full-time education – 'I learned one important betting lesson at college. I had three months' allowance on Shebeen at 8-13 in the Yorkshire Cup and she finished fifth of six. I've never bet odds-on since.'

63. MONKEYING ABOUT

I've heard of people monkeying about while gambling. I've even heard of them gambling with monkeys – slang for a £500 stake.

But for the first time I heard about a poker-playing monkey when, in 2006, 'Mikey', a chimpanzee professionally trained to recognise colours and shapes, was entered for the World Series of Poker main event. The ape's backer, Max Wright, of PokerShare. com, said: 'We will sponsor him because we know a chimp can beat a chump.'

The WSOP did not want to be made a monkey out of, although he did take part in an exhibition game with Dutch pro Marcel Luske, who said: 'He was well behaved and the game was a lot more civil than other games I have played in.'

The chimpanzee, whose usual dress is red trousers, red braces, red bow-tie and red glasses, was banned, with WSOP's Gary Thompson insisting: 'We are not letting any chimpanzees in. It would be cruel and unfair to our players.' One wonders what US pro Lee Watkinson made of all this – after all, when he won a WSOP gold bracelet in 2006 he donated his prize-money to the Cortland Brandenburg Foundation, which is dedicated to rescuing captive chimpanzees.

64. 'THIS MAKES THE GREAT TRAIN ROBBERY LOOK LIKE SMALL FRY'

'An attempted betting coup at Dagenham Greyhound Stadium, Essex, yesterday, could have involved bookmakers throughout the country in the loss of more than £10m,' declared the *Daily Telegraph* on June 30, 1964.

When betting on the 4.05 race, over 840 yards, at the dog track had begun, a well-organised group of men had descended on every window selling tote tickets and begun to place a pre-arranged set of 11,757 forecast bets, predicting which dogs would finish first and second.

The men had deliberately concentrated their bets on three of the 25-1 or longer odds outsiders in the race (Lady Of Kintail, Lamberts Cross and Chestnut), and placed just one each on the potential combinations involving the other three, well-fancied runners.

This meant that when two of the three fancied dogs – second and third favourites Buckwheat (2-1) and Handsome Lass (9-2) duly finished first and second (there were eight lengths between them) from traps five and one, leaving 4-6 favourite Dancing Nell out of the frame in fourth, the declared dividend on the forecast paid a monumentally large £987 11/9d for each 2/- ticket.

The gang had earlier toured betting shops placing forecast combination bets on the three fancied dogs, meaning that each one accepted for 5 to beat 1 was now worth the £987 11/9d payout. To prevent word of what had been happening either entering or getting out of the stadium, telephone lines on the switchboard had been sabotaged.

Bookies soon became aware that they had taken hundreds of bets on the result, placed in an estimated 400 betting shops. They were not best pleased: 'This makes the Great Train Robbery look like small fry,' declared Ron Pollard of Ladbrokes. 'We alone stand to lose £250,000 on the race.'

Other bookies were worse off; most were hard hit – Jack Swift stood to pay out £300,000; Joe Coral £200,000; City Tote £160,000; William Hill £50,000.

As soon as they realised what had happened, bookmakers, via their National Sporting League and National Association of Bookmakers organisations, and the Dagenham management declared that they were withholding payment while enquiries took place. Bets on the race were finally declared void.

Despite court cases lasting two years, few punters received the full payout – except the person who had placed the one winning ticket at the track. Some bookmakers paid out at a reduced level of around £50 per ticket – and then only to customers they knew and could vouch for. Most bets struck by 'strangers' were never settled.

'In one respect the Dagenham syndicate could easily have fallen down on their coup,' said *Evening Standard* greyhound editor Willie Wicks, 'If one of the runners not included in the forecast bets placed away from the track had come in first or second.'

Indeed, but by unlawfully stopping punters from placing legitimate bets at the track, the plotters had, by all acceptable standards, crossed the line between cunning and crooked.

Romford-based John Turner was believed to be the 'brains' behind the coup, revealed the *Sporting Life* writer Bob Betts in 1989. It was alleged that he employed 100 men in his syndicate and stood to collect £280,000 in winning bets. He and three other members of the syndicate were prosecuted for fraud, but the judge ruled there was nothing illegal about the coup and the four were each awarded 50gns costs. The Dagenham management was instructed to pay out on the one on-track winning ticket.

Writing about the scam in the *Sporting Life* in 1990, respected greyhound expert Reg Potter declared: 'The Dagenham coup simply went hopelessly over the top – even in the different atmosphere of 1964 there was no way bookies would pay out a £987 dividend on fancied runners. Though I should mention that some did pay out a lower dividend to their regular, innocent clients.

'Greed has been known to spoil the most carefully laid plans and the Dagenham coup is a supreme example.'

High-profile racecourse bookie Barry Dennis, today noted for his outspoken views and flamboyant gestures such as giving racegoers free Christmas puddings when they race at Lingfield near Xmas, confessed in January 2005 that he was connected with the Dagenham coup, helping to spread the money around the betting shops – 'I won £50,000 and it was the day of the start of my honeymoon. What a start to married life that would have been. I found out that John Brown, later to become chairman of William Hill, was their office tea-boy at the time. He mentions me and the episode in his autobiography. So near, yet so far.'

Brown did indeed comment about the coup, recalling that William Hill himself had put in a rare appearance in the office that day – 'He pulled out this huge silk handkerchief, blew his nose loudly and said 'I'm going fishing'. And he did, but he talked to the company's lawyers and the perpetrators never got paid.'

65. HOWZAT FOR A BET?

Cricket was a betting sport from the time it was invented. According to the *Daily Telegraph Chronicle of Cricket*: '1646 – first recorded cricket match – at Coxheath in Kent – betting involved.'

In 1697 a match in Sussex was 'played for fifty guineas apiece'.

In 1731 'many thousands' were at Richmond in Surrey, where a game was played for a 200-guinea stake. Within 20 years an estimated £20,000 in side bets rested on a game played at Newmarket for a £1,500 stake per side.

The 1778 laws of the game included a section headed 'Betts', declaring: 'If the notches of one player are laid against another, the bett depends on both innings unless otherwise specified.'

By 1783 allegedly crooked games were appearing – one in particular, between Hambledon and Kent caused suspicions after the Hambledon scorer 'accidentally' mislaid his scoring stick on which run notches were marked and two easy catches were missed, according to the *Hampshire Chronicle*.

A 100-guinea-a-side game at Lord's in 1793 between Five Gentlemen of the Globe, and Four Gentlemen of the MCC ,didn't last long after the former were all out for 2.

66. ODDS ON THE AUSSIES

Bookmakers were banned from cricket matches in Australia in 1878 when England's captain Lord Harris was assaulted by one who faced a £1,000 loss if they won the match!

However, the Aussies can still boast a unique cricketing and betting distinction – the only Test skipper also to be a bookmaker.

They went close with Arthur Coningham, a bowler for Australia who took a wicket with his first ball in Test cricket, and then went on to stand as a bookie at Randwick flourishing a large bag bearing the legend: 'Coningham – The Test Cricketer'.

But H.L. 'Herbie' Collins went one better. An inveterate gambler, who played the favoured Aussie coin-gambling game 'two up' during the First World War in the French trenches, and was also an avid poker player – 'the only bookmaker who ever captained Australia was noted for the composure with which he won or lost matches and fortunes,' recorded Ray Robinson and Gideon Haigh in their book, On Top Down Under adding, 'His eyelids would not flicker nor his mouth twitch, no matter what happened when he had 100 runs or £1,000 at stake.'

He became skipper in 1919. Contemporary bowler Halford Hooker recalled: 'He would bet on anything – waiting on a railway platform he would bet on how many trains would pass through the opposite platform, how many carriage windows would be open.'

A photo of the skipper featured in Jack Pollard's Australian Horse Racing shows the trilby-wearing, sharp-suited operator with a handkerchief in his top pocket at the races, holding a handful of betting slips with a bag around his shoulders declaring 'Bert COLLINS. Reg. A.R.C.'

67. AUSSIES BACK THEMSELVES TO LOSE

Just what Aussie skipper/bookie Herbie Collins would have made of opponents England being quoted at 500-1 to win a 1981 Test match at Headingley we will never know – but Ian Botham spotted the odds and declared: 'Bloody hell, that's got to be worth a punt.'

In his 1994 autobiography Botham bemoaned the fact that he never put on a bet, but recorded that Aussie fast bowler Dennis Lillee 'gave the team bus driver a tenner to do the necessary'. Admittedly, England looked down and out in the game, but within two days of their stirring comeback victory, inspired by Botham, The Sun headlined its front page with an article alleging 'Two Australian cricket stars allegedly netted £7,500 between them by backing England.'

Rod Marsh, the wicketkeeper, later admitted: 'I had a five quid bet, I mean, big deal.'

Only in 1998 did Lillee comment – 'I never had any qualms over the matter. I had never seen such ludicrous odds for a two-horse race and told everyone in the dressing room I was going to have £100 on the rank outsider. They all said I was mad and demanded that I put it on the bar at the end of the Test instead. . . when the odds were still there with England 135 for 7 after being forced to follow on, and still needing 92 to make Australia bat again I had a rethink.'

He then sent bus driver Peter Tribe to put the £10 on.

Shortly after this controversial incident a clause was added to the contracts of Aussie players – 'The player undertakes that he will not directly or indirectly bet on any match or series of matches in which he takes part.'

68. 'ANG ABOUT, LOUGHRAN

Angus Loughran became well known for covering the betting action during race meetings for BBC TV.

His own betting interest began at Amplethorpe, the Catholic public school he attended in Yorkshire, where he would offer odds on how many monks would turn up each week for Sunday mass – the results being posted up on the hymn board by an altar boy.

In 1982 he made a big betting breakthrough when he won £300 thanks to a unique proposition.

Sitting at the Oval watching Chris Tavare batting – very slowly – for England against India, Angus bet several spectators that he would take a stool out to the wicket and sit on it.

He accepted odds of up to 10-1, told boundary fielder Kapil Dev what he intended to do, then sauntered on clutching the stool, sat on it, and was arrested.

69. BRO, DEAR

Winning £67,000 in an afternoon's punting at the races is pretty good going.

On October 5, 1971, the subject of this story staked £20,000 on course at Sedgefield on Vimy Rock to win a 2m chase, which it duly did at odds of 1-2, giving him a profit of £10,000. 'Using my brains to boost my bank balance,' he said.

He then played up his winnings, two days later, when he was at Ludlow – sticking the £10,000 on Crackaseal, who was backed from 5-2 to even-money favourite. It lost, though.

Undeterred, on October 9 he had £5,000 on easy 6-4 winner Whistling Sea in a novice hurdle at Uttoxeter.

Now £7,500 to the good, he headed for Sedgefield, and a £10,000 bet on 8-11 favourite Nice Shoe. It won, adding some £7,500 to his winnings.

An hour later and £5,000 on 20-1 outsider Strident, backed down to 9-1, was another winner.

Half an hour later he bet £10,000 on 5-4 winner Red Ruler.

'In just 90 minutes that day, I pocketed £67,000' – not bad for a punter.'

But this was no ordinary punter – it was champion jump jockey Barry Brogan and, as he wrote in his 1981 autobiography, 'Remember, jockeys aren't allowed to bet'.

Brogan raced against Vimy Rock; he rode the beaten Crackaseal; he partnered Whistling Sea to victory; he was second behind Nice Shoe; he rode Strident, but wasn't on board Red Ruler.

Brogan contravened a host of racing rules. And not for the first – or last time. He once turned over £250,000 in a six-month betting spree and over 20 years reckoned he lost £600,000.

An alcoholic, Brogan wrote, 'I was so successful as a jockey I should never have needed to bet, but it fascinated me.' He rode in his last race on May 1977, finishing sixth on Captain Nolan at Worcester.

70. BEAUTIFULLY DOPED ROYAL RUNNER

It was hushed up at the time, so few know the story of the time one of the Queen Mother's horses was the target of a ruthless gang of dopers determined to ensure that he would not win – thus enabling them to benefit financially, presumably from losing bets placed on the well-fancied contender.

Laffy, a promising jumper trained for the Queen Mum by Peter Cazalet, was being aimed at the Monaveen – named after her first ever chaser – Chase at Hurst Park in March 1962.

The race was a high-profile contest with Laffy certain to attract massive betting support from the public.

When a chauffeur-driven limousine arrived at Cazalet's Fairlawne yard, head lad Jim Fairgrieve had little reason to feel apprehensive.

Cazalet was racing at Newbury and Fairgrieve greeted the beautiful young woman in the car, who told him in a foreign accent that she was sending two horses to be trained there.

She also said Cazalet had given her permission to look around the stables, so he escorted her and the chauffeur around before they left.

Cazalet hit the roof when he heard about the visitors, about whom he knew nothing. He increased security around the yard and particularly around Laffy.

Overnight, Laffy was checked on but when he was visited at 9am the horse was struggling to stand up.

The vet was called and a blood sample showed the horse had been doped.

Police were called, but it seemed the doping plan had gone awry as Laffy was now to be withdrawn from the race, whereas the plan was presumably to dope him overnight, allowing the effects to wear off so that they would only become clear with a poor display in the race itself. Fairgrieve was convinced it was an 'inside job'.

Laffy suffered no long-term ill-effects and bounced back to win at Lingfield within days, with the racing public none the wiser about his absence from the Monaveen, in which the newly installed favourite, The Finn, crashed through the first fence and fell at the second, leading jockey Derek Ancil to claim his horse had been nobbled.

Six months later a trial was held at Lewes Assizes in Sussex. A gang of five was accused of doping up to 40 horses. Among the defendants was Micheline Lugeon, the beautiful daughter of a Swiss cemetery superintendent and former au pair, identified by three Fairlawne stable staff as the woman in the limousine.

Prosecutor, Mr Owen Stable (!), told the court: 'A young and attractive Swiss beautician working in league with the horse-doping gang exploited her good looks and got into 23 stables.'

The gang were sentenced to between one and two years each.

71. DIRTY SCOPE PUNTER CLEANS UP

Kicking King was one of the leading contenders for the 2005 Cheltenham Gold Cup, trading at odds of 6-1 – until the shock announcement by his owner Conor Clarkson just 17 days before the big race that the horse was unwell and very unlikely to run.

'Kicking King didn't work well at all and when the vet scoped him afterwards he was dirty,' announced Clarkson, meaning that the horse had an infection that required a week-long course of antibiotics, which would virtually spell the end of his chances. There was 'no way he's going to make it' said Clarkson, so mainstream bookies like Coral, Hills and Ladbrokes removed the horse from their betting lists.

Betfair, the internet betting exchange, allowed customers to offer their own odds about the horse's chances – and several put up odds of 999-1.

When Newbury gambler Chris Trinder saw that price available he decided to risk £25 on the horse – 'I had no inside knowledge but thought there was a chance he could recover.'

Other punters followed him in and staked a further total of £69 on Kicking King.

And ten days later there was another major reverberation in the betting market for the Gold Cup as the news was announced that the horse's condition had improved so much that he was now a definite runner – and what's more, on the same day the winner of the race for the past three years, Best Mate, was withdrawn.

Now Kicking King's odds shortened dramatically and when the race came under orders a few days later he had been the subject of the most drastic shortening of odds of any horse ever – from 999-1 to 4-1 favourite.

Kicking King, trained by Tom Taaffe, stormed through the field to win the race convincingly – to Trinder's joy. He was £25,000 better off as a result of his foresight.

Not so happy were the nine Betfair customers who had offered the 999-1 odds.

'It goes to prove there's no such thing as free money,' observed Betfair spokesman Tony Calvin.

Others raised an eyebrow at what had happened. Daily Mirror gambling expert Derek McGovern took a very cynical viewpoint on the events of the past 17 days.

'I've no idea what 'scoping dirty' means, but if I've any scope I'd love it to be absolutely filthy judging by what it did for Kicking King's wellbeing.

'While there is nothing to suggest the Kicking King camp was anything but truthful in their bulletins about the horse's ill health, what is to stop less scrupulous figures adopting a similar approach for dishonest purposes?' asked McGovern, putting up the scenario in which the owner of a fancied Grand National horse might be tempted to issue pessimistic bulletins about the health of his contender – whereupon 'those odds on Betfair would drift like the Marie Celeste. Once my money was on at 1000-1 I could then simply say that recovery had been far swifter than expected.'

And McGovern pointed out that: 'If I was on a runner at 1000-1 that should only be around 12-1 I could then lay the beast on Betfair at, say, 16-1. Happy days, no matter what the result.'

It transpired that one of the Betfair clients who had laid 999-1 about Kicking King and accepted £15 at those odds, had done something similar during a race at Southwell in 2002 when a horse got rid of its jockey on the way round and was offered at 999-1, only to be remounted and go on to win.

'Do you think?' asked McGovern of the layer, 'he's got the message now that gambling is not for him.'

72. GOOSEY, GOOSEY GAMBLE

Racegoers visiting early race meetings in Queensland, Australia in the late 19th century had the option of betting on the horses or on the 'gambling goose'.

This popular feature involved punters buying one of 15 cards for 'a bob' – 5p – with a ten bob prize on offer, decided when the goose selected the winning card on the instructions of his owner.

73. BACKING A WINNER

In 1722 renowned German author Count de Buckeburg was reported to have laid 'a considerable wager' that he would ride a horse from London to Edinburgh – backwards.

He set off with his face pointing in the direction of London while his horse's head was pointing towards Edinburgh.

The count made it in four days.

74. PRIDE BEFORE A FALLON

It might be the greatest ever example of an impeccably organised betting coup.

The Druid's Lodge Confederacy's astonishing triumph with Hackler's Pride in the 1903 Cambridgeshire was punting perfection personified.

The confederacy collected a reported £250,000 – the equivalent today of a sum well into eight figures.

The confederacy was a group of five specialists who came together for the express purpose of relieving the bookies of copious quantities of cash.

They were City financier Percy Cunliffe; Irish stud owner and West End impresario Wilfred Purefoy; celebrated huntsman Frank Forester; Edward Wigan, wealthy in his own right from his family's hop merchants' business; and Irish vet and stud manager, Holmer Peard.

The five had installed brilliant young Irish trainer Jack Fallon, in specially constructed stables on Salisbury Plain – away from prying eyes. This was Druid's Lodge.

Here the syndicate created a powerful stable of horses to be aimed at all manner of targets, from sellers to Classics.

The genius of their system was that the outside world rarely knew which race was a true Druid's Lodge target. They were not above running horses over the wrong distance, short of fitness and with the deliberate intention of losing if it suited their purpose.

Who could possibly imagine such things happening these days?

The group were also brilliant at spreading their betting money about to confuse the market. They had many coups before and after, but Hackler's Pride represented the pinnacle of their achievements.

The horse was acquired in 1902, under the ownership of Frank Forester, after being 'spotted' in Ireland. She was aimed at, and duly won, a late season five-furlong sprint.

1903 plans were initially fluid as the stable considered various options. Unfit, she ran down the field at Sandown in a 16-runner sprint in April.

Tried over a mile in June she finished a close-up second to a decent winner, conceding 4lb and still short of fitness.

This was the crucial juncture that saw her aimed at the Cambridgeshire.

The filly, as intended, now made no impression in the Wokingham Handicap before finishing mid-table in the Stewards' Cup.

Allotted an eminently satisfactory 7st in the Cambridgeshire weights, hard training of the horse now began.

A small hiccup endangered the whole scheme as trainer Fallon took some of the fancy early prices offered about the horse, without telling the rest of the conspirators. Purefoy was incensed and threatened to withdraw the horse.

A network of agents was now set to work to distribute the money – they even used a parish priest in Birmingham to put some on.

By mid-October, the horse was still a 25-1 chance. The money was going down, but other horses were also being backed to prevent the true picture emerging.

The first inkling the public had of the stroke about to be pulled came when the Sporting Luck newspaper reported the horse had been backed to win 'something like £10,000'.

Now the gloves were off and cash poured on the horse.

Hackler's Pride was still being backed on the day of the race, from 8-1 to 6-1, which made her second favourite behind 9-2 shot Kilglass.

Now the group revealed that – to his own surprise – their favoured jockey, Jack Jarvis, was being switched from another of the stable's horses.

The filly was so tuned up that she almost bolted with Jarvis as they went down to the start.

The race was virtually a formality – 'I was one of the first away, and after a hundred yards I never saw another horse in the race,' said Jarvis as they cruised to a three-length win. Only after the race did bookies begin to realise the cost of the coup. Cunliffe's commission agent handed him £63,000 – equivalent to some £5m now; Fallon admitted to winnings of £32,000. The rest collected similar amounts.

Not content with this, Hackler's Pride was promptly aimed at the 1904 renewal, for which she was backed from 33-1 to 7-2 – and won again, landing almost as hefty a blow on the bookies.

The Druid's Lodge Confederacy was finally brought to an end by the intervention of the First World War.

75. GONZO SETTLES UP

Hunter S Thompson, the legendary writer, author of Fear And Loathing In Las Vegas, shot himself in February 2005, causing equally legendary sportswriter Hugh McIlvanney to recall the time he won a bet from the 'wild pioneer of gonzo journalism'.

The pair were in Las Vegas in 1980 for what turned out to be Muhammad Ali's last fight – an ill-advised encounter with Larry Holmes when 'the Greatest' was well past his best, as most pundits were aware.

Despite the fact that Ali had lost two stones for the fight and that 'in the mirrors he consulted endlessly he appeared to have recovered much of the physical impressiveness of his youth' McIlvanney sensed that 'the effect was entirely cosmetic'.

Hugh believed that Holmes 'was a certainty' and had no truck with rumours doing the rounds that an 'arrangement' would give Ali victory and spark a return match which would then be won by Holmes.

'However, if there was one man in town who would embrace the fantasy wholeheartedly it was Dr Thompson, whose head was usually as full of conspiracy theories as of hallucinogenic drugs.'

McIlvanney bumped into Thompson in, inevitably, a hotel bar. 'He was scripting the imminent action in detail and offering to bet with anybody who disagreed.'

Hugh was keen to take some of the action along with a number of others – 'several in our company struck 100 dollar wagers'.

Next night with the bet won, Hugh was concerned that maybe the debt would slip

Thompson's ever-swirling mind. 'Unsurprisingly, he was nowhere to be seen.'

Eventually though, 'I collided with Hunter back at the hotel and asked tentatively if we'd had a bet.'

'Not only did we have a bet,' he said, 'but you are one of the early callers and that means you get cash. Others will receive cheques, and that is no privilege.'

McIlvanney reflected that their meeting 'had the distinction of being thoroughly pleasant and mildly profitable, a double claim not available to many who crossed his anarchic path. I found him good fun – and a good payer.'

Although Thompson definitely enjoyed a bet, it was not clear what his attitude to horseracing might have been – he once wrote: 'Derby week in Louisville is a white-knuckle orgy of booze and sex and violence. . . Horse people have very short attention spans for anything involving humans. The best thing about the Kentucky Derby is that it is only two minutes long.'

76. CUDDLY CLARIDGE AND THE BEAR-BRAINED SCHEME

Footballer Steve Claridge once resorted to dodgy methods to avoid being on a losing bet, after getting a tip for a greyhound running at a south coast track in the 1980s.

He and several friends decided to plunge on the dog, although they had been warned that it would win easily given a fast start, but if it should be baulked on leaving the traps, would lack the determination to work his way through to the front.

They hatched a plan: two of them would stand close to the traps. If the dog missed the break they would signal to their mates standing in front of the grandstand.

The hare started running, dashed past the traps which flew open, only for the dog to tumble out slowly. The signal was made.

'One of the lads, mingling with the crowd, threw a cuddly toy on to the track. It had the desired effect of sidetracking the dogs who went for the toy instead of chasing the hare, disrupting the race which was then declared void. We got our money back.'

Claridge told this tale in his autobiography, but it bears a remarkable similarity to what happened in 1990 when racegoer Colin Eastick caused chaos as favourite Swift Fox challenged rival Where's The Limo in the final stages of Sunderland's Mailcom Northern Puppy Derby in November of that year.

Twelve-hundred fans were enthralled as the two dogs battled it out with just 30 metres to run – only for Eastick suddenly to hurl a teddy bear on to the track. It hit Swift Fox, just as that runner had looked like grabbing the lead.

Instead, 'panda'monium broke out as racegoers chased after the culprit, who was trying to escape through the main gate of the stadium to a waiting car. He was finally caught by two plain-clothes policemen. A police spokesman later declared: 'If we hadn't taken him away the crowd might have lynched him.'

Eastick reportedly claimed: 'I did it because I think it is cruel to the dogs,' but many racegoers believed there may have been a far more sinister motive. He was later fined £100 by Sunderland magistrates, with £82 costs, a sentence that caused John McCririck to rage: 'Such oddly incomprehensible leniency will only encourage a rash of similar 'jests'!'

77. SUICIDAL BET

Lord Montfort and Sir John Bland eyed the frail figures of 80-year-old renowned dandy and gambler, Beau Nash, and his friend, noted actor Colly Cibber, three years older – and decided they were the ideal subjects for a morbid bet.

The two noblemen were at their London club, White's, in November 1754 when they gambled 100 guineas on which of the two elderly gents would be the first to pass on. Montfort took Nash to survive longer; Bland was with Cibber.

But neither of the toffs would ever collect on the wager. Both – over gambling debts, ironically enough – committed suicide before either of the old-timers shuffled off this mortal coil.

78. THAT'S THE PITTS

George E Smith – who became known as Pittsburgh Phil – was a successful professional gambler who frequented Saratoga racecourse in the States during the very late years of the 19th and early years of the 20th century.

A fearless bettor with an impeccable reputation for settling his debts, Smith had first appeared on the scene when he began betting big on racing through poolrooms in his native Pittsburgh.

At one time he was laying out around $1,000 per day to 'encourage' racing insiders to feed him valuable information from the stables.

He was doomed to an early death, though, succumbing to tuberculosis at the age of 43.

Even while confined to a sanatorium he could not resist a final punt. When his doctor informed him gravely that he had just 24 hours to live, Phil insisted on a bet of $10,000 that he would exceed that prediction.

He and the doctor both wrote out cheques.

Twenty-four hours, 30 minutes later, Phil breathed his last – happily clutching the doctor's cheque in his hand.

79. LADY LUCK

'Nine months ago I was playing online for 50 cents and a dollar. It's an unbelievable turnaround,' beamed Sky TV's Soccer AM star Helen Chamberlain after collecting a £270,000 prize in the August 2005 Ladbrokes Poker Million final.

'I love it and I hate it,' said the excited presenter, who added that she would be spending the cash on paying off her mother's mortgage and buying herself a second-hand Aston Martin. 'Your insides are going all over the place. You cannot jump up and down all over the place like football.'

Helen finished runner-up in the six-player final, which took place on familiar territory – Sky's Isleworth, Middlesex studios, behind 42-year-old Romford fork-lift truck driver Tony Jones. He took the £560,000 top prize, despite having only started playing 18 months earlier.

After the game, Helen commented: 'Before the final the eventual winner said that I was the opponent he feared most because he had been watching me in the heats and the semi-finals and he couldn't work out my style.

'The point was, I didn't have one.'

80. PREGNANT PAUSE

When pregnant single mother-to-be Elise Harp put up advertising space on her belly for sale on eBay in 2005, an online poker site won the bidding war.

SunPoker paid $8,900 for the right to place an ad on the Atlanta, Georgia woman's midriff area and were very happy with the deal after it generated considerable media coverage. You could even say they were so pleased they were belly-laughing all the way to the bank.

81. DODGY TRAINERS

Passengers on the 8.25am Grand National Special train taking them from London's Paddington to Aintree for the 1931 running of the great race were delighted to find at their seat a neatly printed, gilt-edged card offering an on-board betting service.

They were even happier when they learned that a female representative of the company would come round to their seats to take bets at either starting price or tote odds during the journey, with winnings to be distributed on the way back.

Many passengers took advantage and handed over hundreds of pounds in bets.

Third favourite Grakle, a 100-6 shot, won the race and passengers duly returned for the trip back and their winnings.

But there was no sign of the female bookie on the way back.

Arriving at Paddington, passengers tried to call the company on the numbers printed on the card they had been given – no such numbers existed. Nor was the company to be found at the Regent Street address given.

It was a masterful – mistressful(?) – scam, leaving rueful punters wishing they had considered more carefully the telegraphic address printed on the card – 'Gladofit'.

82. DERBY DUPES

Another brilliantly conceived scam cost gamblers attending the 1933 Derby when a gang of crooks constructed a portable totalisator on the chassis of an old lorry, hired for 30 bob, which they drove to the track and set up for business near Tattenham Corner.

Punters flocked to bet at the separate windows available for 5/-, 10/- and £1 tickets, handing over cash to the smartly dressed staff.

As the runners milled around at the start the 'National Totalisator' closed its windows ready, thought racegoers, to calculate payout dividends.

After the race queues formed as successful gamblers waited to be paid out. And waited ... and waited.

The perpetrators were long gone, leaving behind them a worthless wreck of a motor, and taking with them an estimated haul of £1,600.

83. WHAT'S DOWN, DOC?

Louis Theroux was shocked when he met Dr Martha Ogman while he was filming his 2007 TV documentary, Louis On Gambling.

For the elderly fruit machine fanatic confided to Louis on camera that 'I have lost $4m in seven years – but I enjoyed every moment of it'.

Louis seemed more upset than did the wealthy widow, whose son, Seth, was philosophical when Louis asked him whether he felt she was losing his inheritance: 'If there's nothing left, there's nothing left. What can you do? She loves to gamble.'

Louis, who decided to empathise with casino losers by withdrawing $3,000 of his own money with which to gamble (and promptly made a profit of $1,500!) reflected: 'Her gambling seemed less about winning or losing, and more about filling her days.'

84. POKER'S GREATEST BLUFF? LOOK, NO HAND!

It must have been the greatest bluff in the history of poker – winning a hand despite having no cards to play.

Irish player Nicky Power was taking part in an event, when, reported *Poker Europa* magazine in May 2007, 'Roland de Wolfe raised from the small blind after everyone else had passed. Nicky on the big blind raised all in – and then to his horror noticed that his cards had been swept into the muck by the dealer.

'The quick-thinking Nicky cupped his hands in front of him to hide the fact that he had no hand to play – and Roland passed, allowing the Irishman to take the pot.'

85. ALF'S WORLD TURNED UPSIDE DOWN

A bizarre finish to a dog race literally turned 70-year-old Alfred Alchediak's potential £750 winnings upside down.

In 1988 Alfred was sure he had landed the tricast at his local Tampa, Florida track. However, one of his selections, Oshkosh Zest, actually crossed the line backwards, completing a back-flip after tripping on the heels of the dog in front of him as he raced for the line. As a result the track stewards disqualified Oshkosh Zest 'for completing the course upside down' thus making Alfred's bet a loser.

Outraged, Alchediak launched a doomed, two-year legal battle, attending court five times in a fruitless effort to get his winnings.

86. STIFF TASK

The website www.stiffs.com invites visitors to gamble $15 on being able to tip as many celebrities as possible who will die each given year.

As the site boasted – 'the list with the most dead celebs wins a sh*tload of cash'.

And the entrant successfully selecting the greatest number of expired notables wins the prize-money. When I checked the site in May 2008, there were 644 entrants battling it out for honours with 'Comas Are Overrated' leading the way, having already correctly predicted the demise of Charlton Heston, Georgia Frontiere and Suzanne Pleshette.

He or she was hoping that Efrem Zimbalist jnr, Yves St Laurent and Annette Funicello and/ or a few other celebs would soon be heading skywards to help towards a payout of over $1,000.

Among those who contestants were anxious to appear on the obituaries page were Posh (but not Becks), Bowie, J K Rowling and John Travolta, to name but a few.

The site also contains betting advice – 'You don't want to ruin your chances by throwing in the name of someone you simply wish would die.' And there's a 'sick ticker' giving updated medical bulletins on ailing stars.

A few years back one contestant included Sir Peter O'Sullevan in his list, but as he has now proved he will comfortably see most of us off, he no longer figures.

87. PAPAL BULL?

On March 21, 1591, Pope Gregory XIV issued an instruction threatening excommunication for anyone found gambling on the identity of his successor. Maybe this was just a coded tip – he died on October 15, 1591.

88. HARRY HORSING ABOUT

He died in 1817, aged just 37, but Harry Mellish packed a great deal into his short life, and built up a reputation for being a fearless, and sometimes foolish, gambler.

The story was told by contemporary sources of the time he undertook a remarkable wager while serving under the Duke of Wellington:

'It was while he was in the Peninsula that Mellish made one of the maddest bets in the annals of wagering.

'He appeared one morning on a wretched-looking horse who made him the subject of unlimited chaff – "Why, the brute wouldn't fetch a fiver," said one of his brother officers.'

This was the opportunity Mellish had been seeking – 'I'll bet you a couple of ponies [£50 in total] that I get £45 for him,' declared Mellish.

'The wager was promptly taken by half a dozen officers. Mellish quietly booked all the bets, and then, putting spurs to his charger, galloped straight for the enemy's nearest picket.

'As soon as he was in range, the French sharp-shooters began to blaze at him; but, regardless of the bullets, Mellish rode on till his horse was shot under him. Then, waving his hand to the Frenchmen, he walked coolly back to the British lines.

'Now, the government then allowed £45 for every officer's horse killed in action.

So, Colonel Harry Mellish won the wager – for which he had deliberately risked his life.'

And, of course, albeit not even commented on then, deliberately sacrificed that of his steed.

89. STRICTLY FOR THE BIRD

A much-respected judge of racing, Alex Bird was a professional punter who built up his war-chest with which to take on the enemy, by the simple, but stunningly effective tactic of teaching himself to be an almost infallible judge of photo-finishes.

In the days when photo-finish outcomes would take several minutes to be announced, he would position himself in line with the winning post, waiting for the virtual dead-heats when he would use his own judgement to bet big on the horse he almost knew to be the winner.

He came up with his scheme in 1948 and it did him proud – 'My winnings were to bring me a mansion home, Daimlers, my own plane, a string of racehorses, a private dining room at Aintree and a box at Manchester United.'

Bird first tested out his idea at Newmarket, refining it bit by bit. He took up position and imagined an imaginary tape across the course – 'I practised my method, trying different positions and stances. Finally, I got it right, with an extra ingredient. I kept my left eye closed, and that was to be my stance on courses throughout Britain, wherever the photo-finish was operated, for 20 years.'

In 1954 he narrowly missed out on one of the all-time betting coups when he backed his own Tudor Line to win him £500,000 in the National – only to see the 10-1 shot come up agonisingly short, going down by just a neck – close at it was, Alex would have been the first to know he'd been beaten on the line. He later wrote, 'As the judge was positioned on the line I knew it could be just an optical illusion.'

A very expensive one.

90. WHO COTTONED ON?

In August 1984 'Fine Cotton' won a race at Eagle Farm in Queensland, Australia – but before backers of the winner, the subject of what one writer would call 'the biggest ever betting plunge in Australia', could collect their cash, the stewards had examined the horse and had decided that all was not as it seemed, and disqualified the heavily backed runner.

It transpired that another horse, Bold Personality, who looked nothing like him, had been substituted for Fine Cotton. Following investigations by the Australian Jockey Club, nine people were warned off, including two high-profile Sydney bookies – who always protested their innocence – and a Roman Catholic priest.

Racing author and historian Jack Pollard put forward an alternative, and novel, explanation for the scam in which Fine Cotton was backed from 33-1 to 7-2 with a potential payout of over A\$1 million: 'It has been suggested that whoever did organise the ring-in always intended that Fine Cotton/Bold Personality be disqualified.

'This presupposes an ingenious plot by other bookmaking interests to incite, by deliberate pre-race leaking, a massive Australia-wide plunge on the part of a gullible betting public.

'No bets are refunded after a disqualification in the above circumstances, and this would have meant a 'skinner' of undreamed of proportions for the bookmakers concerned.'

Fine Cotton himself had a song written about him, and a pair of underpants named after him.

91. WHO NUDE ABOUT IT?

It was the greatest hand of poker those around the table had experienced for, although they weren't playing strip poker, Russian gymnast-turned-wannabe poker pro 'Catgirl' was starkers at the table during the 2008 PartyPoker.com World Open.

She had wanted to play completely and utterly naked, but officials of TV station

Channel 5, who were filming the tournament, refused to allow her to do so – so she appeared artfully 'wearing' body paint as she took on Dave 'Devilfish' Ulliott and a number of other top-ranked players.

The 33-year-old Catgirl was philosophical after finishing second in her heat: 'Poker is about entertainment as well as being a very serious business. I want to go forward as a professional player, so why not give the world something to talk about.'

92. FOOTING THE BILL

Poker player William Rockwell has made a big impression on the game, after suffering a motorcycle accident that left him without the use of his arms.

The American now plays using his feet to control his cards – and picked up $25,000 in the 2006 Five Diamond Classic event.

93. TOT-ING UP THE WINNINGS

Andy Totham, betting columnist for *The Sun*, believes he was responsible for a self-fulfilling prophecy that landed perhaps his greatest ever winning tip and wager.

The occasion was the 2003 FA Cup final, between Arsenal and Southampton.

Creating his column for the big match, Totham spotted – 'hidden deep among the multitude of markets from William Hill, one called 'Massage Parlour'. Quite simply, it was 9-2 for the Gunners' Ray Parlour to be treated by the physio on the pitch.'

Totham duly headlined the bet – with a cunning motive in mind. 'On the morning of the game we knew, just knew, that someone in the Arsenal camp would spot our Sun headline urging Mr P to hit the deck. It wasn't match-fixing, just a small manipulation of a 30-second spell during the game.

'Come on, Ray – do it for us punters' begged our article.'

At half-time of the match, Parlour had been the recipient of a number of hefty challenges and tackles – but had stayed resolutely on his feet, to the distress of Totham and Sun readers everywhere.

'Keep the faith,' said Totham as his mobile rang continuously during the interval.

Twenty minutes into the second half Parlour was still upstanding.

Then he and Saints' Chris Marden made contact with each other – and down went Parlour. And stayed down – until, to cheers from the crowd, on rushed physio Gary Lewin to treat Parlour.

'Years on, we still have the widescreen TV and top-of-the-range music system we bought on the back of that Cup final bet. The kids called the TV Uncle Ray,' laughed Totham, a Colchester fan. 'I'll never know if Parlour read the article, but the memory of that cheering still brings on a warm glow, and proves that hundreds of others certainly did read it. And bet it, too.'

94. TOP HATS

Kwong Lee, Martin Fitz and Shuhal Miah became the first people found guilty of 'cheating at play' under the 1845 Gaming Act when, in 2005, their tactic of 'top hatting' – dropping chips on to a roulette table after the ball had landed – was deemed illegal.

95. AT YOUR CONVENIENCE

The Earl of Dudley was a somewhat eccentric backer of the 19th century who once struck two simultaneous bets with his bookmaker, one of which won him £3,000; the other of which lost him £100.

The Earl immediately paid over £100 for the bet he lost. Contemporary writer W A C Blew takes up the story. 'As he never asked for his winnings, the bookmaker hoped that he had forgotten all about them, until one fine day the well-known carriage drove up to the bookmaker's house and Lord Dudley entered to claim his winnings, with the remark that he did not claim on settling day as he heard the bookmaker had had a bad week, and he thought his demand might perhaps inconvenience him.'

96. DWYER CONSEQUENCES

Dwyer was the name of the bookmaker who, according to a contemporary report, 'kept a cigar and betting house in St Martin's Lane, London, in 1851 and was in the habit of laying a point or two more than the regular odds, and in consequence did the largest business of any 'list-man' [so called because of the lists of runners displayed at their premises]. He was considered to be absolutely safe.'

It was the custom in those times to pay punters on the day following a big race and in that year's Chester Cup there was a hefty gamble on Nancy – perhaps by those who had relatives or friends bearing this popular name of the times. She duly won, returning a starting price of 12-1. Successful punters flocked to Dwyer's, but 'his doors were found to be closed and the house being broken into by an enormous crowd of infuriated creditors, everything valuable was discovered to have been removed. Dwyer, as a matter of fact, had bolted with about £25,000 of the public's money.'

97. JACKIE GETS THE BIRD

Formula One ace Jackie Stewart was a world-class clay pigeon shooter in a previous sporting incarnation.

But he was stunned when he suddenly found himself taking part in an event on which huge amounts of money were being gambled and in which he was required to shoot live birds. In his 2007 autobiography, Stewart recalled 'one grotesque occasion' when he was in Barcelona and 'a promoter appeared and invited me to take part in a live pigeon-shooting contest'.

Stewart added: 'The 'sport', if it could be called that, was reportedly associated with some serious gambling.' Stewart reluctantly took part but insisted 'this was the first and the last time for me. I didn't enjoy it'.

98. DAVID BETFORD

One of Britain's greatest distance runners, David Bedford is now equally well known as the man who organises the London Marathon each year, and 'that old runner who looks like the 118 118 blokes'.

On the eve of the first ever London Marathon in March 1981, and somewhat the worse for wear after enjoying a long night's carousing in the Luton nightclub he owned, Bedford was offered, and promptly accepted, a wager of £250. To win he had to complete the Marathon next day or, more accurately, later the same morning.

Not even officially entered, 'Bootsie' called in a favour from then race supremo Chris Brasher to get himself in.

Then he rounded off his preparation with an early morning curry, retiring to bed at around 4.45am.

Up a couple of hours later to be driven to Greenwich by mate Johnny Brookes, a legitimate entry, Bedford arrived at the start feeling fine and set off.

He told me: 'At 16 miles my curry was threatening to put in a reappearance. At 22 miles, I was on all fours, leaning over a manhole cover being sick, losing the curry into a drain, and on the TV Brendan Foster said, "There's Dave Bedford looking, er, not quite as fit as we might have expected".'

Bedford somehow got round in three hours 45 minutes and returned to Luton for a kip. 'When I finally got up I could hardly walk,' he said, before setting off to claim his winnings.

'The guy who made the wager was nowhere to be found – the bloke never showed up again, so I never got the winnings.'

99. LEGAL EAGLES

Three Australian solicitors got together to take on the bookies in 1958, and for the next 15 years Bob Charley, Clive Evatt jnr and Don Scott ran the layers ragged.

The 'Legal Eagles' were the first high-rolling punters to eschew tips and inside information, and to operate purely on their own judgement and research.

'The extent of their winnings remains a secret,' wrote Aussie racing historian Jack Pollard. 'But their impact on the Sydney betting ring during their years of operation certainly startled bookmakers, as well as giving fresh hope to embattled punters that scientific study can be rewarded.'

100. TITANIC'S SINKING FEELING

Alvin Clarence Thomas, born in Missouri in 1892, would change his name to Titanic Thompson and become one of the sharpest, most ruthless gamblers of his day.

By the age of 15 he had pulled one of gambling's most devious and cunning strokes.

Sitting by a fishing pond, Alvin persuaded a passing stranger to stake his expensive fishing rod against his spaniel on a bet in which the odds seemed stacked against the youngster.

He was willing to bet that the dog could retrieve a marked stone from the bottom of the pond where the stranger would be allowed to throw it.

The wager was agreed upon, the lad marked a small rock with his knife and the stranger lobbed it into the deepest part of the pond. Carlo the spaniel jumped in, swam out, dived down, and came up with the rock in his mouth.

He dropped the rock at their feet – on it was the knife mark.

The stranger tried to bluster his way out of the bet and found himself looking down the barrel of a .22 gun. He handed over the rod and left.

'That dog of mine was good at that trick,' recalled Thompson years later. 'But I ain't one for taking chances. A few days previously I'd covered the bottom of that hole with dozens of marked rocks. That sucker never had a prayer.'

When he left home to seek his fortune by gambling, Thompson became a notorious card sharp but better known as the king of such proposition bets – he would dive over a full-size pool table without touching it for a wager. In 1917 in Arkansas he pulled another master-stroke when he bet he could throw a walnut over a hotel, inviting his opponent to select any of the nuts from the bag he was clutching.

They agreed on a 100-dollar bet at odds of 3-1 – and Thompson promptly hurled the walnut up and over the five-storey hotel.

It was an amazing feat – but somewhat easier once he had switched the ordinary walnut for the one he had prepared earlier by inserting into it enough lead to give it the necessary bulk to be hurled a great distance.

He once deliberately moved a signpost pointing to a town 20 miles away a couple of miles nearer, then engineered a car trip during which he expressed surprise at the distance displayed and offered to bet it was wrong.

Noted American gambling expert John Scarne recorded that Thompson 'bet some Broadway wise guys he could drive a golf ball over 300 yards. He did it all right – off a hill where the drop was nearly 300 yards'.

He also recalled how Thompson 'clipped a crowd of big-time horse bettors including Arnold Rothstein and George McManus' who had a standing bet on the number of white horses they would spot during a train trip from Pennsylvania Station in New York out to the Jamaica racetrack.

Thompson joined them one day, suggesting 'it looks like a good day for white horses' and betting that there would be more sighted than the highest number already tipped by any of those present.

'He won that one in a walk,' noted Scarne, 'because he had made a deal with a livery stable and arranged to have eight white horses planted at a crossroads which the train would pass.'

Legendary pool player Minnesota Fats wrote about one of Thompson's strokes in his autobiography, recounting how he bought a farmer's entire stock of watermelons for a high price, had them counted one by one and placed on a truck, which the farmer was told to drive slowly past a local hostelry, frequented by high-rolling gamblers, at an appointed time.

Thompson was in position as the truck chugged up the road. 'Ty gets the show on the road by allowing he will wager any amount that he can estimate exactly how many watermelons the farmer has on the truck. The high-rollers all got down real heavy and when they stopped the farmer to inquire about his inventory, Titanic just happened to have hit the precise number. He won a fabulous bundle, but I obligingly relieved him of most of it at pool.'

Thompson achieved a kind of immortality when legendary US writer Damon Runyan based his character Sky Masterson on Thompson, commenting: 'The Sky is a great hand for propositions, such as are always coming up among citizens who follow games of chance for a living. And no-one ever sees The Sky when he does not have some proposition of his own.'

Thompson's own father was a gambler who left his family. Thompson tracked him down and played and beat him at cards before handing him his money back, telling him when he asked why, 'I have my reasons'.

And in 2005 I discovered that Thompson's own son, Tommy Thomas ('my dad left when I was four years old') gave up his life as a gambler – 'I had a Porsche, a BMW, and a speedboat. I became one of the best card mechanics, or card cheaters, in the world' – to work with gambling addicts.

101. CATHING IN

Catharine Unsworth, a Liverpool doctor's wife, went racing to Haydock Park on November 30, 1929 and fancied a bet on the 15-runner selling handicap hurdle, in which 100-8 outsider Coole caught her eye.

Noticing that the beast seemed to be entirely unsupported on the tote Catharine purchased a two-shilling (10p) each-way bet on the horse, who proceeded to storm home.

Mrs U was somewhat gobsmacked when it was announced that the win dividend was £341 2/6d – world-record win odds of just over 3,410-1. She was the only person to have backed Coole to win. Even the place part of her bet – although others had also backed this option – paid 100-1 – £10 2/- to her stake.

102. WHIP ROUND FOR BET

Alice Thornton took on her brother-in-law Captain Flint – who was secretly in love with her – in a public race at York for a side-stake of 500gns on August 25, 1804, in an event that really captured the public imagination.

10,000 spectators turned out to see Alicia, riding Vinagrillio, beaten by Thornville, over four miles.

Alicia's husband, Colonel Tom Thornton, refused to pay the stake money over and Flint later horse-whipped him for his dashed cheek.

Alicia went on to challenge the top jockey of the day, Frank Buckle, to a match and this time she won.

103. O'DEAR

Linda O'Neill, wife of trainer Owen, reckoned that the two runners they were saddling at Bath in August 1993 might be worth the small financial interest of a fiver win double.

'I was all set to place the bet but Owen told me to keep the money in my pocket,' fumed Linda after the two won at 66-1 and 50-1 – a 3,416-1 double that would have netted her £17,080.

'You wouldn't be able to print what she said to me when I arrived home,' said Owen.

104. COULD CHEETAHS PROSPER?

Kenneth Cecil Gandar-Dower (1908-1944) has a unique place in greyhound racing history.

He – and 1,296 others – met an untimely end when the ship he was on, the SS Khedive Ishmael, was torpedoed by a Japanese submarine near the Maldives.

A poet, explorer, journalist and double international for England at both tennis and squash, he had attended Harrow School, who he played for at cricket.

He attended Cambridge University, representing them at seven sports.

Aged 23, having already competed at Wimbledon, he became a competitive flyer – eventually undertaking a trip from London to Madras in his Puss Moth plane.

In 1934 he led an expedition to Mt Kenya, writing a book, *The Spotted Lion*, as a result in 1937.

Back in England when the book was published, Kenneth came up with a corker of an idea – to introduce a unique gambling opportunity for punters by racing the 12 cheetahs he had captured in Kenya and brought back with him against each other and whippets at greyhound racing tracks.

The first race took place at White City in August 1937. 'There were immediate problems – cheetahs are more shrewd than greyhounds and they will not chase an inanimate object,' recalled author Jeremy Halies, 'and when one of their number gets ahead it is allowed to pursue the quarry alone.'

The introductory race at White City was notable for the way in which the cheetahs 'disgraced themselves by cutting off corners'.

Gandar-Dower was also allowed to race his big cats at Harringay – 'he was now confident that the cheetahs would not bite lumps out of the handlers or the greyhounds'.

But the curved track was a problem 'and when an oblivious punter, quietly marking his card on the rails, was knocked over by one of the cats which had missed a bend, the authorities at White City decided that the circus was no longer welcome'.

The cheetahs were shipped back to Nairobi – but greyhound racing had a unique feature for old-timers to recall to this day.

105. WHAT A W***ER

Mario Puzo, the writer who created *The Godfather,* had an unusual memory of a very strange way in which greyhound racing punters were fleeced, which he revealed in his 1976 book, *Inside Las Vegas.*

Discussing various forms of gambling, Puzo mused: 'Greyhound racing, which I always thought of as particularly English because of its enormous popularity there, was actually invented in America.'

Puzo declared that 'the first patent was taken out in the United States in 1890 and the first track opened in Oklahoma in 1923'. He recalls that Belle Vue was the first

English track to open and remembered: 'In 1943 I was billeted there as a soldier in World War II. There I met one of the many girls who worked as greyhound trainers and she told me that sometimes the girls masturbated the dogs to make them lose.

'I flinched and never tried to get inside information again.'

106. STIFFING THE BOOKIES

The bookies feared the man they called 'The Big Stiff'. The racing public loved his efforts to put the layers out of business and dubbed John Warner Gates, who had amassed a huge fortune by selling barbed wire to Texas ranchers, 'Bet-a-Million', in honour of his legendary stakes.

Gates would regularly gamble $50,000 on a race, enjoying Saratoga in particular where, in August 1902, he lost $400,000 in one session – but then won most of it back playing the card game, faro. So extreme was his gambling that Gates was once requested by American Jockey Club chairman August Belmont II to limit his bets to $10,000 a time as he was encouraging the anti-gambling lobby with his wilder punts. Gates refused point blank – 'There's no fun in betting a few thousand. I want to lay down enough to hurt the other fellow if he loses.'

And hurt the bookies, if not humiliate them, did Gates later in 1902 when he strode into the Saratoga ring to back a horse called High Chancellor.

Starting with $10,000 at 12-10, he piled on $50,000 and more, forcing the odds down to evens and lower.

High Chancellor duly won and Gates returned to the ring, together with a huge, hired servant pushing a wheelbarrow, which was soon stuffed full of the $100,000-plus which he had to collect. The Big Stiff took great delight in accompanying the massive cash collection past his deadly ring rivals.

107. HARD TO SWALLOW

French gambler Adrian Marque, from Nice, became jealous when his fellow poker player Louis Guilhot scooped a hand with three kings. Marque murdered Guilhot by stuffing poker chips down his throat, reported the media in June 1998.

108. HOW CARL BET HIS FINGER ON A HAND

Carl Valentine staked his right index finger on a hand of poker in apparently the most bizarre wager of its kind.

The machine shop labourer from the American Midwest was provoked into the wager following a visit from a childhood friend made good, who had become a multi-millionaire via internet marketing.

The pair got to talking about the internet and the friend offered to bet Carl $1 million that he would be unable to direct two million unique visitors to an individual website by April 18, 2006 – the friend's birthday.

Knowing full well that his labourer friend did not have that kind of money, the friend may have been a little shocked to have his bluff called when Valentine announced that he would accept the bet – and put up his right index finger as his stake. The destination of the stakes was to be decided by a heads-up poker game between the pair at the PokerRoom.com site on April 18.

Now, cynics may suspect that this entire story was a neat publicity stunt for an internet poker site, but on December 12, Carl's supposed website, Savemyfinger.com, duly appeared online and began to attract hits. On it, Carl mused: 'Am I kidding? No. Am I nervous, Hell yes. This is seriously not a joke.'

There is, though, a get-out for Carl – 'I told him [the friend] I would bet my finger against his money. If I send two million visitors to the site I will be playing to win $1m, if not I am playing to keep my index finger.'

Valentine told pokerlistings.com: 'Obviously I am a bit crazy for accepting the proposition, but it's just a finger – I have plenty more. Besides, this is the only opportunity I will probably ever have to win $1m.'

However, as Carl's story spread around the web, fingers were pointed accusingly by digital doubters, alleging that his yarn should not be so handily accepted.

As the hits mounted, passing 1.5 million, Valentine's conscience was pricked, and he confessed – 'I don't think it is a big surprise to most that this was just a funny story.' Declaring that the intention had been to engage in an experiment with viral marketing, he knuckled down and made a decent fist of calming detractors:

'If you were offended, I apologise.' Still, you have to hand it to him!

109. URI JOKING?

Spoon-bending is a pretty amazing talent claimed by Uri Geller – but a gambling feat he claimed seems even more startling.

In his autobiography, the Israeli showman told how he used his psychic powers to net £17,000 from a London casino.

That's remarkable enough – but Geller went on to declare that he felt so guilty at exploiting his gift in this way that, to salve his conscience, he threw all the money out of his car window.

110. FIVE YEARS WITHOUT A WINNER

Glenn Ford began backing horses in 2002.

He staked a £5 bet each week – and lost an estimated 250 times in succession before finally nailing a winner for the first time FIVE YEARS later on August 31, 2007, when 20-1 shot Fandasil finally won for him at Hamilton Park.

The closest the 45-year-old from Southsea, Hants, had ever come to a winner before was 66-1 runner-up Thought Is Free, beaten in a photo-finish at Newmarket.

Bookie Richard Meek, of Portsmouth's Betting Room, commented: 'It usually hurts me deep inside when I have to pay out on winning bets – but I made an exception for this one.'

111. WHITE VAN SCAM

Three members of a casino-busting gang won a total of £250,000 from six different venues before they were convicted of 'cheating at play' in 2007.

Bit Chai Wong, 39, prompted suspicions in a London casino when she won 34 hands of three-card poker in a single hour.

When security officials checked her out it led to the discovery that the woman and her two accomplices were using miniature cameras woven into a jacket sleeve and handbag, concealed earpieces, transmitters and a van full of video monitors to win thousands by discovering what cards the croupier was playing, and passing the information to Wong.

Wong, heard the jury at Southwark Crown Court, had devised the scam after suffering heavy losses.

With the scam proving effective, more than one of the casinos targeted had noticed a parked white van outside of their premises when the gang won.

Eventually they were caught on CCTV and arrested.

Wong, a waitress from Bedfordshire, and Fan Leung Tsang, 41, received suspended nine-month sentences, 150 hours' community service and were banned from casinos for two years. Chef, Yau Yui Lam, 45, was jailed for nine months.

The judge, Geoffrey Rivlin, commented: 'The crime of cheating at play may be over 150 years old but as has been demonstrated in this case, it is still alive and kicking.'

112. ROMANCE ISN'T DEAD

Busty actress Pamela Anderson, 40, married her third husband, Rick Salomon, 38, in October 2007 after a whirlwind romance sparked by Anderson's disastrous poker playing.

The former Baywatch star had reportedly accrued debts of $250,000 at the green baize tables in Vegas. However, the chivalrous Salomon stepped in to offer to pay off the debt. What a gentleman! There was, though, one condition. She must offer him 'sexual favours' in return. Aah. Who said the age of romance is dead?

Anderson saw no problem with the arrangement and was soon explaining: 'I paid off a poker debt with sexual favours, and I fell in love.' Yes – but she soon also fell OUT of love. In December she filed for divorce, citing irreconcilable differences.

The marriage was annulled in March.

113. BAD LOSER

Austrian gambler Josef Reiner was too scared to tell his wife that he had lost thousands of pounds in a casino – so the 26 year old broke his own nose, jaw and arm with an iron bar and told her that he had been attacked and robbed.

However, suspicious doctors at the hospital to which he was admitted in August 2008, called the police, to whom he confessed. A police spokesman commented: 'He must have been very afraid to inflict so much pain on himself.'

114. THE WARRIOR THROWS DOWN GAUNTLET

Akio Kashiwagi from Tokyo was, in June 1990, reportedly betting £120,000 per hand at Baccarat in Atlantic City casinos – staking up to £10m per hour in sessions lasting 14 hours. As he played, a chef prepared his favourite food – bacon, lettuce and tomato sandwiches and marinated monkey meat. No sign of sushi, apparently.

The *Wall Street Journal* reported that 'The Warrior' had assets of £600m and a £60m annual income.

Records showed a £4m win at Donald Trump's Plaza Hotel and Casino in early 1990 – but also listed a £5m loss. He once lost 11 consecutive £120,000 hands. One of The Warrior's aides, commented, 'He plays only for fun.'

115. FAT CHANCE

Reclusive billionaire Fouad al-Zayat was, in early 2007, ordered to pay Aspinall's, the London club, £2m plus £50,000 costs in a dispute over an alleged bounced cheque.

It was revealed in court that Syrian born al-Zayat, known as The Fat Man, had staked £91m at Aspinall's over some 600 visits spread over 12 years. He had reportedly lost £23m.

And he was not best pleased when the casino took him to court over what he claimed to be one night's gambling bill.

'If my name was an English name not an Arabic name this would never have happened' he claimed to *Daily Telegraph* reporter Malcolm Moore, in June 2007. He claimed he had asked for the croupier to be changed during the course of the session in March 2000 and therefore not dated his cheque so that negotiations could take place. He had subsequently continued to gamble, losing a further £10m which was paid.

Zayat, believed to be one of the legendary group of mega-gamblers known to casinos as 'Whales' said he would never gamble in London again.

In September 2008 the 'Fat Man' won a High Court battle over the disputed £2m payment, which meant he avoided having to repay the sum - although his counter-claim for the return of the additional £10m was rejected.

116. TO BE FRANK, HE'S A WHALE

The original 'Whale' or mega-gambler, is believed to be Frank 'Lefty' Rosenthal, a Las Vegas gambling tycoon portrayed as Sam 'Ace' Rothstein by actor Robert de Niro in Martin Scorsese's film *Casino*.

Rosenthal defined 'Whales' as gamblers who could raise instant credit of up to $5m when they arrived at a casino.

'Whales' have spawned a species of casino employee whose job is to schmooze, entertain and retain the loyalty of such players for their gambling house. Best known of these 'Superhosts; is probably Steve Cyr, whose Vegas career is documented in the 2004 book, *Whale Hunt In The Desert* in which Deke Castelman wrote, 'The largest table-game bet currently taken in Vegas is $250,000, but only seven or eight human blue whales can handle that kind of action.'

He reckons up to 50 more can bet $150,000 per hand and another 100 $100,000.

How does Cyr keep his Whales swimming around him? 'Whales can receive as much as $250,000 in free play … scribble their names on $20,000 dinner and drink tabs … cases of $600 a bottle champagne. Boxes of $100 hand rolled cigars. Thank you cards attached to Beemers and Hummers.'

117. MICHAEL CRAWFORD IS NO FRANK SPENCER – HE'S BETTY

A former accountant claimed to be Britain's biggest ever betting shop customer, according to specialist gambling reporter Brian Radford in a *Daily Express* article of 14 February 2008.

Radford reported that Crawford, in his early forties, staked £5m during 2007 and wrote that 'he currently employs seven hand-picked agents, using gadgets straight out of James Bond, to place bets for him in towns across the country.'

Apparently, Crawford's crew deliberately dress up – 'down' Radford called it – in shabby clothes, to encourage betting shop staff to regard them as mug punters. He also equips his agents with ear-pieces through which he sends them last minute betting instructions.

Crawford explained his system of selecting his horses by vaguely telling Radford that: 'It's based on getting to know what horses are being bet, particularly trainer-jockey combinations. And I've got the means to know just before a race.'

One of Crawford's agents described himself as 'a pensioner with dodgy legs' and said that was why he had been hired – 'Crawford is an absolute genius. Betting shop managers think I'm a mug who has picked up a few quid from a rich aunt. I act a bit daft, saying things like 'I really fancy that horse. It's got a great name. I'll have £3,000 on it. Managers pay with a smile because they're convinced I'm an idiot who has struck lucky and will soon be giving it back.'

Liverpool-based Crawford admits that gambling destroyed his marriage, but said: 'It was after my divorce that I decided to concentrate my mind on beating the bookmaker. I was angry with them. Then I hit on a formula. For my operation to work all seven have to be in a betting shop at a precise time to receive my late information.'

118. HOW TO COCK UP A CERT

In his autobiography, *Farewell But Not Goodbye*, former England manager Sir Bobby Robson told the tale of how he set up a betting coup by entering one of the players from his then club side, Ipswich Town, in a professional athletic sprint race and then backing him to win.

The player was Kevin Beattie, who 'could run a hundred yards in ten seconds in football boots, never mind spikes. So we entered Beattie, placed our bets and waited for the inevitable pay-out. We thought he was a cert.'

The Powder Hall Sprint took place at Newcastle and Robson sent Beattie with youth team coach, Charlie Woods who he told: 'Call me after the race to confirm that Kevin has won.'

The call came through at 9.30pm, and Robson demanded, 'We won, then?'

The answer didn't please him.

'You'll never guess what happened. I got him there, he got changed, got to the starting line, the pistol fired and off he went, but halfway through the race he just started walking.'

Robson waited for the explanation: 'Kevin wore a pair of tight shorts and didn't put a slip on underneath. He was halfway down the track, way ahead, when his penis popped out of his shorts. It just all came out. So he stumbled the last 40 yards clutching his shorts and trying to run with one hand free. He got pipped at the post.'

119. TROUBLE FREE CONSERVATORY

Trainer Noel Chance has kept the 50-1 voucher about his 2000 Gold Cup winner Looks Like Trouble, who stormed clear of Irish favourite Florida Pearl to land chasing's most coveted event at 5-2.

'He had won the Sun Alliance Chase the previous year, and I thought that 50's was an insult, so I helped myself and it paid for a new conservatory,' said Chance.

120. THE BIRCH DESK

Future ace *Racing Post* tipster Richard Birch was still cutting his punting teeth at the Press Association agency when he became convinced that his equine pin up, the 1990 1000 Guineas and Oaks winner would also win the Irish Derby.

He steamed in, staking his maximum £500 on the filly at 9/4 and proceeded to bore everyone in the office about how easily Salsabil would win. When the horse drifted to 5/2 and 3/1 on the day he was goaded by his office colleagues into backing her again – splashing out another £500 which he could not really afford.

When Salsabil backed up his boasts and quickened to victory, the celebrating Birch leaped on to his desk to celebrate his £2.475 winnings – 'And broke it.'

121. POST-MAN DELIVERED FIRST CLASS WINNER

On the Flat, the Autumn Double – the Cambridgeshire and the Cesarewitch – has always proved popular with turf aficionados.

One of the great successful plunges for the nine-furlong cavalry charge was with Sir Mark Prescott's Pasternak in 1997. Pasternak, part-owned by the late Graham Rock, former *Racing Post* editor, and one of the shrewdest judges of horse flesh in the pressroom, is reckoned to have taken £5m out of the bookies' satchels.

Rock told anyone who would listen that they could 'have what you like on Pasternak,' and, though he was offered at 11-1 on the morning of the race, the *Racing Post*'s front page headline 'Why you must back Pasternak' captured punters' imagination, and bookies were virtually knocked over in the rush to get on, and he eventually did the business at 4-1.

122. GREAT SCAM? OR GENUINE REQUEST

Now, call me an old cynic ('You're an old cynic') but I am not entirely convinced that the letter I received in January 2006 was being entirely open and genuine about the matter in hand. The letter, from a lady giving a Brighton address, was asking me to send her £5,000 as settlement for a winning bet.

Fair enough – up to a point. The winning bet was, she said, placed by a gentleman, subsequently deceased and whose executor she now was. The bet in question, she wrote, had been '£5,000 to £1 bet that Prince Charles and Princess Diana will never become King and Queen of England.'

Ah. Well, that would clearly be a winning bet – in the event that any bookmaker had ever been misguided enough to quote such odds to anyone. She suggested that the bet had been struck at some unspecified date before the gentleman who had placed it had unfortunately 'died in an accidental fall' in 1994.

Okay, so, let's have a look at the betting slip, then.

Now, that's a problem – 'the betting slip has so far not been found (search continuing).'

I see, so here we are, discussing a bet which noone can prove ever existed?

'He did initially show me the betting slip when he made the bet. When the Royal marital problems eventually received wide publicity he told me the betting shop had offered him £1,000 for the slip and he refused it. That was about 1988 or 1989.'

I informed my correspondent that when she managed to locate the slip, of which we seemed to have no record whatsoever, I would be delighted to establish its bona-fides and, if fully satisfied, to settle it in full.

At time of writing I have yet to receive any follow-up correspondence.

123. HOUSEY, HOUSEY

The FitzGerald family, the Dukes of Leinster, owned the 67,000-acre Carton House estate in Maynooth in Kildare, Ireland – now a luxury hotel – from the 1730s until in the 1920s when, according to the house's official history, the 7th Duke had to hand it over to Sir Harry Mallaby Deeley to cover his £67,500 gambling losses.

124. SAME OLD STORY?

The cash was down for Coriolanus to win the 1883 Adelaide Cup.

The horse's owner, R Kelly Maitland, a one-time handicapper at another Aussie course, Caulfield, had seen his horse slaughter fancied stablemates Sting and Mistake in a pre-race trial.

The owners of all three had decided to get behind Coriolanus and they poured money on the horse, only for the rain to come on race day, turning the going heavy and resulting in a reversal of trial form as Sting came through to win – upsetting his owner, Teddy Weekes, all of whose money was on Coriolanus, beaten into second.

With the owners all sulking, top-hat clad Maitland had to persuade Weekes to go up to accept the trophy from the Governor.

He did so and launched into a speech of thanks before his frustration finally got the better of him and he blurted out: 'But the bloody bookmakers got all the money, my Lord!'

125. BEN'S AFFLECK-TION

Ben Affleck, the superstar actor, became the first high-profile A-list celebrity to win a major poker tournament when he landed the $356,400 first prize in the Commerce Casino California State Poker Championship on June 23, 2004.

Affleck had to see off a field of 90 players in the $10,000 buy-in event – among them another major movie name, Tobey Maguire, who went out on the first day of the three-day contest, but stayed around to watch the outcome.

Affleck left poker pro Stan Goldstein in second place as he used a pair of jacks to land the spoils.

Not all of Affleck's gambling exploits have furthered his reputation, and his stormy, on-off relationship with actress Jennifer Lopez often allegedly faltered due to his love of a wager.

In August 2001, it was reported by LA showbiz reporter Gary Morgan that 'film star Ben Affleck booked himself into a clinic after winning $50,000 at a boozy all-night gambling session'. Morgan also quoted 'Vegas columnist' Norm Clarke as saying 'he has a $150,000 betting limit at the Hard Rock Casino, but I'm told owner Peter Morton allows him some flexibility. He is allowed to bet double the house limit of $10,000 per play'.

Affleck, who improved his technique after being bought poker lessons from southern California pro Amir Vahedi, is reportedly a generous presence at the gambling tables – once, in August 2000, tipping employees a total of $140,000 after a successful session at the Hard Rock. In 2004, Victoria Coren wrote in the Observer of an occasion on which Affleck 'deliberately folded a winning hand for $13,000 because he felt his young opponent couldn't afford to lose'.

126. BET HE'S A WINNER

'I've never seen this kid before in my life. But I'll bet you £1,000 he's won more than a million playing online poker.'

Poker writer – and successful player – Victoria Coren was eavesdropping on a conversation between poker pros Ted Forrest, winner of $5.1m at the game, and Erick Lindgren, $5.6m, in September 2007.

They were discussing the teenage-looking male sitting alongside them.

Forrest accepted Lindgren's bet.

The 'kid' was asked the question – he 'nodded silently and performed a little hand mime. Yeah, he'd won a little more,' Coren told *Guardian* readers.

'Forrest removed a fresh, sealed packet of £50 notes from his trouser pocket and tossed it across the baize to Lindgren.'

127. HOW COREN CASHED IN

Victoria Coren, who told the story above, has had the experience of winning a life-transforming amount of money at the poker table.

She contested the 2007 European Poker Tour event in London, along with 500 others, expecting to be quickly eliminated.

But somehow the hours became days and the field shrank from 500 to 300, 200, 100 – 'until there were just two of us left'. The other was a 'macho' Lebanese-Australian player called Emad Tahtouh.

Coren, sister of TV celeb Giles, was level on chips and decided to 'use Emad's aggression against him'. She found herself with a straight – 'all I had to do was bet it weakly, and Tahtouh could not resist the temptation to shovel in his chips and try to bully this nervous girl out of the pot'.

The strategy worked, and three hands later she had clinched the victory.

'The money I could take or leave.'

She left it on deposit at the casino for a month – then put it in the building society: 'I haven't bought a flat, a car, new breasts or a ticket round the world. I bought quite a nice top from Selfridges, took a lovely week's holiday, gave some of it away.'

128. MILLION DOLLAR CHEAT

Having won $1.2 million, the first prize in the 2007 PokerStars.com World Championship of Online Poker event, the UK-based winner, a player identified as 'TheVOid', was disqualified.

PokerStars issued a statement: 'We have determined, based on the totality of evidence, the tournament winner 'TheVOid' was in breach of the PokerStars Terms of

Service.' The winner was rumoured to be a UK player who was playing on someone else's account.

129. TYSON'S KNOCK-OUT BET

Mike Tyson's manager revealed to him minutes before his 1988 heavyweight title showdown against Michael Spinks that he had staked both of their purses on a first-round knock-out win.

'So I went out and knocked him out in the first round,' said Tyson, whose purse was an estimated $20 million.

'Later,' continued a rueful Tyson, 'I found out he was joking.'

130. ARGY BARGY

Nowadays, bookmaker concessions are everywhere – money back if your selection is beaten a neck on a Sunday when there is an R in the month; money back if Thommo calls anyone 'Big Fella' before the off, etc, etc.

But there was a time when no bookie had ever dared refund cash to losing punters.

Then England played Argentina in the 1986 World Cup. Maradona punched the ball into the net and also scored one legitimate goal and England were officially beaten 2-1. Both William Hill's then MD, John Brown, a West Ham fan, and I, felt the nation's sense of injustice.

I suggested that we could demonstrate our depth of feeling by refunding stakes to all punters who had bet on the game being a draw – effectively disallowing the Maradona 'goal' ourselves. Brown gave the go-ahead.

It cost us tens, if not hundreds, of thousands – but earned us millions in goodwill and PR dividends.

131 BOOKIES' FREUDIAN SLIPS

When Clement – not then, Sir Clement – Freud won the 1973 parliamentary by-election in the Isle of Ely for the Liberal party, he was a 33-1 outsider.

Yet he fancied his chances strongly – and made Ladbrokes pay for writing him off, to the tune of 'four years' parliamentary salary before taking my seat on the green benches'.

'My reason for backing myself,' he explained, 'was that I was Clement Freud, anti-Conservative, with no affection for socialism, who cooked and did panel games and Jackanory and Panorama and a dog food commercial on television.'

He has since cleaned up in political betting on a number of occasions – in the 1979 general election he placed a Canadian on five Liberals to retain their seats – four won, of whom he was the shortest priced at 6-1. 'My winnings came to six figures.'

When Martin Bell, the campaigner in the white suit, stood against the less than universally popular Neil Hamilton, Freud bought Bell's majority – offered by a spread-betting firm at 200 – for £2 a vote, then watched contentedly as Bell romped home by 11,000.

132. PLEASURE SEEKING

Sir Clement's older brother, the artist Lucian Freud, also has an interesting relationship with gambling – a friend of his once told the Sunday Times that Lucian loved gambling, but 'he used to do it for the sheer pleasure of losing'.

Freud the elder was reportedly warned off British racecourses by the Jockey Club in 1983 over an unpaid debt of £19,000 and, according to the *Sunday Times*'s John Cornwell, 'betting only began to lose its savour, he has confessed, when he became so rich that losing no longer hurt'.

In June 2008 Freud told the Sunday Telegraph's deputy editor Richard Eden that 'he no longer gambles', adding that he had not spoken to brother Clement for more than 50 years!

133. SINGULAR WAGER

Thomas Hodgson and Samuel Whitehead struck a bet in 1806 at the Castle Yard, York, as to which of them 'should succeed in assuming the most singular character'.

The precise amount at stake is lost in the mists of time, but umpires were selected, whose duty it was to 'decide upon the comparative absurdity of the costumes in which the two men appeared'.

Hodgson duly arrived for the settlement of the bet – 'decorated with banknotes of various value on his coat and waistcoat, a row of five-guinea notes, and a long netted purse of gold round his hat, whilst a piece of paper bearing the words 'John Bull' was attached to his back.'

Whitehead, not to be outdone, turned up 'dressed like a woman on one side; one half of his face was painted, and he wore a silk stocking and a slipper on one leg. The other half of his face was blacked to resemble a Negro; on the corresponding side of his body he wore a gaudy, long tailed linen coat; and his leg was cased in half a pair of leather breeches, with a boot and spur'. So recorded writer John Ashton, adding: 'One would fancy that Whitehead must have presented the most singular appearance, by far.'

Hear, hear – but the umpires thought differently, awarding the stakes to Hodgson. Perhaps they had laid Whitehead on Ye Olde Bettefayre.

134. POXY BET

Two young 18th century bucks, members of the famous White's Club in London, were making their way from the club to the nearby brothel run by Mrs Comyns, according to chronicler of the club Henry Blythe, when they struck a bet as to whether one of them would contract venereal disease as a result of their evening's entertainment.

'One member wagered that he would, and then went to a great deal of trouble to discover a pox-ridden young harlot who could ensure that he won his bet.'

135. TIMELESS ADVICE

Racehorse owner and breeder Sir Hugo Cunliffe, whose Felstead won the 1928 Derby, was born in 1870, but he left behind him gambling advice that is as relevant today as it was in his day.

Sir Hugo's 'code of rules for the benefit of punters' included:

Use your eyes and not your ears.
If you lose, find out why.
Accept no tips.
Never back a horse that sweats.
Cut your losses – don't chase them.
Don't try to make a living out of betting – you can't.
Don't plunge on the last race.
Watch your fancy throughout the race.
Don't change your mind at the last moment.

136. NOT A LEG TO STAND ON

The *Racing Calendar* for 1763 reported that there was betting at Huntingdon Races when 'a Quarter of a Mile Match was run for 100Gs, between a Gentleman and a Grey Gelding with one Leg tied, and won by the former. The Horse's Leg untied in running.'

The matter of just what the horse's leg was tied to or with is not addressed.

137. PLACE GOING TO POT?

Enjoying a trip to Newmarket races on October 3, 2003, a member of a party from the Wheatsheaf pub in Bedfordshire decided to risk eight quid on a Placepot bet – which made him the only person to land the dividend of £63,284.30, a record that has stood until at least the day I wrote this!

138. FIRST FEMALE £1 MILLION POKER WINNER

Annette Obrestad from Norway became the first woman to win a World Series of Poker main event; the first woman to win a £1 million tournament, and at 18 years old the youngest person to win a World Series bracelet.

She did it at the 2007 WSOP Europe event held at the Empire Casino in London, and it made her the biggest female prize-money earner, overtaking Annie Duke.

Poker writer David Flusfeder also reported that 'she once played a 180-player, $4 sit-and-go internet tournament without ever looking at her own cards. She just played position and her reading of her opponents – and won the tournament.'

139. KING OF PUNTERS

If my family name were King, I'm not sure that I would be inclined to name my first-born son Arthur. Or, for that matter, Wayne. However, Arthur King may have launched a whole new gambling trend.

It's a little bit on the late side for Arthur, 91 at the time, to start anything new, I suppose, but he became the first person to place a bet with William Hill that he would die within six months.

Somewhat morbid, I grant you. But Arthur, from Exeter, was of sound mind and relatively sound body, and it was he who approached me about the bet.

What's more, he had a thoroughly practical reason for wanting to place it – he wanted to avoid the possibility of his surviving family becoming liable to inheritance tax of £3,000 should he shuffle off this mortal coil on or before 6 December 2005.

As I am no greater fan of the tax-man than former soldier Arthur, that struck me as an entirely understandable motive to wish to place a bet on one's own mortality.

It was something of a unique bet for a bookie to accept – after all, how often will I get the chance to say of a punter: 'Well, if he wins, that's HIS funeral'?

Anyway, we agreed on a price of 6/1 and Arthur was happy to hand over 500 quid. If he survived past 6 December everyone would be delighted that good old Arthur was still around. If he didn't, then everyone could give him a jolly good send-off, remember him fondly, then those who benefited from his will would discover that thanks to his foresight, that £3,000 which had become due to the Inland Revenue because of inheritance tax would taken care of by the good old bookies.

There's only one scenario which could confuse the matter, and I think I made sure that didn't arise by stipulating that the bet would be void in the event of suicide! You'll be relieved to hear that Arthur remained alive and was delighted to lose his £500!

140. GREATEST FOOTBALL LEAGUE GAMBLE

Bookmakers throughout the country were astonished at the huge gamble which was launched on an apparently insignificant League Two game towards the end of the 2007/8 season.

Bury were backed from 11/5 to 10/11 to win hundreds of thousands of pounds for punters by beating Accrington Stanley in the match, with some bookies even suspending the market as money poured in.

Word had circulated well before kick off. I was on holiday in Guernsey at the time and visited a tiny betting shop up a flight of stairs in the island's capital, St Peter Port – and even there was a notice scribbled up informing customers that no bets would be accepted on the match.

The Football League were informed in advance of the game that there were suspicious and unusual betting patterns surrounding the match. Officials set to officiate at the game on 3 May 2008 were reportedly changed, and media attention was focussed on the game and its outcome. There were rumours that Accrington players had been at a stag party shortly before the game. These were denied by club officials.

Bury duly obliged with a 2-0 win. Both clubs insisted the conduct of the game was above reproach. Accrington manager John Coleman said: 'We gave our very best for 90 minutes.'

Most bookmakers paid out on the result, albeit with reservations, some after initially withholding payments, while Betfred took the decision to refund stakes to punters, pending the outcome of an FA investigation.

'All of our clients who backed Bury have been issued with a receipt and if the investigation confirms that the game was above board then they will eventually be paid out.'

The Association of British Bookmakers published a statement: 'ABB advises members to make their own commercial decisions based on their specific circumstances and published rules but advises that payment of winnings on the game may continue to be withheld until the outcome of this investigation is known.

'In the meantime ABB sees no reason to withhold the return of stakes on bets placed on Bury to customers and recommends that when making such payments, members should ask customers to supply sufficient information to ensure that any subsequent settlement of outstanding bets can properly be made in the future.'

141. NUT SO SILLY

The 'Squirrel' gambling syndicate won £3m by betting on the Scoop6 bet in a three week period in October and November 2007.

Run by Richard Brocklebank, from Hyde near Manchester, the syndicate won a record £1.5m on the bet in October 2007 and then collected a further £425,000 in early November, collecting an additional £1m bonus on the bet at Doncaster a week later.

The syndicate boasted 30 members and acquired their nickname in 1994 when Brocklebank, eager to make contact with other Scoop6 winning ticket holders hoping to win the bet's bonus, dressed in a squirrel suit at Goodwood racecourse.

142. YOU BET BOOKIES ARE COURTING CONTROVERSY

Bookmakers usually fight shy of accepting bets on court cases for fear of being ruled in contempt of court, or of being accused of influencing the opinions of jurors. But there have been high profile cases where they have taken a chance and opened a book, regardless.

One of these occasions was in June 2005 when online company Gamebookers began betting on whether pop star Michael Jackson would be found guilty of child sex abuse charges – going 1/2 that he would; 6/4 that he would not. Spokesman, Luke Brill, said: 'We thought long and hard about whether to do this, but, after consulting our lawyers, decided to go ahead.' They also offered odds about the length of his sentence if found guilty, which he wasn't.

Several years previously, Sporting Index had been criticised when they started to quote odds about the verdict in the infamous O J Simpson murder trial. It was reported at the time that one of the jurors on the case was thrown off the panel for gambling on the outcome.

143. GAMBLING THIEVES' FATAL ERROR

The greatest gambling-related criminal disaster may have occurred when two Chinese thieves gassed themselves to death with cyanide which they had brought along to overpower their victims, whilst carrying out a raid on a gambling den in the city of Ruichang in June 2005.

The survivors of the five strong gang were arrested and, in May 2006, sentenced to death by a court in Jiujiang.

144. CEE WHIZZ

Top Cees was one of a string of big-race gambles to come off in the 1999 Cesarewitch, but he will always be remembered more for his 1995 Chester Cup triumph ,which landed some huge bets for trainer Lynda Ramsden, and her owner husband, Jack.

The win led to a High Court against *The Sporting Life*, which, it was claimed, had libelled them in an article about the horse's previous down-the-field run, prior to the Chester Cup win. The plaintiffs, including Top Cees' jockey, Kieren Fallon, emerged triumphant, having been cleared of any wrong-doings in the horse's prep-race at Newmarket. Libel damages of £195,000 were awarded against the Life.

145. FOR FOGG'S SAKE

Josh Fogg, pitcher for top US baseball side the Cincinnati Reds, struck a bet with teammate Ken Griffey jnr. The details of the bet are unclear, but the stake was $1,500. Griffey was somewhat miffed about losing, but realised he had to settle the debt.

So, reported website dailycamera.com in May 2008, he came up with a novel idea, which resulted in Fogg opening his locker one morning – to find in there 60 boxes, each weighing one stone, containing in each $25 in one-cent coins.

The Griffey settlement found favour with Daily Mirror betting columnist Derek McGovern, who commented: 'I love that kind of gesture – settling a debt while raising two fingers to the winner. The only thing better is not settling a debt.'

146. CHINA WHITE

White House kitchen staff were dismayed when President Warren G Harding, in office from 1921-23, gambled away a set of their finest, priceless china, during a poker game.

147. HOUSE THAT?

Chris Boyd sold his house in Wycombe for £147,000 in 1994, then took the cash to Las Vegas and staked it all on the roulette wheel coming up red. It did, and he doubled his money, before coming straight home.

148. QUEEN VICTORIA WAS AMUSED

Queen Victoria awarded the game of poker an unexpected seal of approval in 1871 (some sources say 1872) when it became obvious that she was, indeed, amused by the game.

General Robert Cumming Schenk (born 1809) had been appointed as US Envoy to England by his president, U S Grant. Schenk was an inveterate poker player, and when Her Majesty invited the president's representative to her summer estate in Somerset, Schenk decided to lighten the atmosphere by suggesting a game of poker to some of the assembled male guests.

The game was under way when in walked Queen Victoria, who insisted on sitting in on the game, despite her complete ignorance of its rules.

Schenk, as it was later reported, 'under strict orders from President Grant to create no incidents', duly agreed to teach his royal hostess how to play.

'The amount is unrecorded,' says an account of the occasion, 'but Victoria must have been a healthy winner, because she announced immediately after the game that she was delighted with it.'

She was so delighted that she requested Schenk to supply her with a written set of rules. Schenk complied and in so doing sparked the very kind of incident Grant had feared.

Delegations descended on the White House, demanding his recall and letters were written to newspaper editors in the strongest possible terms condemning him – he was even burned in effigy.

What could be responsible for such outrage? Was it because he was encouraging the monarch and, by implication, her subjects, to gamble? Partly, maybe, and also partly because poker was very much a male game in those days, not considered suitable for ladies, particularly ladies of breeding. But the real cause of the uproar was a phrase that Schenk had included in the written rules he had supplied to the Queen and which had been printed for all to see in his original pamphlet of 1875, Draw Poker.

'It is a great object to mystify your adversaries up to the call, when hands must be shown. To this end, it is good practice to chaff (or talk nonsense), with a view to misleading your opponents as to the value of your hand.'

Good grief! The fellow was positively encouraging and endorsing bluffing or, as it was then known in the States, the art of 'coffee house'. Poker purists felt this was tantamount to cheating, and an immoral practice.

Schenk survived the storm and remained as envoy for several more years. Although Queen Victoria did not become a professional player her interest in the game meant that it became very much in vogue in court circles and if she happened to play, she always had at least Queen high to gamble on!

Schenk's pamphlet was expanded into book form and was privately printed and published in 1880 – the year of his death.

✴ Royal interest in poker was rekindled in 2005 when England rugby union player Mike Tindall revealed that he was trying to interest his girlfriend, Princess Anne's daughter Zara Phillips, in the game. 'She has played it a couple of times online,' he revealed.

149. WINNING STREAK

Michael O'Brien, 26, shed his clothes and streaked across the Twickenham pitch as England were playing France in an April 1974 international.

The Australian-born accountant was doing it to win a £10 bet – and under the terms of the wager he needed to reach the opposite touchline fence.

As O'Brien reached his target, he was stopped in his tracks by Police Constable Perry. He was about to arrest O'Brien, when O'Brien told him about the wager. The understanding copper permitted O'Brien to touch the fence – and then nicked him!

A famous photograph of the bearded O'Brien, with his modesty being shielded by a policeman's helmet, was published all over the world.

150. WRITTEN IN THE STARS

Belief that astrology can predict winners is not only as modern as Mystic Meg, but dates back at least as far as 1669.

In a letter dated March 22 of that year, King Charles II told his sister, Henrietta, about his recent trip to the races. 'I came from Newmarket the day before yesterday, where we had as fine weather as we could wish, which added much both to the horse matches as well as to hunting.'

Charles explained that with him at Newmarket was the renowned astrologer to Louis XIV of France, L'Abbe Pregnani – 'he lost his money upon confidence that the stars could tell which horse could win, for he had the ill luck to foretell three times wrong together, and James [Duke of York, later to be King James II] believed him so much as he lost his money upon the same score'.

151. TELEGRAM SCAM

At the turn of the 19th/20th century, bookmakers would accept bets by telegram, provided that they were date-stamped before the 'off' time of the race.

Sporting newspaper of the day, *The Winning Post*, described how a coup was pulled off by trainer Captain Percy Bewicke and stockbroker G A Prentice, with a two-year-old, Stratton, in a race at Nottingham.

'A little village was found. A small shop was discovered in it, which had added to its everyday affairs that of a telegraph office. At a given moment, a huge bundle of telegrams were handed in, piled on top of one another, to back Stratton, addressed to various bookmakers scattered all over England. Well, how plain it is! One female telegraphic operator, one instrument, and sheaves of wires! Result? Stratton won at 10-1. The bookmakers were congratulating themselves at not laying the winner, when the wires began to come in, and they continued to pour in till nightfall.'

This scheme was small beer compared with that operated by a gang of punters who went to the lengths of purchasing a post office of their own, and then setting their own times into the telegraph machine – a real licence to print money.

152. JULES' FORECAST

The face of BBC TV racing for years, Julian Wilson's 'most spectacular win' came in 1970 when his great friend, Nigel Angus, was training a 'very moderate and not very genuine' three-year-old called Arco Star.

It had run five times, showing little, and was the forecast 25-1 outsider of eight in a 1m5f handicap at Hamilton. Angus told him the horse had worked well: 'I'm not saying that he will win but I'm sure that he'll run a great deal better than he has so far.'

Wilson wondered how best to profit from this information, and opted 'to place a £5 dual forecast with the field'.

The dual forecast required the punter to name first and second in either order.

Ridden by Tony Ives, Arco Star 'ran the race of his life to finish second' beaten by 5-1 shot Moor Court.

Wilson's bet had come off. He waited nervously for the returned dividend, and rang the Tote to find out: 'That was £94 14/-, sir.'

And that dividend was to a 4/- (20p) unit.

'The winning entry in the Wilson ledger was £2,332 10/-,' he recalled in May 2008. 'To convert to today's currency you should multiply that figure by about ten.'

Arco Star never did win a race.

153. KIWI KAPERS

Gamblers at the Waikato greyhound track near Wellington in New Zealand could not believe their eyes and ears at a meeting in January 1993 when, even after the races had been run, the tote betting system at the track continued to accept wagers with the results already known.

This happened on two races and in each instance a systems malfunction meant that bets on the race just over were being accepted for a full three minutes.

Racegoers rushed to get their after-time wagers on, and on one of the races, 36 bets were laid on the tricast, which meant a payout of some £3,000.

But the most incredible statistic associated with this incident was that, despite just having witnessed the races take place in front of their eyes, some punters were either extremely honest or extremely stupid – as 153 bets were placed on dogs who had already LOST!

In April 1999 punters at Newbury were able to back Thirsk winner Diamond Promise on the Tote – even though the 15-8 shot had already won. A systems malfunction on staff computers meant that Tote staff were being told that the race was not yet off and to continue accepting bets, even though the result was already showing on TV screens.

The Tote admitted to paying out almost £2,000 from 25 bets as a result.

154. STU-PID BOY

Stu Ungar dropped out of school on New York's Lower East Side in 1967, aged just 14 – to become a professional gambler.

He was still a professional gambler – and a three-time world poker champion – when he was found dead aged 45 on November 22, 1998 in an Oasis Motel room on the Las Vegas Strip.

Within weeks of turning pro in his early teens, Ungar had won $10,000 playing gin rummy – only to blow the stash at the Aqueduct racetrack.

He had become a much-respected gin rummy pro before, fleeing a bookie to whom he owed a substantial sum, he arrived in Las Vegas in 1978 and began to take a serious interest in poker.

His baby-faced appearance rapidly earned him the nickname of 'The Kid'. He was rarely to be seen without his trademark round, blue-tinted glasses. He became a cocaine addict.

Having won the world championship at Binion's Horseshoe Casino for the first time in 1980, aged 26, becoming the youngest winner, he repeated the feat the very next year. He won the Super Bowl of Poker three times, along with many other major tournaments. But in 1997 he had to be bankrolled to enter the world championship again – but he won again.

By now, many rated him the greatest poker player ever and this triumph, which followed a spell in the wilderness, prompted him to pledge: 'I decided to wake up. No-one has ever beaten me playing cards. I have only beaten myself.'

But he squandered his $1 million winning purse within two months and started to fail to turn up to tournaments. He was reportedly back on drugs.

Ungar's biographer, Mike Sexton, said of him: 'He had a genius IQ and a photographic memory. His talent at card games was truly incredible. In No Limit Hold 'Em he was relentless. Describing how Ungar played No Limit poker is like talking about someone who is a fearless warrior with a combination of the artistry of Mozart, the moves of Michael Jordan and the focus of Tiger Woods.'

Some of Ungar's success could be attributed to his single-mindedness at the table – 'Away from the table I'm really not that bad a guy. But when the cards are dealt I just want to destroy people.'

That single-mindedness came at a cost. He was unworldly: 'He did not understand much about anything except poker,' said casino owner Bob Stupack. 'Stu would not know how to pay an electricity bill. I don't even know if he had a driver's licence.'

Licence or no, he did once own a car that was wrecked when he failed to top it up with oil. 'Why the hell didn't they tell me you had to put oil in the car?' he asked plaintively.

He was as bad a golfer as driver – and once lost $80,000 on his way to the first tee, on the putting green. 'I would estimate that Ungar lost several million dollars playing golf,' said Sexton.

Stupak arranged a deal to bankroll Ungar for the 1998 world championship. He gave him some spending money, which Ungar took before checking in at the Oasis Motel. Two days later he was dead – a mixture of narcotics and painkillers reportedly triggered the heart condition that killed him. There was $800 in his pocket – apparently all the money he owned in the world.

Daughter Stefanie poignantly recalled Ungar refusing an invitation to the White House. 'What would I talk to the president about? We have nothing in common,' he told her.

155. DEAD LOSS

Donald McLeod made what was literally a fatal mistake when, in 1906, he turned up and bet at Flemington, in Australia, without the necessary wherewithal to meet his liabilities when a good thing obliged. Attempting to 'do a runner' without paying up, he was caught, beaten up, and killed by a pack of enraged punters.

156. MARCHING ALONG

The Earl of March, aka William Douglas, 4th Duke of Queensbury, wrote his name into gambling history on August 29, 1750 at 7am.

Born some 25 years earlier in Peebles, Scotland, he was about to endeavour to win a 1,000-guinea wager that it was possible to cover 19 miles in one hour in a four-wheeled carriage pulled by four mounted horses.

Having claimed that this hitherto unthinkable – thanks to the state of the roads and weight of carriages – feat could be achieved, Count Taaffe and Andrew Sprowles esq, had duly stumped up the stake money to take him on.

March commissioned Wrights of Long Acre to build him a streamlined carriage – little more than a seat strung on leather straps. He trained racehorses – three of them winners – to pull the contraption, to be piloted by his groom.

A course was created at Newmarket Heath and a crowd gathered to watch.

The carriage required just 53 minutes, 27 seconds to win the bet.

March's next high-profile wager was to 'cause a letter to be conveyed 50 miles in an hour'.

Impossible, scoffed fellow gamblers, and one put up a hefty stake against him.

Once again, showing himself to be an early master of what are now known as 'proposition' bets, March had a cunning plan up his – or others' – sleeves.

The nobleman hired 20 expert cricketers, famed for their skill in throwing and catching.

He put the letter inside a cricket ball and on the appointed day the players stood in a circle and hurled the ball one to another, swiftly covering the specified distance, well inside the 60-minute limit.

Now March cashed in again by backing his London coachbuilder to outpace a renowned professional runner while rolling a coach wheel alongside him.

March had a track of planks laid down for his man to run the wheel on – and collected again.

A 500-guinea, life or death bet March made with a certain Mr Pigot – probably no relation to Lester – ended up in court, after March nominated Sir William Codrington, and Mr Pigot selected his father. The winner to be the one whose nomination lived longer. It transpired that, unbeknown to both gamblers, Pigot the elder had expired on the very morning on which the wager was struck.

Pigot jnr claimed this rendered the bet void – March asserted that he was the winner.

March brought an action in the King's Bench for the stake money – and the jury duly found in his favour.

In 1809, by which time he was a venerable 83-year-old, March struck perhaps the oddest bet of his life – 500 pounds that he would 'die at a certain hour on a certain actual Saturday'.

He was relieved to lose – and paid up happily.

He died on December 23, 1810, a week after his 85th birthday.

157. ONLY KIDDING?

It was on the front page of the *Sunday Telegraph* in May 2004, so it must be true, mustn't it?

'A British father who has sold his 15-year-old daughter for £15,000 to pay off his gambling debts is being investigated by police.'

Bafflingly, the story added: 'Police have declined to comment on the case, although it is understood that they have so far been unable to discover any offence.'

The story contained echoes of a more ancient tale from 1735, which was detailed in an 1824 collection of Local Records of Remarkable Events by John Sykes of Newcastle in which he noted: 'A child of James and Elizabeth of Chester le Street, was played for at cards, at the sign of The Salmon, one game, four shillings against the child, by Henry and John Trotter, Robert Thomson and Thomas Ellison, which was won by the latter and delivered to them accordingly.'

158. BOWLESED OVER BY ELTON

In 2006 former footballer and inveterate gambler Stan Bowles, of whom it was said 'if only he could pass a betting shop like he could pass a ball', commented that if he had been in his prime during today's high-earning era instead of his 1970s heyday, 'I'd be pretty disappointed if I hadn't lost somewhere in the region of £10 million'.

However, he added: 'What I would find impossible to resist today would be the temptation to wager on any game I was involved in … I'd be buying or selling on spread betting, whether it be bookings or corners.'

Bowles will bet on almost any opportunity that presents itself, but is still incredulous at losing what he regarded as a certainty when he was in a pub watching Princess Diana's funeral.

As Elton John sang *Candle In The Wind*, Bowles said to a pal: 'I bet you an even £50 that he'll cry during the funeral.'

'In my mind I was getting even money about a 1-8 shot. There was just no way Elton wouldn't well up, break down and cry. I couldn't believe my eyes, after flawlessly executing the song, Elton sat on his stool as if he was waiting for an order of fries to arrive. I mean, he almost looked happy.'

159. HAPPENIS?

A 42-year-old Romanian man stuck a metal ring on his penis after losing a bet in a tavern, but was unable to get it off, reported the Ananova news website on September 7, 2004.

'Although he was in agony, he waited two days before coming to hospital because he was embarrassed,' said Dr Stelian Belu of Pitesi Hospital. 'The blood supply had been cut off for too long and we told him we would have to cut it off so that necrosis didn't spread to the rest of his body.'

The man fled, leaving doctors concerned he would die without urgent treatment.

160 REMIND YOU OF ANYTHING?

In 1891 jockey Monk Overton became the first US rider ever to win all six of his races on a single day's card, in the process almost bankrupting bookies at the Chicago course where he achieved the feat – 'for some, it was a near-death experience' wrote US racing historian Ed Hotaling, writing about the occasion – 'some lost as much as $6000, a pile in those days – a bookie nicknamed The Ghost took on the appearance of one as his and other firms lost a 'combined, jaw-dropping $120,000.'

161. ANOTHER DEAD CERT

A gentleman had what seemed a particularly unusual bet with me during early 2006.

He received odds of 1000/1 to his tenner that an authenticated case of someone being brought back to life having been medically dead for 24 hours or longer would be officially confirmed within the next couple of years.

Within a week he was back on the phone demanding to be paid out. But I could not recall having heard of a story of any such miracle resuscitation – albeit Easter was not long gone. Surely, I asked, the media might have been interested in such a story and given it extensive coverage. He was convinced he had indeed heard the story being reported – at about midnight on a radio station.

Anyway, we eventually tracked down the story but sadly had to decline his suggestion that a Japanese soldier who had hidden away on some obscure island over half a century ago awaiting the end of the War and had just turned up again constituted conclusive proof that someone who had once been dead was now alive.

162. THERE'S GRATITUDE FOR YOU

Believe me, this is true. One of our betting shop managers was feeling charitable and decided to reward a regular punter who was about to celebrate his 90th birthday,with a free £90 bet.

He duly offered this nice present to the punter,who replied, 'I only ever bet in fivers – can I have the other £85 in cash?'

163. CONTRASTING FORTUNES

A few weeks before the 2005 Champions League Final I spotted a bet we had laid back in the previous December. A customer had staked £500 on Liverpool to win the tournament at 80/1.

Mm. A nice potential payout of £40,000. I wondered whether the chap who had placed the bet fancied talking about it.

His account details had no telephone number with them so I dropped him a line to see whether he'd be agreeable to a little media attention on his unlikely long-shot.

He rang me, we chatted and I asked him when – because by now Liverpool were in the Final – he would be hedging his bet with a few grand on AC Milan.

He assured me he was going to do no such thing. As a loyal Liverpool fan who had followed them to European Cup glory in the past he had no intention of diluting his would-be winnings. It was all or nothing.

I thought of David Bushell, a Preston solicitor, at half time of that Champions League decider, when they were 3-0 down. 'Bet he wishes he'd hedged now' I observed to my son, explaining the bet.

At the time I was doing this there was a Manchester United fan - Alan Fairhurst

– sitting at home in, unusually enough for United fans, Manchester, deciding that he would rub Liverpool's plight in well and truly by having a bet on AC Milan. Even though Milan were, at that time, 1/100 to win the game in 90 minutes play, he was going to shell out ten grand – £10,000 – just for the pleasure of being able to say he had backed them to lose, and to pick up a risk free hundred quid in the process.

You'd have thought that a United fan might have thought back to his own team's Champions League triumph a few seasons earlier when they overturned the odds with minutes to go, or of the day when they trailed Spurs by 3-0 yet came back to beat them 5-3.

My own thoughts turned briefly to the long suppressed memory of a Luton Town match where we were three up against Wrexham, only to lose 4-3.

You know the rest, of course, after Liverpool's dramatic comeback to win, Bushell collected his £40,000, minus no hedging money at all, returned to his home to find the media camped outside – well, I might have mentioned it to one or two members of the Fourth Estate in passing – and promptly took himself off to the South of France for a few days celebration.

Our Mancunian – rather like the Norwegian who had the same bet for £10,167 (I wonder if he could a-fjord it!) – was left with the problem of how to explain to his mates that he'd managed to do ten thousand quid in some style, courtesy of the hated Anfield Reds.

164. WOULDN'T GIVE TUPPENCE FOR HIS CHANCES

The eccentric Dorothy Paget – of whom more in story five – paid a record 6,600gns at the 1931 yearling sales.

As a two-year-old the colt by Derby winner Spion Kop out of Waffles, dam of 2,000 Guineas and Derby winner Manna, ran unplaced five times – after which Ms P named him, somewhat ironically, Tuppence.

However, despite his apparent lack of ability, he was aimed at the 1933 Derby, but on the day of the race was an unconsidered 100-1 shot with most bookies – even longer odds with some.

On Derby day, an extraordinary and inexplicable gamble began as cash flowed on to Tuppence, who had become what is today known patronisingly as 'the housewives' choice', a horse picked on by the occasional gamblers, often just because they like the name.

Tuppence suddenly frightened the life out of bookies – 'there has never within memory been any development in the final stage of the Derby betting to compare with this business,' wrote racing writer of the day Eric Rickman.

Incredibly, Tuppence was backed with hundreds of thousands of pounds, if not millions, down to 10-1 fourth favourite – but once the race started, he ran like the 100-1 shot he deserved to have been!

Tuppence finished last but five in the field of 24.

Later that season he won for the only time – well, half won – when dead-heating at Hamilton, winning his proud owner all of £53 as a result.

He was sent over hurdles, winning twice and becoming involved in a Whit Monday 1934 incident at Huntingdon in which a man died after Tuppence ran into a group of racegoers, knocking one of them down.

165. MY GREATEST BETTING LAUGH

It really was the funniest experience I have had on a racecourse – and I've had a few of those over the years.

It was at Epsom in 2006. We were in a box with a collection of people, all of whom could loosely be described as well connected media types. One of them is a veritable doyen of his trade who, over the years, has mingled with the greatest names in sport and built up an absolute encyclopaedia of contacts. So, when he sat down in the box for lunch and happened to mention that a certain high profile trainer had suggested that he should give him a call to find out whether he had any fancied runners that afternoon, we all waited expectantly.

The phone call was duly made, and the news imparted that although the handler was being represented in several of the races that afternoon, he believed his best hope of success would come in the last race.

Everyone around the table and in the box made a mental note of the name of the beast and carried on enjoying what was a very pleasant afternoon in interesting company.

As the card continued I became too busy mingling to bother about betting and it was with something of a start that I realised there was only one race remaining. So I quickly slipped away to invest a very small proportion of the Sharpe family fortunes on the previously advised nag, noticing most of my box companions making the same journey for the identical purpose.

Meanwhile, the bringer of the glad tidings was deep in conversation with a fellow guest. He had clearly taken the precaution of getting on early.

The horses were going down for the last race and there was a pleasurable anticipation in the air as my box companions discussed how much they stood to win if the hotly tipped runner, a 6/1 shot, obliged. The stalls crashed open, the runners charged out and all eyes turned to watch – including those of our 'tipster' who had a panic-stricken look in his eyes. 'Are they off? Surely not yet. I haven't got my bet on.' A note of despair had crept in to the normally strident, flawless voice. They were indeed off. He had indeed forgotten to put his bet on.

There was a feeling of inevitability as the tipped horse made its way confidently through the field to run out a comfortable winner, going away, to the joy of almost everyone in the box.

Our benefactor stomped off from the balcony to find a drink with which to drown his sorrows whilst all around him people high-fived and thanked him. He was distraught, gutted, choked, peed off – and about a grand worse off than he would have been had he taken his own tip. It was hilarious.

166. THE GREAT MOROCCAN TOTE RIP-OFF

It took some finding, but I was determined to do it – discover a 2007 Derby which Frankie Dettori wouldn't win.

So in mid June of that year, following the Dettori dominance of the English, French and Italian Derbies, I headed for Morocco and the Souissi racecourse where the Derby was the fifth event on an eight race turf card. It attracted ten runners to do battle for the first place prize money of 22,000 dirham – approximately fifteen hundred quid. Unlike the opening race on the programme, which was finished before it actually started – having been down to start at 1pm, but actually going off early and finishing at 12.59; the Derby did go off at its proper time. Like all the other races, there was no commentary whatsoever, which made it a bit tricky to work out what was going on and demonstrated just what a breakthrough it must have been when the first commentaries were introduced to British racing.

Anyway, my optimism was justified and Frankie signally failed to ride the winner. The fact that he wasn't even booked to ride any of the horses and was probably thousands of miles away from the racecourse, may have had something to do with this dismal failure by the diminutive Italian. But the best betting experience of my first exposure to Moroccan racing was yet to happen.

I decided not to play the last race of the day. Everyone else got very excited about the fact that the favourite in the final event was owned by a member of the Moroccan Royal Family – descended directly from Allah, they are, if I understood the explanation of the guide who showed us around the city of Rabat, correctly. After all, he did invite all 26 of us into his house which boasted, he declared proudly, 'a very big toilet.'

So, concluded everyone else, the Royal runner must be a certainty. My misgiving was based on the fact that if every horse with a Royal owner were to win every race they contested, even the most slow-on-the-uptake Moroccan punter might soon figure that something was amiss in the conduct of the sport.

The Royal horse, Rubiszo, won the race.

Much celebrating and hilarity abounded, reduced only a fraction by the stern admonition of our own private Tote operator that he would not be able to pay out on the last for a few minutes. This was the same Tote operator who had introduced clients to the bizarre rule that only bets placed in multiples of six dirhams would be acceptable. So that instead of, for example, one hundred dirhams, he would insist that only 96 be staked. And would then discover that, frustratingly, he didn't have the four dirhams change immediately to hand. Odd, huh?

The few minutes dragged on for a few minutes more, then Tote man gestured the punters over. One or two of them had a strange expression on their face as they returned to our table. Well, how much did you win, then? I asked. 'Er, apparently, nothing. He's given me my money back.'

The trickle of punters treated this way became a stream. Noone had been given any winnings. The race had been voided, went one rumour. The winner was so heavily backed that noone had bet against it so the win dividend was the stake money returned, went another.

That rumour was scuppered by the undeniable proof that many people had indeed bet against the Royal runner. And that there appeared to be no punter riot going on amongst the slightly, shall we say, more excitable element of the crowd.

Whatever the explanation, Tote man had now become 'former Tote man'. He'd disappeared. Just about at the same time as my companions had realised that if everyone backing the winner was only getting their money back and/or the race was void, anyone backing a loser must also be refunded.

But, our coach was waiting, Tote man had done a runner and suddenly noone else on the racecourse seemed to be able to speak English, or understand what they were being asked. And most people had only gambled a hundred or so dirhams which they were not going to be allowed to take out of the country with them, anyway.

I know what I reckon was going on, but I do not wish single-handedly to end the apparently flourishing diplomatic relationship between Morocco and England by explaining it in detail.

So if I ever do go back there I shall again avoid betting on the last race on the card.

167. ANOTHER PLACE WHERE WINNERS ARE HARD TO COME BY

Peter Haynes, the Grand National starter, who took so much stick for his 2007 performance in getting the runners underway might have wished he could go somewhere for a quieter life. Well, I would suggest he might find a more tranquil reaction to his exploits on the beautiful island of Jersey, whose racecourse, Les Landes, I visited not long after that National.

On the racecard the Starter was named as Mr T Germaine. So presumably it was he who oversaw the start for the Bloodstock Advisory Services Handicap, the initials from which spell 'BASH' which is what Mr Germaine promptly did to those punters who had supported the well fancied Treat Me Wild – whose name was also very appropriate – in this 5f 110 yard sprint.

Without starting stalls to set out from, Mr Germaine had the runners wandering around, until deciding they were ready, whereupon one runner got a flying start while poor old Treat Me Wild, partnered by experienced Vince Slattery, was left flat-footed and without the ghost of a chance as the runners headed off. Even the next day's *Jersey Post* commented that: 'As is often the case in races over the minimum distance, the start left a lot to be desired.'

The next race was the big race of the day. Former Royal Ascot winner, Persian Majesty, now seven and in less exalted company, was backed to a shade of odds-on for the Jersey Guineas – a handicap run over 1m 100yards, for three year olds and upwards.

Favourite backers knew their fate the moment Mr Germaine sent the 12 strong field off – minus Persian Majesty, who was left standing on the spot, making no effort to take part whatsoever, but having come under orders.

I thought all this was rather amusing as I hadn't backed either horse, unlike plenty of those around me. But I was laughing on the other side of my face after the fourth race, the Geoffrey Edwards Memorial Handicap over one and a half miles, in which I and all the racegoers around me believed they had seen Khuzdar, which I was on, narrowly get the better of last year's winner, Off Minor.

So you can imagine the language when Off Minor was declared the winner. My pals who had backed him were so startled at the result that they doubted whether the bookies would pay them out. They did. I went off in search of a copy of the photo-finish to verify with my own eyes that the result was right. There didn't appear to be one. I understand that such sophisticated treatment was not currently available at the course.

The only thing which finally calmed me down was the announcement that one of the horses in another race was carrying a stone overweight. My dear friend Babs Bishop wandered over to the paddock to look at the runners, then came back and told us: 'That horse doesn't LOOK like it's a stone overweight.'

168. BINGO, GO, GO ...

Ninety three year old Lily English claimed she had gambled on more games of bingo than anyone before when, in June 2008, she clocked up her 60,000th game in Andover, Hants.

169. A GLOVELY 20/1 WINNER

Derek McGovern, the *Daily Mirror*'s 'Betting Guru' once found a very handy 20/1 winner: 'In 2007 England travelled to Russia for a crucial Euro 2008 qualifier. They flew in on the Monday (for a Wednesday game) and Moscow was covered in snow. Sky Bet, clearly believing that the temperatures would be freezing on match night, offered 20-1 for no England outfield players to be wearing gloves.

'Now this would have been a great bet even if temperatures were below freezing. The England players were being crucified by fans in the build-up to the match and we all know what the average English fan thinks of players who wear gloves. Imagine losing while wearing gloves – you would never be forgiven. More importantly, Sky Bet had not checked the weather forecast.

'An unseasonable mild spell was predicted for Moscow, starting on the day of the match, and by kick-off time, the temperatures were as mild in Moscow as they were in Market Rasen. 'No outfield players wore gloves.'

170. RONALD MACDONALD THE SPONGER

The 1901 Boston – scene of the Tea Party – Marathon was one of the hottest betting races ever run. The previous year's winner, James Caffery, down from Canada, was even-money favourite to see off the local challenge of the 1898 victor, Boston's own Ronald J MacDonald, believed to be back to his best and backed down to 2-1 second favourite.

Huge crowds turned out and according to contemporary reports 'thousands of dollars changed hands on bets. A public used to betting on boxing and horseracing practised the same sort of support for marathon runners'.

Canadians had flooded to Boston to support their man not only to win, but to lower the 2hrs 32min record time.

Caffery made his big effort a few miles from home – with MacDonald launching a bid to reel him in. As the latter ran he was handed a sponge by a spectator with which to mop his brow, but shortly after he appeared distressed and slowed to a stop, stricken with cramps.

His medic, Dr Thompson, immediately diagnosed chloroform poisoning, blaming the sponge. MacDonald had been nobbled.

However, MacDonald's coach accused the doc of prescribing pills that had crocked the runner, and of covering up by blaming the sponge.

Then a rumour began that MacDonald had backed Caffery and thrown the race – blaming the sponge.

But Caffery wasn't worried – he'd gone on to smash the record down to 2hr 29min 23sec and, reported the Boston Herald, 'those who came south to bet on Caffery returned to Canada happy and richer'.

171. HEAVY WAGER LADE

Sir John Lade accepted a 'trifling wager' in October 1795. To win the bet, Lade, described in contemporary reports as 'diminutive', had to carry a weighty local, Lord Cholmondeley, on his back from Brighton Pavilion to a well-known landmark.

The odds were believed to be heavily against Lade as a crowd gathered to watch, and Cholmondeley declared himself ready to be transported, whereupon, reported The Times, Lade 'desired him to strip', pointing out that 'I engaged to carry you, but not an inch of clothes'.

Cholmondeley declined to appear naked, and Lade won the wager.

172. GAMBLING GHOST?

Troy Taylor, author and founder of the American Ghost Society, may well have tracked down a very rare and elusive phenomenon – the poker ghost.

In autumn 1996, Troy was called in to investigate when strange and unaccountable noises and the occasional inexplicable sighting were reported at premises that had once operated as an illegal gambling house during the days of prohibition in Decatur, Illinois.

Troy took a look around the third floor where the unaccountable events had been witnessed and 'noticed there was a sharp chill to the air – it was odd that on the third floor of an old building on a very warm afternoon it would be cooler than the lower floors'.

Troy recalled: 'I had been inside one of the rooms and had left for a few minutes. I returned a short time later and discovered two vintage playing cards had mysteriously appeared on the floor. They had not been there previously, but I still could have written the whole thing off to coincidence, if not for the fact that I discovered them in the same corner of the room where I had felt the 'presence''. On an earlier visit he had felt a 'chilling, tingling sensation' only to learn that it had been the location of a man's death in the 1930s.

'It made me wonder, if a man had really been killed in that corner, just what cards had he been holding in his hand? I remain convinced that this location is truly haunted.'

All the indications in this case are that the cards he found were being used in a game of poker, so I contacted Taylor to ask whether he had discovered any additional details.

Troy, whose activities are chronicled at www.prairieghosts.com, told me: 'Thanks for your message, and the two cards that I found were a jack of spades and an eight of hearts. I don't know if he was playing poker or not but it seemed a good bet, based on the reported use of the rooms. The only other poker-related ghost story that I know of would be the famous story of Wild Bill Hickok, who was shot in the back while playing cards. His ghost is still reported to be haunting the saloon where he was murdered.

173. CHEEK OF THE DEVIL

The greatest cheek ever shown by a gambler must have emanated from the man who called me on Friday, June 27, 2008 – genuinely asking what price I could lay him about Robert Mugabe winning the controversial, uncontested elections in Zimbabwe.

174. BY GEORGE

Ricky George has hit the headlines in two sports – first, when he scored a spectacular extra-time winner for minnows Hereford against giants Newcastle in the 1972 FA Cup third-round game.

Then, a quarter of a century later, he returned to the front pages when the horse he co-owned, Earth Summit, won the Grand National, landing him a string of hefty bets in the process – 'I started backing him just before the Welsh Grand National which he won. The first bet was £100 each-way at 25-1, and I followed up with £1,000 each-way at 16-1. Then, on the day, I had £1,000 to win at 9-1 and another £500 at the same price on the rails.'

175. EX-CELLENT BET

Multi-millionaire racehorse owner and punter Robert Sangster attended the 1996 Melbourne Cup with Andrew Peacock, Australia's ambassador to the USA.

Both had a well-fancied runner in the opening race and they had struck a bet involving no cash but whose outcome was of vital interest to both of them.

The pair had both been married at one time to the same Susan (later Lady Renouf, born Susan Rossiter) and, reported racing writer Marcus Scriven, 'Nothing as trivial as money was at stake.' He revealed just what depended on the outcome of the race within a race of their two runners – the bet was that whoever lost would have to take 'The Sheila' (as they both customarily referred to their mutual ex-spouse) away for a week.

Scriven reported a friend who watched the race in Sangster's company as saying: 'There was great tension as they came towards the last [furlong] with Andrew Peacock's in front. Then Robert's overtook Peacock's – and won.'

176. CONGRATULATIONS! CLIFF LANDS 6479/1 WINNER

A 40 year old night-shift worker from Newport, South Wales walked into his local betting shop on 30 December 1989 and staked £30 on an accumulator for a series of events to happen before the turn of the millennium.

The punter's predictions were: Cliff Richard (4-1) being knighted; U2 (3-1) staying together as a rock band; Eastenders (5-1) still being around as a BBC soap opera, and both Neighbours (5-1) and Home Away (8-1) remaining regularly on British television screens.

All of his predictions proved accurate, and two days into the new millennium he walked back into the shop and asked for his winnings, which amounted to £194,400. Nobody had thought it was worth passing on the slip to head office, but the bet was confirmed as a bonafide transaction, and the punter was duly paid out, his 6,479-1 accumulator still being the largest novelty 'killing' of its genre.

177. SEXED-UP WAGER

I defy you to discover a more bizarre betting yarn than the one that unfolded in the Court of Justice in July 1777, when a surgeon called Hayes demanded £700 in winnings from a broker called Jacques.

The pair had bet six years earlier on the matter of whether the former ambassador to England from the Court of France, the Chevalier d'Eon, was not the male he appeared to be, but a woman.

This had reportedly been a matter of much speculation with an estimated £300,000 gambled on the subject.

Hayes claimed to have irrefutable evidence that d'Eon was female – and called a surgeon, M de Goux, who claimed that he had treated her and therefore knew her to be a woman.

A second witness swore that in 1774 d'Eon had made a 'free disclosure' of her sex to him. The chevalier had, he swore 'permitted him to have manual proof of her being, in very truth, a woman'.

The Lord Chief Justice, Lord Mansfield, hearing the case, stated to the jury that d'Eon had 'publicly appeared as a man, had been employed by the Court of France as a man, as a military man in a civil office and as a Minister of State here and in Russia'.

The Russian interlude was puzzling – as he had reportedly worn a dress while there, but had also sported a beard.

Having deliberated on all the available evidence, Lord Mansfield found in favour of Hayes.

He won his £700, but an early 19th century review of the case revealed: 'When d'Eon died in London on May 22, 1810, it was proved without a shadow of a doubt that he was a man.'

The former dragoon had been in drag for the final 39 years of his life.

His name entered the English language as a result – 'eonism' meaning to have transvestite tendencies.

178. ANOTHER WINNER FOR LESTER

Lester 'Benny' Binion was the man who unleashed the World Series of Poker – now justifiably described by veteran player Doyle Brunson as 'the grandaddy of the poker tournaments' – on to an unsuspecting world back in 1970.

To be scrupulously accurate, Tom Morehead (also reported as Moore) of the Riverside Casino (other reports say Holiday Hotel) in Reno had first come up with the idea in 1968, when it was dubbed the 'Texas Gamblers' Convention', and involved stud, draw, lowball and hold 'em and produced, by vote, a 'King of Cards' who was awarded a silver cup. For its first two years, Johnny Moss won and retained the cup, but, rather like the way certain record companies turned down the Beatles in their early days, so Morehead allowed Binion to take the concept forward, eventually creating the most prestigious and wealthiest contest in poker, even though at the time he began staging the event, poker was not normally played in his casino, Binion's.

Having been a booze bootlegger and craps game organiser, Binion, who survived pneumonia-related health scares in his Texan childhood years, and therefore managed to avoid the stress of ever attending school, had arrived in Vegas in 1946 (having along the way been found guilty of first-degree murder in 1931 and shot and killed another man five years later – self defence, this time) when, according to writer Andy Bellin, he carelessly 'lost about $400,000 playing poker'.

Nonetheless, he kept going, and eventually opened his Horseshoe Casino there in 1951 – attracting tourists in by displaying $1m in a horseshoe-shaped glass container.

In 1953 he was imprisoned for four and a half years for tax evasion and forced to sell his interests in the casino, although he remained closely associated with it as a 'consultant'.

Binion, born in Texas in 1904, was buried during the Christmas holidays in 1989, and fellow casino supremo Steve Wynn paid him a thoughtful tribute: 'He was either the toughest gentleman or the gentlest tough I ever met.'

All of the winners of the WSOP have been characters, but not all of them are the type of fellow you would like to live next door to you. Writer Andy Bellin summed it up well in 2002: 'I've met some of the greats, even played with a couple. Some are polite and humble, others are absurd and seem like cartoon caricatures of themselves.'

See whether you can sort the polite from the absurd yourself – here are the stories of some of them:

179. 1970: MOSS ROLLS IN

Johnny Moss, real name John Hardie Moss (38 runners; players gambled with their own money. No official winning purse.). Moss was born in 1907 in Texas and became a pro player aged 19. He won the inaugural title (and a trophy), which was played over a variety of poker variations – California Draw; California Lowball; Seven Card High; Seven Card Low, or Razz; Seven Card High-Low Split; Five Card Stud, and what was, at that time, the little-known Hold 'Em. Moss won via a vote by the other players for the overall best player. He later commented: 'A lot of gamblers hate me, but they still vote on me being the best player in the world.' The world didn't seem much bothered, however, and media coverage was sparse.

Moss had learned how to play poker by the age of ten. He'd also decided how he would make his living when his father told him that he either had to give up work or give up gambling.

'But if I don't work how can I get money to gamble?' he asked his daddy. 'That's what gamblers got to figure out,' came the reply.

So, the young Texan quit work and decided to become a professional poker player.

Before hitting the road, and at the tender age of just 18 in 1925, he wed childhood sweetheart Virgie Ann, who travelled along with him, keeping tabs on their gambling money. On their wedding night, Moss had played poker and during the course of the game been losing so badly that he had to 'borrow' his new wife's engagement ring to stake another hand. She gave it up voluntarily – 'If I hadn't Johnny would have ripped my whole finger off.' The ring put Moss back on track in the game, and 60 years later she still had the engagement ring to show off while telling the story.

But, as Johnny headed for the East Texas oilfields, where he played poker 'with the roughnecks and the drillers', Virgie Ann became pregnant.

Johnny was already becoming worldly wise, and realised that not everyone was happy being beaten by a greenhorn kid.

There were 'more cheaters than oil wells', he discovered. He was asked in one dodgy game:'What do you have to take this pot?', to which he replied 'Two sixes', pulling out just that – a pair of six-guns.

The arrival of the first Moss offspring was imminent, and Virgie Ann booked into a $35 room in the local hospital to prepare to give birth. Johnny saw her safely installed before popping out to play a pre-birth game of craps and a hand or two of poker.

He lost all of their ready cash and had to head back to the hospital to take Virgie Ann back home as he could no longer afford to pay for her stay.

Their daughter, the interestingly named Eleoweese ('My daddy gave Eleoweese her name. She must have been ten years old before I learned how to spell it.'), was born at home with Moss acting as midwife to the doctor, who waived his $35 fee when Moss explained his lack of finances. Moss went to work as a security guard to earn the money to pay back the medic.

Still, Virgie Ann probably consoled herself, that's the worst he can do to me.

Well!

Moss, then living in Dallas, decided that he would spend a spectacular 1939 $250,000 winning poker hand on buying a new house. He sent Virgie Ann out to check out the local property market.

After a thorough search she came up with the ideal house for them, and happily told Moss the search was over. 'Sorry, but you looked too long,' he said, confessing he had lost the money.

Virgie then began to exercise more control over their finances and their position improved to the point that, in an effort to get him finally to settle down, he recalled: 'She said she'd pay me a thousand a week if I was to come and lie around the house in Odessa and drink whisky all day.'

He was tempted, but then realised, 'What would I do with a thousand a week if I couldn't gamble?'

But he did go on to become the first man ever to win the world championship of poker – the WSOP title – three times, securing poker immortality for himself.

180. 1971: MOSS DOUBLES UP

Johnny Moss (six runners; $30,000 first prize). The method of deciding the winner had changed – Benny Binion felt that the players were too egocentric. When they voted for the best player they invariably voted for themselves and 'second-best' votes had to be counted. So, a $5,000 buy-in was introduced for the hold 'em section, from which the world champion would emerge. Benny was by now running the Horseshoe with his sons, Jack and Ted.

181. 1973: PUG'S POT

Walter Pug(gy) Pearson (13 runners, $130,000). Born in 1929, Pearson – a former top-flight Navy frogman – learned how to play poker the hard way, hustling on the road. 'I got so good I could play with folks that used marked cards and signals and God knows what and beat 'em every time.'

Guns were much in evidence in those early 1950s days and Pearson would have to ensure his money was well hidden – 'My favourite trick was to lay my bankroll on the ground, then drive my car on top of it, so that it was buried under the tyre.' Pearson won the title by seeing off his final challenger, the veteran Johnny Moss, who told him: 'If it had to be anybody other than me, I'm glad it was you, Pug.'

Mrs Moss was not as gracious in defeat, telling her husband, 'I think you simply gave it to him.'

At this time there were evidently moves afoot to create a rival to WSOP, albeit in a somewhat different style. Gambling writer J Philip Jones wrote in 1973 that 'in an effort to improve the image of poker and to take the game out of its traditional saloon atmosphere, the World Poker Federation organised a world championship, to be held in Cannes. Preliminary contests took place to find good national representatives, and it is hoped that the championship may become a regular event.'

182. 1974: MOSS'S HAT-TRICK

Johnny Moss (16 runners; $160,000). Moss once explained: 'The difference between a good player and a great player is that when a good player gets lucky, he'll win a big part of the table. When a great player gets lucky, he'll win the whole table.' One of Moss's problems was that, great poker player though he undoubtedly was, he was nowhere near as brilliant at other games – as his biographer Don Jenkins observed: 'He lost enormous sums of money on the dice tables waiting for poker games to begin.' The 1978 media guide to the WSOP would state: 'Moss pocketed ten million dollars from the tables in 1950 – and lost it all shooting craps.' But in this year he managed to turn back the clock to produce some of his best form and outlasted his final rival, Crandell Addington, in a four-hour heads-up. The defeated Addington described it as the 'greatest four hours of my life'.

183. 1976: HELLO, DOLLY

Doyle 'Texas Dolly' Brunson (22 runners, $220,000). Brunson won with a 10-2 hand. He faced Jess Alto, a non-pro in the ultimate showdown. Brunson bet $4,000, Alto raised $7,500. Brunson called. The flop produced jack of diamonds, two of hearts and ten of spades. Alto now bet $8,500. Brunson called. The fourth community card was the ten of diamonds. Alto went all-in for $67,000. Brunson paused for a minute then called. Up came the final card – ten of clubs, giving Brunson a full house to beat Alto's apparently winning hand of two aces, two jacks. He was champion.

Brunson later admitted: 'I thought Alto was bluffing and I was going to try to outbluff him and steal the pot. So I got lucky and made a hand.'

He won it again – again with a 10-2 hand – in 1977 when 34 runners contributed $340,000.

184. 1978: BOBBY'S THE BOY

Bobby Baldwin (42 runners, $210,000). Baldwin, from Tulsa, Oklahoma, and therefore the first non-Texan winner, was credited with the shrewd remark 'it takes a special kind of woman to be married to a gambler'.

Baldwin gave runner-up Crandell Addington – a man with a penchant for a Stetson and a cigar – a feeling of deja-vu by subjecting him to his second runners-up position, in a similar heads-up finish to the one he had received from Johnny Moss in 1974.

★ Amateurs entered for the first time, and the tournament welcomed its first female runner – Barbara Freer. The prize-money rules were changed to give the winner half of the buy-in cash with 20 per cent for the runner-up; 15 per cent to the third; ten per cent to the fourth and five per cent to the fifth.

185. 1980: THE UNGARDOG

Stu Ungar (73 runners, $385,000). By the end of day two only 12 players were left in – the lowest financed of them was Johnny Moss, with just $7,000 of the $730,000 total. But a reminder of his status in the game appeared when the on-site bookie was foolish or misguided enough to chalk Moss up as a 100-1 no-hoper.

When the dust from the stampede of spectators – and, perhaps, players – wanting to get a piece of that action had cleared, the bookie found himself facing a potential payout of one million dollars.

Johnny gave his supporters cause for optimism when he won the first pot of day three, taking $15,000 in the process, and by the end of day three Moss had moved ominously back into contention rather like an early day Tiger Woods, sitting third of the remaining seven contenders. The bookie panicked and began to try to buy up some of the bets he had accepted. One player, Pat Callihan, reportedly refused to sell his $500 wager, even for $40,000.

Moss went to bed early that night. But it was asking just too much of the legendary three-time champ to rise to the heights again, and a $200,000 hand lost to Doyle Brunson just about left Johnny down and out. He was finally eliminated in a 'changing of the guard' moment by the eventual winner, the young, flamboyant Stu Ungar, who had idolised Moss since he was a 16-year-old in 1970.

With the field down to youngster Ungar and established star Brunson, Ungar was confident enough to look to stake $50,000 on himself when he heard he was the 6-5 underdog – Brunson himself laid him the bet. After his win a reporter asked Ungar what he would do with his prize-money. 'Gamble it,' he said.

But before he could do that he had to overcome a minor hitch – they couldn't pay him without a Social Security card and he didn't have one. He had to rush to a nearby federal building and tip the clerk $100 to get one so that he could be paid his winnings.

Photographer Ulvis Alberts, who would use the results in his book, Poker Faces, was at the event taking shots of the contestants, some of whom asked him for copies of the prints, for which he was charging $75 a time. 'Suddenly there was a problem,' said Alberts. 'Nobody had change.' His solution was typically poker, typically Vegas – 'So I charged them $100 and everyone was happy.'

Stu retained the title in 1981.

186. 1982: TREE-MENDOUS

Jack 'Treetop' Straus (104 runners, $520,000). At one stage Straus was down to a single $500 chip. And it wasn't that long after his triumph that he was again down to just a few dollars, for Straus, a former basketball player, managed to go through his winnings in the space of a mere two months.

'Hell,' he was reported as saying, 'if they had meant man to hang on to money, they'd have put handles on it.'

Straus – whose Treetop nickname was not unrelated to his reported size of 6ft 7in – did not only bet on poker: 'For my money, there is no thrill in life more exhilarating than listening to a ball game with half your bankroll bet on it.' But when he was concentrating on poker he did not mind pushing out the boat. He once bet $250,000 on a pair of hidden nines in a seven card stud game – sadly, Benny Binion, who called him, had hidden jacks.

187. 1983: SMOKIN'

Tom McEvoy (108 runners, $580,000). McEvoy, who had moved to Vegas in 1979 to become a pro, was really smokin' as he won this tournament – but he later turned his attentions to ridding casinos of smoking. He was a prime mover in getting non-smoking events instigated, the first of which in Nevada took place in 1999, and then in the WSOP in 2002. McEvoy, who learned to play poker aged five when he relieved schoolmates of their lunch money ('If little Johnny is dumb enough to lose his money there is nothing I can do about it,' said his supportive mum), became a prolific poker author, having read virtually everything published elsewhere on the subject – 'Even the really awful ones have something to offer. I try to take at least one really good idea or concept away from every book I read.'

188. 1984: TRUE GENT

'Gentleman' Jack Keller (132 runners, $660,000). Keller was born in 1943, spent his early years in Philadelphia and joined the US Air Force, but in the early 1980s became a poker pro.

The 'Gentleman' nickname was acquired while working at the Chicago options stock market. He had problems with substance abuse, and died in December 2003. His poker style was summed up by his friend and fellow player, Bob Ciaffone of Card Player magazine – 'He did not make probing bets. He bet the full size of the pot like it was part of his personal religious credo never to bet less than the maximum.' Ciaffone also believes 'if one were to make a list of the top ten greatest all-round poker players, Jack Keller would have to be on it.'

189. 1985: WORLD CHAMP JAILBIRD

Bill Smith (140 runners, $700,000). T J Cloutier, beaten by Smith in the latter stages, when he took on Smith's pair of threes with ace-three, erroneously thinking his opponent to be the worse for wear, commented of the new champ's playing style: 'Squeaky tight when sober, possibly the best player in the world when half-bagged, and horrible when drunk.'

Anthony Holden said in his book, *Big Deal*, that Smith, now deceased, 'doggedly drank his way to victory'. Holden was there to research the bestselling book, which centred around his performance in that year's WSOP, in which he claimed to be 'the only Englishman taking part'. On his table, Holden played against both Telly 'Kojak' Savalas and former champ Stu Ungar, before going out in 90th place.

Smith, who also finished fifth in the event in 1981 and 1986, claimed to hold an unusual record – for being arrested more times than anyone else within 24 hours for playing poker.

While taking part in an illegal game, he and the other players were arrested and banged up, only to secure their release by the afternoon. Some of them set up another game with a predictable result – they were soon back in the slammer. Out by evening, Smith went for the hat-trick – and duly achieved it.

190. 1988: CHAN PIPS OPPONENTS

Johnny Chan (167 runners, $700,000). For his second consecutive WSOP triumph, Chan kept an orange by him on the table, occasionally stroking it for luck. The final hand of this event, between Chan and Erik Seidel, would eventually be immortalised in the poker movie, Rounders.

191. 1989: HELL, YEAH

Phil Hellmuth jnr (178 runners, $755,000). Hellmuth, aged 24, was the youngest winner. Chan, who had by this time dumped the lucky orange, was runner-up. 'Many have compared him to tennis bad boy John McEnroe,' said Inside Edge writer Roland de Wolfe of the temperamental Hellmuth, who became known as 'Poker Brat'. 'But to me he's more, well, David Brent.' To which Hellmuth responded: 'Being humble is a great thing, it's just not me.'

Hellmuth was notoriously arrogant early in his career and poker expert Nic Szeremeta said: 'Phil's ego is the biggest I've ever come across.' But, in 2001, leading Scottish player Brian McNally conceded that Phil's 'cockiness has mellowed to superciliousness'.

Hellmuth later recalled his triumph here and that he had 'made a deal with my dad that if I won the championship I would buy him a new car. It was the first poker tournament he ever attended, and it was also his first Mercedes-Benz! I'll never forget the dealer turning up that last card. Yes! I was world champion of poker. I looked around the room for my father. There he was running up to embrace me. Luckily I have the whole scene on video.'

192. 1994: MINE HOST

Russ Hamilton (268 runners, $1,000,000). Additional to the prize-money was an ounce of silver for every pound the winner weighed. Hefty Hamilton weighed 330lb, although there were rumours he had secreted cans of beer about his person for the weigh-in!

Writer Al Alvarez contested the championship – he was busted out in 232nd place, ahead of three former world champs – and boasted: 'I suspect I am the only published poet to have done so.' In 1983 Alvarez had published his classic book about the event, *The Biggest Game In Town*.

Winner Hamilton reportedly learned to play poker in a real dirty environment – a West Virginia coalmine.

193. 1996: HUCK OFF

Huck(leberry) Seed (295 runners, $1,000,000). Aged 27 at the time, Huck was hoping the win would improve his sex life as he complained about his relationships with women – 'When I say I'm a poker player they think I'm some kind of bum.'

The 6ft 6in champ, known for playing in shorts and trainers worn without socks, reportedly did a deal with the other two players who made the final three, to split the prize-money and play for the title.

194. 2000: JESUS, HE WON!

Chris Ferguson (512 runners, $1,000,000). Ferguson was nicknamed 'Jesus' because of his supposed physical resemblance to the Son of God!

Commissioned by *Harper's* magazine to cover the event for them, poet-novelist James McManus put his advance up for grabs by entering a satellite tournament, which he won, to earn himself a $10,000 place at the main event – where he managed to finish fifth, winning $250,000.

Top female player Annie Duke finished tenth – either because of, or despite, the fact that she was eight months' pregnant at the time. Ferguson won on the last card from T.J.Cloutier, when the nine he needed duly arrived.

In third place was Rabbi Steve Kaufman, who collected $570,500 and fifth, properly enough, was Jim 'writer of Positively Fifth Street' McManus, in which volume he refers to the Rabbi as the 'Satanic Prince of Noodges [one who pesters or annoys, apparently] who forked me down into the pitch'.

195. 2002: HAIR-RAISING WINNER

Robert Varkonyi (631 runners, $2,000,000). 'If Varkonyi wins, I'll shave my head,' vowed former winner Phil Hellmuth, and so he did (allowing Varkonyi himself to remove some of it), leaving the winner to muse: 'Only Phil could miss the money yet steal the limelight.'

His favourite poker game is Hi-Lo Stud and, asked for his favourite famous person, he named 'Leonardo Da Vinci, Albert Einstein and Halle Berry'.

Varkonyi started playing as an undergraduate at the Massachusetts Institute of Technology, from whence he became an investment banker in Brooklyn, New York, before moving into big-time poker.

Varkonyi made an instructional poker video – which also featured members of the cast of The Sopranos.

196. 2003: LIVING UP TO HIS NAME

Chris Moneymaker (839 runners, $2,500,000). He qualified initially via a $39 internet stake qualifying tournament. What's more, he had borrowed half his initial outlay – and duly handed over half his prize-money to his benefactor.

British gambling writer Derek McGovern felt that Moneymaker's success, having learned his trade on the internet, was something of a kick in the teeth for the high-flying pros, whose success had always been held to emanate from their face to face skills. 'An internet dude winning the World Series – that's like a gelding winning the Derby, a mongrel winning Cruft's, a trans-sexual winning Miss World ... it exposed as subterfuge the notion that the very best poker players have some extra-sensory perception beyond the range of mere mortals like you and I.'

Showing the way that satellite tournaments were influencing the make-up of the event, this year just 63 of the competitors actually paid the full $10,000 buy-in.

197. 2005: JOE'S DEADLY INTENT

Joseph Hachem (5,619 runners, $7,500,000). The event moved to the Rio 'All Suite' Hotel for all bar the final stages– but you can't please all of the poker people all of the time. 'High ceilinged with acres of space, the room had the morbid atmosphere of exam time at a large comprehensive. The enormity of the room sucks out the tension, leaving nothing more exciting than hundreds of mere mortals, anonymous in their very ordinariness,' commented Brett Morton of *Inside Edge* magazine.

Writer Victoria Coren – sponsored by paradisepoker.com – made a pertinent point: 'It is said that the new time (July) and venue will be better for a tournament which has outgrown its humble roots. But, coincidentally or not, room rates at the Rio are far more lucrative than at Binion's.'

Hachem, an Aussie chiropractor from Melbourne, albeit born in Lebanon, who first played the game with his family, aged 15, may have had outside assistance during the course of the tournament. His younger brother, Tony, told writer Michael Kaplan that Joe had been sitting holding Q-10 and needing a pair, at a crucial stage: 'I closed my eyes and prayed to our deceased brother, asking him to give us a Queen. Then it came; he was looking out for Joe and I.' Their brother, Elei, died 18 years previously in a car accident.

After his victory Hachem, whose previous biggest pay-day had been $28,000, returned to his hotel room and slept: 'I woke up a few hours later, walked into the bathroom, looked in the mirror and started bawling my eyes out. It was then I realised "Oh, my God, it's real"!'

In his first tournament after the WSOP, Hachem finished out of the prize-money.

The tournament featured a controversial 'F-Bomb' rule – anyone caught using the swear word beginning with that letter was 'fined' by a ten-minute penalty away from the table. Some were delighted – female pro Lucy Rokach approved and called for further measures: 'All naughty players should be banished, preferably wearing a dunce's cap with an F emblazoned on it.' But player Keith 'The Camel' Hawkins was outraged: 'If someone swears to himself or uses a swear word in conversation, penalising him is ridiculous. We are not playing in a kindergarten. We are adults playing in a casino. Treat us with a bit of respect, please.'

No-one apparently asked Mike 'The Mouth' Matusow for his opinion after he picked up no fewer than five F-Bomb penalties.

The ultimate net prize pool for the tournament was confirmed by accountants as having topped $100,000,000 for the first time – it actually reached $103,000,000.

198. 2006: STRANGEST YEAR YET?

Novelist Martin Amis contested the 2006 WSOP, not lasting past the first day (in common with former world snooker champ Stephen Hendry). He observed that 'in glandular terms, poker is inseparable from the carnal energies: it is all heartbeat and sweaty palms'. His first hand, a straight, was his best, but only won him $200. The tournament, at the Rio, which hosted the final table as well – the first time that the latter stages had not been concluded at Binion's – was won by Hollywood talent agent Jamie Gold, chip leader for an unprecedented four days, who never after day two made a call that risked all his chips, and who picked up £6,337,437 for his pains. He put his success down to the bowl of his favourite fruit, blueberries, which he had in front of him throughout. But Gold then found himself involved in 'discussions' over whether he had agreed to split half of his winnings before the commencement of the tournament. There was also controversy when it was later revealed that although there were 8,773 contenders for the event the chip count by the final table appeared to be $91.3m – much more than should have been there, allowing for the $10,000 entry fee per head.

Many of those players turned up in what they presumably believed to be 'hilarious' fancy dress – and the likes of Wonder Woman, Spiderman and Batman's Robin were all on view, as was pro Joe Sebok, who had lost a pre-event bet and therefore had to play clad in a bear costume with the added bonus of a diaper attached.

In addition: late for day two and without a cabbie, English player Joe Beevers interrupted a gardener at his duties and bribed a lift from him for $100 but found himself $16,000 down when he arrived as play had begun ... Snooker's Steve 'Golden Nugget' Davis finished 579th, somewhat better than former world heavyweight champ Lennox Lewis who was, whisper it, knocked out by a girl, Celia Mortensen ... Richard Lee finished sixth to pick up $2,803,851 and was the highest-placed finisher without a sponsor – intentionally – commenting:'The only thing I'm going to endorse is God, my family and the city of San Antonio.'

In fifth place was 45-year-old insurance agent Rhett Butler from Rockville –but I'm sure he didn't give a damn ... According to Poker Europa writer Nic Szeremeta, this year's WSOP was not even a bog-standard kind of contest – 'The toilet facilities are so inadequate that the field for the 'first days' of the main event had to be split into groups of 1,000 each for 'comfort breaks'. Nic's evidently not a fan – 'I do not regard the WSOP as the world's greatest poker event. It is only the biggest' ... Virgin Atlantic was well aware where many of the people it was flying in from London were headed, and supplied them with in-flight sickbags emblazoned with the message 'We don't want you to chuck in your hands' ... After being knocked out 71-year-old Tory donor and spread-betting specialist Stuart Wheeler commented: 'In 30 years I want to be the first poker world champion over 100'. Another player banned was English pro

Roy Brindley who, according to his column in *The Sportsman* newspaper, was refused permission to enter the States because of what he does for a living – 'A professional poker player going to Vegas to play poker? That could be considered pursuing your profession, that is work and nobody works in America without a work permit.' He didn't have one, so he missed out … 91-year-old Victor Goulding from Florida was the oldest player in the tournament – the previous year he made an impact when he was 'timed out' after swearing – and he made history as son Rick, 52, and grandson Brenton, 22, also competed, making them the first three-generation family to contest the event together.

199. 2007: JERRY GOOD

Winner Jerry Yang picked up a record $8,250,000 despite the field numbers dropping from 8,733 the previous year to 6,358. The American, a 39-year-old psychologist/social worker from southern California, donated ten per cent of his winnings to charity.

200. DEAD OR ALIVE

'As the 18th century waned, White's Club [in London] developed into a great gambling centre; its members indeed professed a universal scepticism and decided everything by a wager,' wrote gambling historian Ralph Nevill in his 1909 tome, Light Come, Light Go.

'There was nothing, however trivial or ridiculous, which was not capable of producing a bet. Many pounds were lost upon the colour of a coach horse, the birth of a child, the breaking off of a marriage, and even a change in the weather.' Nothing changes, does it – I have taken bets on most of these matters over the last few months!

However, we don't take many bets of the type Nevill then went on to describe:

'A favourite mode of speculation was backing one man against another, that is, betting that he would live the longest.

'An actor was pitted against a duke, an alderman against a bishop, a pimp against some member of the privy council. Scarcely a remarkable person existed upon whose life many thousands of pounds did not depend.

'The various changes in the health of anyone who was the subject of heavy betting naturally gave rise to many serious reflections in the minds of people who had wagered large sums.

'Some would closely watch all the stages of a total stranger's illness, more impatient for his death than the undertaker.

'Great consternation was caused by an unexpected demise.

'Considerable odds were laid upon a man with the constitution of a porter, who was pitted against an individual expected to die every week.

'The porter, however, unexpectedly shot himself through the head, and the knowing ones were taken in.

201. CURSE OF 1/100

It is the shortest odds bet available on Betfair, the 1.01, requiring punters to lay out £100 to win £1. It sounds like a nonsensical wager but more money is traded at long odds-on than any other price on the exchange and there is seldom any shortage of takers when the price appears.

Even though some of them may heard the story of the gambler who saw that golfer Neal Lancaster, in the middle of the fairway after his tee shot at the last of the 2002 Canadian Open, needed just a five at the par four to win, so lumped £50,000 on him at 1/100 to win £500. Lancaster three putted on the green to go into a play-off which he lost.

In 2004, the *Racing Post*'s Paul Kealy made a study of 1.01 shots over a three month period, totting up £36m staked – resulting in losses of £200,000.

202. SHE'LL BE RIGHT

An Aussie punter collected A$2.6 million by mistake, reported Melbourne newspaper *The Age*. It happened on Melbourne Cup day in 2003 'after the TAB [Australia's tote betting system] operator mistakenly entered one of his $6 trifecta [first three home] combinations of Makybe Diva, outsider She's Archie and Jardines Lookout 203 times instead of 20.

'The mystery Sydney punter, who had elected not to have his bets read back to him, would have had to honour the wager, come what may.'

203. ESKIMO ALMOST ICED

Playing in the 2007 World Series of Poker event, American pro Paul 'Eskimo' Clark, a 48 year old Vietnam veteran, was twice asked to stop playing and seek medical assistance after collapsing, suffering what was reported in places as a 'mini-stroke'.

He refused, according to some sources, because he needed to win money to pay off his debts. One poker blogger wrote: 'The man was moments away from the Angel of Death sucking out his last few breaths, and the vultures circled his dying mass ready to get paid moments after he busted out in 4th place.'

It was also alleged that the casino, Harrahs, made Clark – a medic in the forces – sign a waiver before allowing him to continue playing.

204. SENSATIONAL

Tony McCoy got the Jonjo O'Neill-trained Mini Sensation home to win at Exeter in December 2004. It was hardly a routine win in the 4m race as Mini Sensation looked to be going so badly at one point that one exchange punter offered the combination at 999/1 – snapped up by one fellow punter for £8.50.

McCoy and Mini Sensation kept plugging away and eventually wore down the opposition to win, landing one happy punter £8,500 for his £8.50 stake.

And McCoy had previous. Back in January 2002 he was unseated on 8/11 favourite Family Business in a novice chase at Southwell. The the other six runners in the race all fell or unseated – one, Eaux Les Couers actually fell, remounted, refused, then unseated.

Realising no runners were left, McCoy dashed back to the track, remounted Family Business and finished alone. The layer who accepted a £4 bet at 999/1 when McCoy was unseated was not best pleased, as he lost almost £4,000.

205. BET YOUR LIFE

'Two fellows were observed by a patrol sitting at a lamp post in the New Road, London; and, on closely watching them, the latter discovered that one was tying up the other, who offered no resistance, by the neck,' wrote Andrew Steinmetz in 1870's *The Gaming Table: Its Votaries and Victims*.

'The patrol interfered to prevent such a strange kind of murder, and was assailed by both, and very considerably beaten for his good offices; the watchmen, however, poured in, and the parties were secured.

'On examination the next morning it appeared that the men had been gambling; that one had lost all his money to the other, and had at last proposed to stake his clothes.

The winner demurred – observing that he could not strip his adversary naked in the event of his losing. 'Oh', replied the other, 'do not give yourself any uneasiness about that; if I lose I shall be unable to live, and you shall hang me and take my clothes.'

206. SOUND STAKE

Also from the Steinmetz book is the story of 'a clerk named Chambers, losing his monthly pay, which was his all, at a gaming table, who begged to borrow of the managers, but they knew his history too well to lend without security, and therefore demanded something in pawn.

'I have nothing to give but my ears,' he replied. 'Well' said one of the witty demons, 'let us have them.'

The youth immediately took a knife out of his pocket and actually cut off all the fleshy part of one of his ears and threw it on the table, to the astonishment of the admiring gamesters. He received his money and gambled on.'

207. GAMBLING TO THE BIT-TER END

It was recorded on 26 November 1772, in the *Gazette de Deux-Ponts*, that having lost heavily whilst gambling, 'a mad player at Naples bit the table with such violence that his teeth went deep into the wood; thus he remained, as it were, nailed to it, and suddenly expired.'

208. DRIVING FORCE

Manufacturer of the still famous car brand which bears his name, Andre Citroen, who died aged 57 in 1935, was one of the most flamboyant gamblers of his day. And it was said of him that he once deliberately lost 13million francs – worth £200,000 at the time – in one session of baccarat, purely to attract publicity for his company and its cars.

209. BETS SCAM XPOSED

'Xposed' was the banner headline on the front page of the *Daily Mirror* on Wednesday, 14 December 2005. The story, labelled 'Exclusive' began: 'A betting scam that raked in a fortune from reality TV shows such as X Factor has been smashed.'

The article went on to claim that BT workers had been giving phone vote pattern information to punters, who were then betting on the outcome of elements of shows like X Factor; Strictly Come Dancing and Hell's Kitchen.

'The gang made £30,000 on X Factor alone,' alleged the story.

By the next day the Mirror was declaring that one group of punters had collected £105,000 as a result of the scam.

Bookmakers had always been aware of the potential for such skullduggery but because of the enormous market for such betting from legitimate punters believed they had to take the risk of being targetted in such a way and stay on their guard to identify any suspicious betting patterns and react appropriately to protect their financial interests.

210. PUNTING'S GREATEST HAT TRICK?

Trainer/owner/punter, William 'Betting Billy' Tindall, was another great Aussie racecourse character, in his prime in the 1920s. He was instantly recognisable by the black hats he wore wherever he went. He also dressed in immaculate suits – which often had to be temporarily pawned when results went against him.

He rode as a jockey, but grew too large and became a trainer noted for tilting at the betting ring.

In the 1920s at the Moorefield course he found himself down to his last 19 shillings (95p). Knowing that his reputation would never survive the sight of him proferring less than £1 for wager he sold his racecard to raise the extra shilling – and then proceeded to back a string of winners, building his betting bank up to £6,000 by the end of the afternoon.

But his greatest betting feat took place at Flemington on Melbourne Cup day, 1934. Rain had turned the going heavy and Tindall knew that his three runners on the day in the lesser races were mud lovers.

'The first of our starters was Sculpin in the Railway Highweight,' he later explained, 'always a great betting race.'

Billy's 'putter-on' grabbed 50/1 about the horse, staking £800 at that price then backing it down to 20/1. The horse won by a neck.

'I rated Nellie's Tip a good thing for the Yan Yean, the 6th race' but to make sure the bookies wouldn't spot who was backing the horse he found three trusted friends to 'invest £9,000 for us.' Nellie's Tip stormed home at 9/2.

'Perfumery was in the last and we slapped it on her until her price fell from tens to 9/2. She had the race won from barrier-rise and we walked off the course with more than £200,000 of the bookies' money.'

Betting Billy died aged 77 in 1953 – he was flat broke.

211. GREATEST BETTING TRAGEDY

Twenty year old Mark Day died tragically after a forfeit for losing during a game of cards went fatally wrong. The University of Essex second year student had reportedly been playing poker against two friends whilst on holiday in Majorca in July 2008.

After losing the game, Day's forfeit was to strip to his underwear and run along the hotel corridor.

As he did so he failed to stop and smashed through a window, plummeting over 40 feet to the ground below. He was pronounced dead at the scene.

212. BIGGEST EVER BET?

J. Fairfax-Blakeborough was one of the greatest chroniclers of the Turf, publishing a series of very detailed books dealing with racing history.

In his 1927 book, *The Analysis of The Turf*, he turned his attentions to betting and named what he considered to be 'the largest amount that was ever stood on one horse' as the £270,000 which Mr Jaqes of Easby Abbey, Richmond (Yorkshire) and 'his confederate' stood to win had Mildew won the 1850 Derby.

But the layers were saved when the 9/2 second favourite was unplaced behind 16/1 winner Voltigeur.

We can only guess at what that £270,000 would be worth today, but F-B declared that 'perhaps the biggest haul which has fallen to an individual was Mr Naylor's £150,000 win over Macaroni in the Derby of 1863.' Naylor was a Liverpool banker.

The most consistently successful 'high roller' of those days would seem to have been Sir Joseph Hawley, who 'on three occasions won between £50,000 and £60,000 viz, on Teddington in 1851, on Musjid in 1859 and Beadsman in 1858. He would also have won as much on Blue Gown (1868) if he had not hedged.'

213. WINNING IS NOT ENOUGH

Most punters are over the moon to back a winner – ANY winner, no matter how far the horse wins by.

Renowned Classic-winning trainer of the mid-19th century, William I'Anson, of Malton, was immortalised for the advice he famously passed on to his son – 'If I was you I wouldn't bet, but if you DO bet – BET!'

But he told the story of a miller friend of his who he told about one of his runners in Newcastle's Seaton Plate, a race he regularly won and in which on this particular occasion he was running two – the outsider of which he rated a certainty.

The Yorkshire miller friend had never before been racing before that day but I'Anson persuaded him to bet £500 on the horse, which won a close-run race by a head. On his way to celebrate in the champagne tent, I'Anson met up with his friend and invited he and his wife along for a drink

'No, thank you' replied the stern-faced man, 'I've just time to catch the next train to York.'

'But you must not go yet, I'm certain to win the next race.'

'I've had sufficient of certainties – the last certainty has cured me of racing for life.'

'You won your money, what more do you want?'

'Ah, but only just – the way you talked I expected to see the horse win by a couple of hundred yards. It's too risky a business for me. I've won about £3,000 by the skin of a horse's teeth, and nothing on earth would make me have another bet, it's too uncertain a game for me, so I'll bid you good day.'

He was never known to have another bet.

214. LOOKING AHEAD

Many punters like to take out long-term bets to give themselves something to look forward to.

A Scottish customer bet £10,000 at odds of 10-1 with me several years ago that Tiger Woods would equal Jack Nicklaus's record of 18 Major titles before the end of 2010.

He'll have been a little concerned when Tiger had to take time off for knee surgery in mid 2008, but he is still very likely to go very close to landing his £100,000.

Then there is the gentleman from Lytham St Annes in Lancashire who, on October 25, 2007, took a punt on the next two World Cups being dominated by the South Americans – and gambled £5,173 at 28-1 that Argentina win in 2010 and Brazil in 2014, along with £8,824 at 16-1 for Brazil to win both.

Don't ask me why he staked those amounts, but the first will win him £144,844 and the second £141,184.

Some look somewhat further ahead – like J W Richardson from California, who, in 35 years time when he reaches the age of 100, can win £500,000 for his £50 bet at 10,000-1 that he will be able to 'father a child by the conventional method'.

He tells me he will offer half his winnings to any amenable female willing to help him land the bet.

Then there is Mr Khanna from Barnet, in his twenties at the moment, but who will win £1,000,000 when he reaches the age of, er, 125.

215. DODGY DICK

Dick England was a late 18th century gambler and all round bad guy – a cheat, conman, highwayman and murderer, to boot. He was involved with a number of other villainous characters who cheated a clerk of the Bank of England, called Clutterbuck, at gambling – causing him to rob the Bank of 'an immense sum' to pay off his debts.

He tried to scam Mr D, 'a gentleman of considerable landed property in the North' when that worthy came to gamble in Scarborough.

England and his cronies got the good gent wildly drunk . 'Dick England and two of his associates played for five minutes, and then each of them marked a card as follows – 'D owes me 100guineas'; 'D owes me 80 guineas', but Dick marked his card, 'I owe D 30 guineas' recorded a contemporary account.

Next day Dick duly met up with Mr D , showed him the card, and insisted on paying him 30 guineas despite D's protestations that he knew nothing about the debt.

Of course, the trap was then sprung as England's accomplices then produced their cards in an effort to con D into handing over to them the money they claimed he had lost to them. Friends eventually intervened to save D from settling up.

England next won £40,000 from 'the son of an Earl' – it is not recorded how honest the play was – but the loser shot himself fatally as a result.

In June 1784 England, by now suspected of highway robberies, became involved in a duel with a Mr Rowlls, who he accused at Ascot races of being a man who 'neither paid what he lost nor what he borrowed'.

This was the pot calling the kettle ebony coloured and Rowlls 'offered to strike' England.

A duel was called – during which England shot Rowlls dead – and then fled to France, avoiding capture for twelve years (and winning a great deal from gullible Parisians), until he was finally tried at the Old Bailey in 1796, where he was found guilty of manslaughter, and 'sentenced to pay a fine of one shilling and be imprisoned in Newgate twelve months.'

This narrow escape from the gallows apparently concentrated England's mind and he retired from gambling.

216. WHO SHOT A.R.?

Arnold 'The Brain' Rothstein was not, perhaps, the most lovable of gamblers. Suspected by many to be the brains behind the infamous fixing of the 1919 World Series of baseball when a number of players went crooked to ensure that the Chicago White Sox lost to the underdogs, the Cincinnati Reds, he was also a big money poker hustler, credited with winning what was at the time said to be the largest ever single hand , worth $605,000, from infamous gambler Nick the Greek.

On September 8 (also reported as 29), 1928, Rothstein was invited to a high-stakes poker game organised by New York bookie George McManus and held in the Congress Apartment building (on the corner of 54th St and 7th Ave) home of gambler and former convict Jimmy Meehan.

Also in the game was inveterate gambler Titanic Thompson and two of his long-term acquaintances from San Francisco, Joe Bernstein and Nate Raymond.

Local high-rollers Sol Fusik, Oscar Donnelly and Abe Silverman also sat in on the game, while other reports suggested brothers Meyer and Samuel Boston, and bookmaker Martin Bowe, were present.

Rothstein was into a number of suspect operations, such as bootlegging, nightclubs and drug running, and it is said that both Damon Runyon – as 'The Brain' – and Scott Fitzgerald – as 'Wolfsheim' – immortalised him as characters in their books.

The game was to be five-card stud and it was not long before the stakes for each hand were running into thousands. Rothstein began to lose. Apparently under-staked with cash, he was covering his losing bets with 'markers' – the equivalent of 'iou's.

As the game wound down, the final hand of what had apparently turned into a 30-hour marathon saw Rothstein offering to cut the deck for a high card against Nate for the modest consideration of $40,000.

'Don't appear to be your night, Mr Rothstein,' declared Nate as the cards were revealed.

As losses and winnings were tallied up it seemed that Rothstein owed Nate $319,000; Bernstein $69,000; Fusik $29,000; Donnelly $20,000; Silverman $8,000; and Thompson $30,000 – which added up to $475,000.

It wasn't all bad news for Rothstein, though – he had at least managed to win $51,000 from McManus, who promptly settled up in cash.

Rothstein left the game, promising to pay his debts within days, saying: 'I'm Rothstein, that name ought to be good for the money.'

Days passed, then weeks. No settlement, and rumours began to circulate that Rothstein was alleging the game had been crooked. He was, though, said to have told Runyon that he was just making them sweat a little by having to wait.

Silverman, albeit having the least to collect, made a scene in public when he bumped into Rothstein, and was told to come to Rothstein's office for his money.

It was being said on the street that a Chicago gang had been hired to collect or to rub Rothstein out. Police later said that he had decided 'I'm not going to give them a cent, and that goes for the gamblers and the gorillas'.

On the evening of November 4, at around 10.15pm, Rothstein visited his favourite restaurant, Lindy's, where he received a phone call from George McManus, organiser of the poker school, asking Rothstein to come to room 349 at the Park Central Hotel where he hoped to broker a deal over the payment of Rothstein's debts.

Rothstein set off to walk there, but at 11.07pm was found in the 56th Street service area of the hotel, suffering from a bullet wound to the groin. Despite asking for a doctor and a taxi, he was rushed to Polyclinic Hospital, still conscious but either unable or unwilling to name his attacker, declaring: 'I got nothing to say. I won't talk about it.'

At 10.15am on November 6, presidential election day, he died, aged 46.

When the result was made known, with Herbert Hoover winning, bets Rothstein had made worth $500,000 had proved successful. But his death voided the bets.

McManus was indicted for murdering Rothstein and brought to trial a year later, but the prosecution had no eyewitnesses and McManus was acquitted.

The case remained 'open' according to NYPD records for many years to come, but those close to the case believed there was little point in searching for another culprit. One of those at the game, Joe Bernstein, later reportedly said: 'It was an accident. George did a lot of people a real big favour, though. But it screwed me out of seventy grand.'

There was also a strong suggestion that Rothstein may well have had a point as to the nature of the game in which he lost all that cash. Gambling expert John Scarne recorded in his Guide to Modern Poker that Titanic Thompson told him: 'Sure, we [he, Raymond and Bernstein] cheated Rothstein out of the $319,000 in markers, and if it wasn't for that drunk McManus shooting Rothstein we might have collected our money.'

Scarne concluded that, having investigated the incident and spoken to most of the principal participants, he was 'of the firm opinion that McManus, Thompson, Nate Raymond and Bernstein as a team had set out to fleece Rothstein at poker with marked cards and stripper decks'.

217. TEESY COME, TEESY GO

'I have maybe lost half a million in the last 12 years. Pounds, that is.' So declared top female golfer Laura Davies in her 1996 autobiography, Naturally.

I like the 'maybe' – classy touch, that. After all, she has earned enough from golf to make that figure relatively insignificant.

Not, though, that she did not enjoy a few winners along the way.

There was the £20 Canadian bet of three horses and two greyhounds – all of which won in February 1995 to land her a £27,691.34 payout.

Two days later she won £6,000 with a football bet. 'I have to say it worried me that I felt nothing – no thrill whatever,' she recalled.

Laura learned to love a bet when her gran sat her on her knee to watch TV racing. Her favourite horse was Desert Orchid.

She once enjoyed a win so big that 'I walked out of a casino in London and ran to the car because I won so much money I was afraid of being mugged'.

Criticism of her gambling is water off a duck's back – 'Christ, I'm not embarrassed. I don't drink, don't do drugs. I like a bit of a punt. Big deal.'

218. THE TRUTH, THE HOLE TRUTH

The talk of golf in the last story reminded me that I once sat in a London pub with two guys who had taken bookies for – well, estimates varied from half to two million quid. And I was delighted to accept a drink from them as, thanks to the shrewdness of my own company's odds compilers, we had emerged unscathed from one of the most audacious, but entirely legal, scams ever undertaken.

Paul Simons and John Carter had come up with an idea so breathtakingly simple in concept, yet so cunningly implemented, that it resulted in bookmakers effectively signing their own financial death warrants.

A close and painstaking examination of golfing statistics had revealed to the punting pair that the incidence of holes-in-one in major golf tournaments was pretty frequent.

Yet, because they were rarely scored by the top players who were in contention for the titles, this was a little appreciated fact.

But if you thought about it logically, it made sense. Every tournament involves up to 100 of the world's leading players, each of whom would have two (if they missed the cut) or four attempts at ace-ing several par-three holes per round.

The law of averages dictates that, given so many of the world's best hitting balls towards the greens, a significant, albeit tiny, percentage of shots will result in a hole-in-one.

In fact, Simons and Carter figured the true odds at most European Tour events to be no longer than even money.

The pair realised that if a bookie was laying over the odds for a single, but could be persuaded to lay that price in doubles, or even trebles, then their chances of a killing would be much improved.

All they had to do was persuade gullible, or unsuspecting, bookies to offer them unknowingly generous odds and then wait for the law of averages to bring the profits rolling in.

They gave their scheme a dry run in Australia in 1990, but were scuppered when they found few bookies prepared even to quote them odds, let alone the ones they were after.

So, it was back to Blighty, where they prepared a list of tournaments most likely to produce aces – the Open; US Open; European Open, Volvo PGA and Benson & Hedges.

They also prepared a list of 2000 betting shops to target.

The first of them was 'hit' on March 18, 1991 – a Hugh Gunning shop in Chichester where Carter was offered and laid 5-1 for a hole-in-one at each tournament, which he played up into 20 doubles at 35-1 to £20 a time.

The very next shop quoted 25-1 for each individual tournament bar the US Open, and accepted four bets of £250.

They were up and running. One bookie, Arthur C Whittaker of Derby, quoted 100-1 for an Open ace as they criss-crossed the country.

Then the tournaments began. In the B&H, Jay Townsend hit a terrible round of 84 – which included an ace at the 11th. One down.

Wraith Grant was down in one at the fifth during the Volvo. Number two.

John Inman – truly – holed in one at the fourth in the US Open.

Brian Marchbank aced one in the Open at Royal Birkdale.

In the European Open, Miguel Angel Jimenez holed in one at the 17th during the first round.

Getting paid out was not always easy, with some bookies suspecting a sting – but The Sporting Life newspaper, the 'bible' of betting in those days, put the whingers in their place – 'Unless a bookmaker who has laid over-generous odds has a clear and unambiguous rule giving him the right to void or amend the bet for good reason, he has no option but to pay up.'

My pal, John Kay, chief reporter of *The Sun*, revealed the truth behind this story and introduced me to John and Paul in the London boozer where we all celebrated their inventive and completely legal sting.

A couple of years later, Simons died.

219. READY FREDDIE

Universally agreed to be the biggest boards bookmaker at the Cheltenham Festival, Freddie Williams became well known for his betting battles with the legendary punter/bookie/owner, JP McManus.

And Williams' reputation was made for good one day in March 1999 (23 years after he had first put his name down for a Cheltenham 'pitch') when McManus approached him and asked for a bet of £100,000 each-way on his own horse, Shannon Gale, in the Pertemps Hurdle Final.

The Scot never flinched and offered 7-1 – leaving him facing a potential payout just a little light of £1 million.

In the event, Shannon Gale finished fourth, and McManus got back all but £25,000 of his stake money.

On the same card, Williams laid a punter £80,000 at 11-8 about Nick Dundee, the Irish 'banker', in the SunAlliance Chase. The punter was staggered when Williams left the price at 11-8. He asked for another £80,000, and was duly accommodated. 'But I still didn't take down the price.'

The horse fell.

He hasn't always got the better of McManus, of course. In 2002 his Like-A-Butterfly carried a £100,000 bet to victory at 15-8. And the Irishman had £200,000 on his 5-2 winner An Muine Muice at Newbury in 2003.

In 2006 at Cheltenham Williams laid a reported £600,000 to £100,000 on Jewson Novice Chase Final winner Reveillez, followed by £50,000 each-way on 50-1 winner Kadoun, which cost him another £325,000.

Williams also offered a clue about the original source of McManus's success, telling writer Jamie Reid in a 2005 interview: 'John was in business as a bookmaker for 15 years. He had a good bet on Dawn Run when she won the Gold Cup in 1986 and that helped him to change his life. However, he told me that if she'd lost he'd have been skint the following week.'

Born in 1942 in East Ayrshire, Freddie was booked for a career down the pits, but failed a medical.

He began betting well before he was 18, and when he was part of a workforce buy-out of the soft drinks company he worked for, he made enough to take a bookmaking pitch at Ayr in 1974, expanding to Hamilton and Musselburgh and opening a few betting shops.

Tragically, Williams died in June 2008 – after spending that afternoon taking bets at Ayr races, and the evening doing likewise at Shawfield greyhound track.

220. BAD LOSER

After losing £400 in a betting spree in two Blackpool casinos in December 1994, a sore loser returned to the Castle Casino in a 40ft Mercedes truck, which he drove into 23 vehicles parked outside, causing £150,000 of damage.

221. OUT TO MAKE A KILLING?

A Huddersfield betting shop offered odds on how many bodies would be discovered at mass murderer Fred West's Cromwell Street house in Gloucester in March 1994.

But after a storm of protest, the odds of 4-7 for 8 to 11 bodies and 6-4 for 12 or more, were hurriedly withdrawn by boss Jack Pearson, owner of the 22-strong chain in Yorkshire.

As the media ran critical stories of 'a bookie trying to cash in on how many victims a mass murderer may have killed', Pearson disowned the reported comments of his general manager John Rangeley that: 'It's fascinating and a bit of fun for the punters.'

222. LIFE OR DEATH BET BEYOND MY KEN

In August 2003, with his favourite club, Hull City, languishing in the lowest division of the Football League, keen fan Ken Jaques, then 53, placed a bet of £50 at odds of 20-1 with me that 'before I die Hull City will reach the Premier League'.

On May 24, 2008, Hull beat Bristol City 1-0 in their Championship play-off final, putting Hull into the Premier League and winning still-alive engineer Ken £1,000.

223. WATCH IT

Trade-Union activist Lech Walesa, who became the first post-Communist president of Poland, was always a keen table tennis player.

When he became president he continued with the ping-pong, which he played for significant stakes – once losing his gold watch.

224. LAST MAN STANDING

The Royal & Ancient Golf Club's minutes record that on November 3, 1820, two members struck a wager – 'Sir David Moncreiffe, Bart., of Moncreiffe, backs his life against the life of John Whyte-Melville, Esq., of Strathkinnes, for a new silver club as a present to the St Andrews Golf Club, the price of the club to be paid by the survivor and the arms of the parties to be engraved on the club, and the present bet to be inscribed on it.'

Thirteen years later, Mr Whyte-Melville, in 'a feeling and appropriate speech, expressed his deep regret at the lamented death of Moncreiffe'.

He duly delivered to the club's captain the silver putter, and lived for a further 50 years.

225. CONGRATULATIONS – I'VE COST YOU A FORTUNE

Frank 'Potato' Dennis was a racehorse owner and punter from Lincolnshire, where he farmed and grew spuds – hence the nickname.

Dennis loved racing and gambling, but found his day-to-day work left him with little time for either.

He came to an agreement with bookmaker Laurie Wallis, who, in the late 1940s, allowed him to ring his bets through in the evening, after the races had been run, keeping clerks late at the office to accommodate him.

The system worked perfectly and Dennis, who would have a hefty bet, usually in the hundreds, often in the thousands (he once staked £65,000 in one session), would go through the card each evening, making his bets, winning and losing.

One night, the clerks in the office told Wallis that they feared he would be in for a battering as they knew one of Dennis's horses had won a race at 100-8 and it was just a matter of how much would be staked on it.

The Wallis man held his breath as Dennis came to the race in question – only to shout down the line – 'I can't have a bet in this one, because my damn fool trainer, Jack Fawcus, has sent me a telegram congratulating me.'

Michael Wallis, who took over his father Laurie's business, also remembered the time Dennis (whose Signal Box was third in the 1951 Derby) landed a huge winning double 'which he knew would stretch my father to the limit – but he told him 'Never mind, my boy, pay me when you can'.'

226. BANK ON BARCLAY

Famous pedestrian Captain Robert Barclay undertook a task extreme even by the standards of 1809 when, on July 13 of that year, he rose from his bed very early to be in Newmarket for the 3.15am start of his bid to walk 1,000 miles in 1,000 hours – at a rate of one mile in every single hour.

'The Captain is backed freely in London at 6-4, although a task equally difficult was never before performed,' declared the London Chronicle pre-race.

There was furious gambling among the thousands of spectators and tens of thousands of others who had heard about the challenge.

Barclay, 29 at the time, went through good and bad spells during the attempt, and on the final morning he could be backed at 100-1 to see it through.

But he did with 45 minutes to spare.

It was recorded that 100,000 guineas (perhaps £40 million today) was riding on the outcome of the walk – of which Barclay won 16,000 for himself, including his original 1,000-guinea bet against James Wedderburn-Webster.

227. NOT A LEG TO STAND ON

It is recorded that in February 1815, 'a journeyman baker' accepted a wager of 50 pounds to ten, laid him by a 'gentleman', that he could not stand on one leg for 12 hours.

A square piece of carpet was nailed in the centre of the room and at 3pm the baker, 'without shoes, coat or hat' took up the position on his right leg.

Eight and a half hours later, with the baker clearly in agony, the gentleman offered him half of his winnings if he would stop there and then.

The baker refused – 'the perspiration was running off him like rain, but he still persisted'. The odds against him, er, stood at 50-1 by now.

'Nevertheless,' we are told, 'he performed what was in its way a wonderful feat [foot, surely – GS], remaining on one leg three minutes longer than the stipulated time – when he was put into a chair and carried home.'

228. THAT'S THE WAY TO DO IT

Lloyd, the 'celebrated pedestrian' of the day, landed a gamble on Monday, March 19, 1826 by commencing at 8am to walk 30 miles within nine successive hours – backwards. He won by 14 minutes.

229. CERTAINLY, SQUIRE

The top jockey and all-round sporting figure of the times, Squire Osbaldeston, staked 1,000 guineas that he could ride 200 miles in under ten hours.

Weighing in on that day in 1831 at 11 stone and at the age of 44, he used 28 horses in the attempt – which he completed in 8hrs 39mins.

230. GREAT LOSERS

'Battle hardened Gurkhas' have been banned from betting shops' reported *The Sun* in July 2008 in an 'exclusive' story by the Chief Reporter, John Kay, which revealed the reason for the ban: 'Their wives moaned they were blowing their pay.'

Astonishingly, the story also reported that the commanding officer of 2 Royal Gurkhas, Lt Col Christopher Darby had banned his 600 men – earning an average of £16,000 per annum – from all five betting offices in Cheriton, Kent, near their base.

A regiment source was quoted as saying: 'The wives sent a delegation to the CO. They said their husbands were going gambling mad and dropping large sums of money.'

I told reporter Kay that if the ban continued we might retaliate by banning our staff and customers from ever joining the Army!

231. HAZZARD BY NAME, HAZARD BY NATURE

One of the most valuable races in the Australian greyhound racing calendar, the Sandown Cup, attracted hundreds of thousands of dollars of bets in May 2007.

The tension mounted as the dogs were being loaded. Veteran trainer Don Hazzard, 79, was loading in his own 11-1 shot, Sky Hazzard, but as he did so, his knee, injured in Aussie Rules games many years ago, gave way. He stumbled forward, grabbing a nearby handle to steady himself. Unfortunately that handle was the emergency starting lever – which promptly sprang the traps, sending the dogs off before the hare had even been sent on its way!

The dogs ran every which-way before they were safely gathered in. Stewards called a 'no race', refused a re-run and divided the $86,000 prize-money among the eight starters. Punters were not happy. Owners were not happy, Trainers were not happy. Nor were the spectators.

'I stood there mortified,' said Hazzard. 'I had gone to Sandown feeling eight foot tall, having my dog in such a prestigious race, but when that happened I wished I was six feet under.'

Trainer Paul Felgate, who fancied his Miss Brook so strongly he had $3,000 on the 4-1 chance, said: 'I was mad because I thought she was a certainty, but now I feel sorry for Don.'

Despite calls for an age limit on trainers, greyhound officials ruled: 'Old or young, people make mistakes.'

232. FAST WORKER

People seem to think it would be fun offering odds to people for the strangest of wagers. Well, if you think that – try pricing this one up:

Dear Graham:
As of November 20 I will be embarking on a fast from food and water for 42 days. The world record, according to Guinness, is 18 days, and according to the christian Holy Bible is 40 days. The question is: What odds are you going to offer me on successfully surviving a period of 42 days, commencing November 20 and finishing December 31 inclusive, without the intake of food or water by mouth – or any other orifice, intravenous drip, injection, etc?
Yours sincerely: Mr J S; North Yorkshire.

I asked for the correspondent to confirm that he would be receiving official adjudication during the attempt, which he failed to provide. And, no, it wasn't from David Blaine.

233. IT WAS IN 'THE PEOPLE', IT MUST BE TRUE!

I find it hard to believe, but the following was reported in *The People* on October 2, 1994, and I'm sure the story will have been checked out thoroughly, so we have to accept it is true:

'Romeo Ray Ladywell (oh, really? – GS) won a million dollar bet after sleeping with a different woman every day for one year. Ray, 39, from Baltimore, is now going on a round the world holiday – alone. "I've had enough of women," he said.'

234. SEAN REALLY MOTORING

Asked about his best ever bet, renowned racing author and journalist Sean Magee explained: 'I not only won my first ever bet, but won big – big enough to buy that D-type Jaguar about which I'd been fantasising for so long.'

Magee then came clean about the true size of his winnings from this school-days (he was eight years old at the time) bet – 'Scarcely had 15-2 favourite Morecambe pulled up after his stroll on the Heath to win the 1958 Cesarewitch than the local toy shop sold me that gleaming blue Jag, top of the Dinky Toys range.'

235. HAT'S NOT THE WAY TO DO IT

The Queen's hat threatened to cause violence to break out among bookies during the 2008 Royal Ascot meeting, when a number of layers – including myself – laid claim to having originated the ever more popular wager on which colour hat Her Majesty would wear on Ladies' Day.

The row was sparked when Irish bookmakers Paddy Power claimed to have started such betting in 1988: 'Everybody rightly associates us with the Queen's hat market as we were the first to launch the bet in 1988.'

This was clearly nonsense as I was well aware that during the mid-1970s William Hill were actively promoting the bet – and I was part of the team doing so, although the original inspiration for us doing so may well have been my boss at the time, Mike Raper.

Even Sporting Index PR guru Wally Pyrah, who had instigated the wager for that company in the late 1990s, admitted: 'I believe William Hill had already introduced it – that would be down to Graham Sharpe.'

Daily Mail columnist Charlie Sale, referring to me kindly (!) as Hill's 'veteran PR spokesman', quoted Coral – 'William Hill started the hat interest long before Power or Sporting Index became involved.'

While I know that we were doing it long before either of those Johnny-come-lately types, I have to admit that I'd be surprised if no-one had ever thought of it even before I came along, and I do know that Liverpool bookie Pat Whelan beat the others, too, as in 1984 he took bets on the colour of the monarch's titfer when she opened the International Flower Festival in that city.

Paddy Power, very miffed at being rumbled in their false claims, ludicrously issued a challenge to all other bookies claiming to have originated the bet to an arm-wrestling contest for £1,000 a go.

With companies reporting major gambles on the Queen wearing a red hat or a fascinator for 2008 Ladies' Day, she produced a skinner for the book when she turned up in blue.

236. DEAD MAN'S HAND

Wild Bill Hickok, sometime lawman and gambler, was a long-haired, flamboyant, well-known figure of the day, known by reputation and deed wherever he went.

He once rode into the lawless Deadwood Gulch and took up residence, deciding to check out the local poker tables. He fancied himself as something of a skilled player. The truth was, though, as gambling writer Carl Sifakis confirms: 'Hickok was a lousy card player and most of his biographers admit that he lost more money than he won at poker.' It was also said of him – 'It is not improbable that his reputation as a gunfighter won for him many a stake over the poker table which his cards could not win.'

Bill played draw poker, playing fairly as a rule. However, an encounter with a less scrupulous gambler named McDonald had already ensured Bill's place in poker lore.

They had played in Sioux City some years earlier. McDonald beat Bill frequently, and Bill was eventually tipped off that his opponent was almost certainly not playing strictly within the permitted rules.

They sat down again in a no-limit, one-on-one game, drinking as they played. Midnight came and the game was still going strong. Bill had picked up what he thought was a winning hand and was betting accordingly.

Finally, McDonald showed his hand – three jacks.

'I have a full house – three aces and a pair of sixes,' declared Bill, throwing his cards face down on the table.

McDonald lifted them one by one. 'I see only two aces and one six.'

Bill whipped out his six-shooter – 'Here's my other six.' Then he produced a knife – 'And here's my one-spot.'

McDonald knew when he was beaten and conceded the pot.

On August 2, 1876, Bill, who had reportedly had a premonition that he would not leave town alive, joined a poker game at the Nuttal and Mann saloon. The three other players were named Carl Mann, Capt William Massie and Charlie Rich. Vitally, and uncharacteristically, he sat in a chair not backed up against a wall.

As he played, a drunken cowboy known as Jack 'Crooked Nose' McCall, with whom Hickok had had a dispute over a 25-cent pot in an earlier hand, entered the saloon and took it into his mind to shoot his 39-year-old victim in the back of the head. Other, later reports would suggest he was acting at the behest of a gambler called Johnny Varnes, who had lost out in a row with Hickok at the Senate Saloon in Deadwood.

Whatever the motive, Bill slid silently to the floor, still clutching his cards – a pair of aces and a pair of eights. The other card has been variously identified, but most reports suggest a queen.

From that day forward, superstitious gamblers have described a hand boasting a pair of aces and eights as the 'dead man's hand'.

McCall was tried, set free, re-tried – and hanged.

237. STRANGELY ENOUGH

Living in Betton Strange, Shropshire, it was no surprise that punter David Gough's winning bet in March 1986 was something out of the ordinary, landing him winning odds of 1,648,959-1 when his five pence, six-horse accumulator parted Coral from £82,521.

238. CORN YOU BELIEVE IT?

The Hon George Lambton, highly respected rider and trainer of his day, is best remembered for the way in which, in 1903, he exposed the use of doping on horses –usually with cocaine – by telling Jockey Club stewards that he intended to dope six of his own animals to see for himself the effect.

He selected six runners. 'I obtained dopes from a well-known veterinary surgeon. They were not injected with a needle, but just given out of a bottle. Their effect on a horse was astonishing. I used five of them, and had four winners and a second. Not one of these horses had shown any form throughout the year.'

Lambton's actions caused a sensation and led to doping being made a criminal offence.

However, he was also aware of other ways in which the results of races could be adversely influenced, and recalled the time he was at Winchester racecourse and 'had been losing a lot of money'. He asked trainer William Day about his runner General Scott's chances in a three-horse race, and was told: 'If you know which of the other two will win, back it.'

Lambton didn't know, but backed both at combined odds of 1-4, then went into the stand to watch the race unfold. 'Coming to the turn into the straight, to my horror I saw William's horse ten lengths in front. There was a beautiful field of standing corn on the left-hand side of the run-in. Whether the horse was hungry or not, I do not know, but instead of coming round the turn he dashed into the cornfield, and there was an end of him as far as the race was concerned.'

239. AGE BEFORE BOOTY

Philip Tilson selected the first three home in the 1993 Derby and placed a Tricast bet with Ladbrokes.

When he went to collect his winnings of £30,000, staff at the shop pointed out that they had never actually offered such a bet.

Believing that they should not have accepted his bet in the first place, if that was the case, he complained to the arbiters of such matters back then, the *Sporting Life* newspaper.

The Life persuaded Ladbrokes to give Mr Tilson his £30,000.

Mr Tilson was still not happy. He'd discovered that another bookie's payout on the bet was even more – so took his case to another arbitrator, Tattersalls. That body ruled Mr Tilson was due – just over £700.

As the disconsolate Mr Tilson contemplated the loss of more than £29,000 following that decision, Ladbrokes discovered that when he had placed the bet he had been under 18. And therefore entitled to nothing other than a refund of his stake money.

240. LOGGING OFF

Brian McGregor, 24, strolled into a betting shop in Hexham with a betting slip on which he claimed to have predicted the outcome of all 61 Boxing Day 1992 matches for a 50 slip.

The jobless woodcutter's bet could have paid out the modest sum of £3,826,470,000,000,000 – had Hexham magistrates not ruled that he had forged the bet, and given him 12 months' probation and ordered that he should pay £20 costs.

241. WILLIAM'S BILL

William Bergstrom, from La Grange, Texas, carried a battered suitcase containing $1 million in 20- and 50-dollar bills into Las Vegas's Horseshoe Casino in 1984.

He staked the lot on one roll of the dice – backing himself not to throw seven.

He rolled a three and a four.

Bergstrom 'shrugged, said he was hungry and went off to find a Mexican restaurant' recalled casino boss Ted Binion.

Three months later, Bergstrom was dead – leaving a will in which he said he wanted to be remembered as the Phantom Gambler of the Horseshoe Casino.

242. GRAY DAY

Gambler Graham Calvert, who took William Hill to court claiming they should have stopped him placing bets, lost his case in March 2008. The greyhound trainer from Houghton Le Spring, Tyne and Wear, sued for negligence as well as compensation for personal injuries at the High Court in London.

The 28-year-old, described by his lawyers as a 'pathological gambler', claimed he had lost more than £2m, as well as his marriage, livelihood and health as a result of a six-month gambling spree in 2006.

He lost around £347,000 in one bet alone when he backed the US to win the 2006 Ryder Cup.

In the landmark case, Calvert's legal team argued the bookmaker had been guilty of 'negligent encouragement and inducement' by not acting to curb its client's gambling, even though he had indicated he wanted them to at least twice.

William Hill instead sought to encourage Calvert to go on huge betting sprees, breaching their own 'self-exclusion' policy, they alleged.

But Mr Justice Michael Briggs said William Hill had no legal responsibility to protect customers from the consequences of their gambling. The judge said by the year 2000 Mr Calvert had become a skilful and successful gambler – his net winnings averaging £50,000 a year for the next five years.

'From 2004 onwards the claimant's gambling began to extend beyond greyhounds, first to horses and later to a range of sporting events, including in particular football and golf. His main reason for doing so was because his growing success as a trainer of and gambler on greyhounds led bookmakers increasingly to place restrictions on his betting.'

Mr Calvert agreed a self-exclusion deal with William Hill but a few months later in August 2006 he opened a new telephone account and began betting again.

'William Hill owed no common law duty in 2006 to its known problem-gambler customers to protect them from the financial and psychological consequences of their gambling,' Justice Briggs said.

The judge added that as far as Calvert was concerned, William Hill's failure to take care to exclude him from telephone gambling in the second half of 2006 did not cause him any measurable financial or other loss.

'Had William Hill taken care to exclude Mr Calvert from telephone gambling for six months, his pathological gambling disorder would still probably have brought about his financial ruin, but over a longer period of time,' he said. 'This is because he would have continued to gamble both at William Hill's betting shops and with other bookmakers.'

Calvert had suffered a deterioration in his gambling disorder during the six months, the judge observed. If the judge had awarded damages for both claims, it could have increased the vulnerability of bookmakers to legal suits. William Hill called the decision a victory for common sense.

'We stated from the outset that there was no case to answer to Mr Calvert and that no duty of care was owed to him in this instance,' said David Hood, director of PR at William Hill.

He added in a statement: 'We, along with the industry, believe that counselling is best offered by those qualified to provide it. We support the Responsibility in Gambling Trust and other charities, who either fund such counselling services or provide them directly, and we will continue to do so.'

243. WALLS HAVE EARS

Former jockey and natural raconteur, Jack Leach wrote two best selling books in the early 1960s. In *Sods I Have Cut on the Turf* he told a splendid betting story about how a professional gambler had got his breakthrough:

'Perhaps the most romantic story about one of this fraternity (pro punters) happened to a man called Hammond. His wife was a charwoman and was cleaning in a trainer's (probably Joe Cannon) sitting room when a big coup was being discussed with the owner. They took no notice of Mrs Mopp, who went home and told her husband, and they put everything they possessed on the animal, which won at a long price.

'Former stable lad Jack Hammond never looked back. He ran into a lot of money and subsequently had a big stable of his own and won the Derby – at least, his horse St Gatien dead-heated for it in 1883.'

In fact, you might say, Hammond, for whom Cannon later trained, cleaned up!

244. FALCON SWOOPED

'The largest sum risked by a backer on one horse in my time must surely be the £16,000 which Archie Falcon had on Mr A Rothschild's Triumph, one of a field of three for the Churchill Stakes at Ascot in 1923,' wrote racing journalist Eric Rickman of the Daily Mail.

Triumph went off at 8-15 and won by three lengths, returning Falcon – described as one of the two heaviest punters since the First World War – a £9,000 profit.

Falcon's only equal as a gambler at the time was Charley 'Old England' Hannam.

245. FUTTER'S FLUTTER

Mike Futter, a 57-year-old Irish bingo chain owner, headed up the five-strong syndicate whose Monty's Pass won him £250,000 when landing the 2002 Kerry National – before being aimed at the Grand National.

Futter, declaring he was 'playing with the bookies' money', started to invest heavily on the horse, shrinking the odds from 66-1 to 50-1 to 40-1, then getting serious with £3,000 each-way at 33-1 with both Hills and the Tote. He had an additional £9,000 each-way at 16-1 with Ladbrokes.

The horse won at 16-1, landing perhaps the heftiest ever individual gamble on the race, after which Futter was said to be £800,000 better off.

'I tipped off all my customers, and the Northern Ireland clubs alone raked in £1.3 million, but I laid a lot of my own bets off to business partners and by the end of the day only £250,000 went into my own ledger, which is not a bad day's work,' confessed Futter with a smile.

In 2004 Futter staked £15,000 each-way on Monty's Pass to repeat his triumph – and was ahead of the game again as he finished fourth.

246. LONGEST ODDS NATIONAL WINNER?

Russian Hero was the shock 66-1 winner of the 1949 Grand National – very good news for owner W F Williamson, who had staked a tenner on him at ante-post odds of 300-1.

247. GEE UP

Owner F N Gee looked set to land his £100 each-way bet on his 100-1 outsider Zahia as the blinkered eight-year-old mare challenged for the lead with two to jump in the 1948 Grand National.

Already calculating his winnings of some £12,500, Gee was then left gutted when jockey Eddie Reavey inexplicably took the wrong course, missing out the final fence and being disqualified.

248. OUT OF STOCK

Stockbroker Edward Paget had landed the first part of a 4,000-1 double when his 40-1 fancy Jerome Fandor won the Lincolnshire Handicap at Doncaster in 1932.

Now Paget needed newcomer Egremont to win the Grand National to make him £4,000 better off for his £1 bet.

And Paget was actually riding Egremont in the National, against 35 opponents, 33 of whom were also-rans as Egremont, who started at 33-1, and 50-1 shot Forbra battled it out for honours.

Amateur rider Paget gave it everything, only to find professional jockey Tim Hamey managing to outdo him by just three lengths.

249. HANSIE FIXED IT FOR US

'It will always be remembered as the Test that was fixed,' insisted England cricket skipper Nasser Hussain, discussing what had at first been viewed as a thrilling victory for England, only made possible by a sporting declaration from South Africa's much respected skipper, Hansie Cronje.

England's January 2000 triumph was made possible only when Cronje set them a last-day target of 249 runs to win in a maximum of 76 overs.

On April 11, 2000, the devoutly christian Cronje confessed that he had accepted substantial amounts of money from bookmakers in India to manipulate a number of South Africa's international matches. He was banned for life in October 2000.

Hussain said of the game against England: 'Cronje had been paid to make sure there was a positive result. Yes, he was trying to make South Africa win, but it turned out that he would prefer us to win rather than the game ending in a draw because he had been paid to make sure that someone won.'

He added that Cronje's actions had enriched bookies, 'all the punters' money obviously having gone on a draw'.

Cronje died, aged 32, in a plane crash although, as *Racing Post* editor Bruce Millington wrote, 'plenty of people suspect he was murdered'.

250. HE'D JUST LOVELL IT

In September 1985, bookie John Lovell permitted his Cardiff betting shop to be used to host long-time customer, 60-year-old Jimmy Peters' . . . wake.

'It is the way he would have wanted to go – he spent most of his life in betting shops,' said Lovell.

251. HALF MEASURES

Michael Halford was delighted but a little surprised in December 1999 to notice a credit from William Hill in his bank account for £438, as he did not bet.

When the 45-year-old computer boss from Winchester, Hants, queried the entry, it emerged that someone had managed to get hold of his bank details and had used them to place a telephone bet of £255 in his name with Hills.

However, the perpetrator was clearly not that bright and had assumed he would be able to draw his winnings from the nearest William Hill betting shop.

Investigating police officer Chris Musselwhite said: 'The offender only found out he couldn't get his hands on the cash when he went to the bookies and was told it had been paid into the account.'

Mr Halford, who was allowed to keep the 'winnings', said: 'Whoever did this must be a bit thick.'

252. THE FIRST COHENCESSION

The grandfather of the bookmaker concession, now a commonplace marketing technique, was Australian bookie Sydney Cohen, who was born in 1890 and only retired from the ring in 1985 at the age of 94.

Cohen was struggling for custom in the 1950s when he came up with the idea of offering slightly reduced 'win' odds to clients, in return for the concession that if their horse finished second or third, they would get the whole of their stake money back.

The first day he launched the offer he reportedly lost heavily. But he stuck with it and was soon coining in a reported £2,000 profit per day.

253. PRIESTLY POKER

Vasile Mihaila, parish priest for the village of Negoesti in Gorj, Romania, was fined and threatened with defrocking after he was caught playing poker in the local pub in February 2006.

The 40-year-old and two of his fellow players were fined the equivalent of £200 each for gambling illegally in an unauthorised place.

A police spokesman told a local paper, Gazeta de Sud: 'There were nine men at the table playing poker, but only three of them had money in front of their seats. I was stoned [sic] when I heard one of them was a priest.'

Church officials said they had begun an investigation and warned that Mihaila could be defrocked for 'activities incompatible with the service of a clergyman'.

The reaction to this incident was somewhat in contrast to the activities of a Canadian pastor, John Van Sloten, a Calgary preacher, who in late January 2006 delivered a sermon to his 300-strong congregation at New Hope Christian Reformed Church, promoting the virtues of poker.

'In my view poker has a lot to teach us about ourselves and even God,' declared Van Sloten, who also spoke about 'how God made us for gambling, how every human is made for the adrenalized-risk buzz of the game and how this is what a real and alive faith should feel like.'

254. WINNY THE LOSER

Winston Churchill travelled on the American presidential train en route to Missouri to make a speech in 1946, and while on board, challenged the president, Harry Truman, to a game of poker – which he told him he had enjoyed playing since the Boer War.

Presidential aide Clark Clifford later recalled that 'Churchill was not very good at the game' and after just an hour's play he was some $300 down, whereupon Truman ordered his fellow players to 'not treat him badly'.

'Finally, however,' remembered Clifford, 'as the evening was drawing to a close, we moved in a little on our guests. When the dust had settled and we tallied up Churchill had lost about $250.'

255. GAMBLING BEHIND BARS

The question of how to keep prisoners occupied during their period of incarceration in Carson City prison, Nevada, exercised the minds of those charged with the job of keeping them content while they did their time.

And they came up with an idea that had not previously occurred to those running any other jails – why not let them gamble? Not only that, why not give them a full choice of casino games to choose from?

Possibly their thinking was influenced by the fact that gambling had just been made legal in the state of Nevada – and from that year, 1932, legalised and open gambling operated in the National State Penitentiary's 'Bull Pen', and only ceased in 1967.

This remarkable social experiment was investigated by Dr Felicia Campbell of the University of Nevada, who reported that prisoners had told her being allowed to gamble 'saved their sanity'.

Writer David Spanier later described this innovation as 'one of the most extraordinary in the whole history of gambling'.

It was championed by one Jack Fogliani, who was at Carson City for a considerable amount of time – serving for 14 years between 1953 and 1967 as superintendent and as warden. While he permitted prison poker and casino games all was calm – there were no reported riots or disturbances.

Those gambling used brass chips to do so, and the prison appointed a cashier who took charge of the money won or lost. The prisoners built their own casino tables.

The Sacramento Bee paper reported, admiringly, in 1962: 'Here behind the old limestone walls of the institution two miles east of Carson City, gambling – legal, above board, sanctioned, aided and abetted by prison officials – is high on the list of approved recreation.'

Fascinated by the story, an Italian paper, Epoca, reported incredulously to its readers – 'In this prison you can become rich.'

When Fogliani departed, so did the poker playing –the day after Fogliani retired, the new man in charge, Warden Hocker, shut the casino down – replacing it with activities such as knitting.

256. SEVENTY FIVE GRAND – SIMON'S EXPENSIVE LESSON

Newly appointed as public relations man for giant bookies, Coral, Simon Clare, now Coral's Director of Communcations, admits that in May 1997 he was 'to put it mildly, a bit wet behind the ears' when he went to the Curragh in Ireland where he was 'killing time in the press room' when an Aidan O'Brien-trained two year old won a maiden race by eight lengths at 2/7.

'I didn't bother going out to the winner's enclosure,' says Clare, but as press representatives returned they began to enquire of him what odds he was offering about the O'Brien winner for the next year's 2000 Guineas. One of them, the late Christopher Poole, then of London's *Evening Standard*, told Clare that if he wanted to outdo his rivals, who had the horse as a 14/1 or 20/1 chance, he should offer 25/1.

'As this was many years before Irish racing was broadcast on the racing channels I rang Coral's senior odds compiler, described the performance as "what you'd expect of a 2/7 favourite" and suggested we offer 25/1, to which he agreed.'

Clare duly distributed the price and 'was suddenly descended upon by every member of the travelling British racing press corps, who immediately formed an orderly queue in front of me, and proceeded to offer up bets ranging from £200 to £400, and even one of £1,000.'

By the time he'd taken them all, Clare had laid the horse to lose £75,000 – at which point it was only then revealed to him that O'Brien had described the horse, King of Kings, as 'very, very special … a potential superstar'.

Realising he had been lured into quoting an extremely generous price to the assembled hacks – let alone any clients who managed to get on, too – Clare arrived back at his office to find the odds halved to 12/1 and irate trading officials anxious to learn why they had been quoting such lengthy odds for such a well touted hot prospect. Clare then broke the news about the additional £75,000 liability, about which he 'hadn't thought to tell anyone.'

Almost a year later, Clare 'winced as King of Kings landed the 2000 Guineas, and in so doing, ensured my initiation at the Curragh proved costly for Coral' and also taught him a valuable lesson – 'to keep my wits about me at all times' – especially when suspecting he was being conned by the racing hack pack!

257. PRINCELY GAMBLER

German nobleman, Prince Puckler-Muskau, was very well travelled around Europe. He came to tour England in 1826, and professed himself astonished at the hold that gambling and horseracing seemed to have over the country at that time. Such an impression did it make on him that he committed his thoughts to paper following a visit to Newmarket:

'In noise, uproar and clamour the scene resembles a Jews' synagogue, with a greater display of passion. The persons of the drama are the first peers of England, livery servants, the lowest sharpers and black-legs; in short, all who have money to bet here claim equal rights.

'Dukes, lords, grooms and rogues shout, scream and halloo together, and bet together till suddenly the cry is heard "The horses have started!"

'In a minute the crowd disperses; but the bettors soon meet again at the ropes which enclose the course. You see a multitude of telescopes, opera-glasses levelled from the carriages . . . and for a few moments a deep and anxious silence pervades the motley crowd.

'Then once more arises the wildest uproar: shouts and lamentations, curses and cheers re-echo on every side, from Lords and Ladies, far and wide. 'Ten to four on the Admiral! A hundred to one on Madame Vestris! Small Beer against the field!' are heard from the almost frantic bettors; and scarcely do you hear a 'Done!' uttered here and there, when the noble animals are before you – past you – in the twinkling of an eye; the next moment at the goal, and luck or skill or knavery have decided the victory.'

It is recorded that the Prince was a heavy winner on his first visit to the sports.

258. DAD KNOWS BEST

Chris Kirkland's Dad and a few of his uncles reckoned that the young teenager was good enough to go all the way in the world of football. So they clubbed together and staked £100 at 100/1 with me on the lad growing up to win a senior cap for England.

Three times he made the squad only to miss out on playing any part in a match, until, finally, in 2006 he was sent on to play between the sticks for his country against Greece – and win his Dad and uncles £10,000.

259. I WAS THE PRATT

Only there as a substitute fielder, cricketer Gary Pratt came on for England – and controversially ran out Australian skipper Ricky Ponting during the Ashes Series, in September 2005, making a name for himself, and landing a £3,400 windfall for a pal of his who has placed a bet with William Hill that Pratt would one day play for England.

The 26 year old Neil Stoker, from Crook near Newcastle in County Durham, went to school with Pratt and in March 2003 placed a bet of £100 with William Hill at odds of 33/1 that his friend – a player for Durham's county cricket side – would make an appearance for the England cricket team within the next five years, and was amazed when he saw him come on to the pitch and run out the Aussie captain, in the process igniting a row over the use of substitute fielders.

Strictly speaking Hills wouldn't have expected to pay out on Neil's bet until Gary Pratt won a cap for starting an England match, but given the extraordinary circumstances surrounding his unexpected starring role they thought it would be a little churlish not to pay out. Neil, a Newcastle fan, said that his winnings would pay for his season ticket for a couple of years to come.

260. FLIGHT OF FANCY

Two hundred and sixty people lost their lives when American Airlines flight number 587 crashed on the morning of 12 November 2001 in Queens, New York City. Hours later, '5-8-7' was the winning number in the New Jersey Lottery's Pick-3 game.

So many players – 27,829 – had used the doomed plane's flight number as a morbid tip for the lottery outcome that the payout was a mere $16 for a 50 cent line.

261. CUSTER'S LAST HAND?

Not only did the US lose one of its greatest generals in June 1876 when Native Americans wiped out George Armstrong Custer and his outnumbered men at the Battle of the Little Bighorn – it also lost a pair of its keenest poker players.

For both Custer and his younger brother, Captain Tom Custer, who was with him in that fateful battle, had a history of controversial poker playing behind them.

George's poker playing had nearly got him into big trouble with the military authorities when, in the late 1860s, he was apparently in the habit of gambling regularly with his subordinate officers in the 7th Cavalry. Worse, he was accused of 'welshing' on his poker debts by at least one of those officers, a charge which, according to historians, created something of a rift between officers in the unit 'that endured until the Battle of the Little Bighorn' according to authority Wayne R Austerman, even though charges were never actually filed against him.

Brother Tom was perhaps an even more enthusiastic – and somewhat better – poker player. Author Carl Sifakis called him 'the best Poker player in the 7th Cavalry, an organization renowned nearly as much for its gambling prowess as for its fighting abilities'.

By all accounts he was something of a reckless player who would play for big stakes and thought nothing of bluffing with abandon in order to bully his opponents out of the game. His most infamous hand saw him dealt the six, seven and ten of spades. He raised the stakes, hoping to draw more spades.

Table rules were that any card accidentally exposed on the original deal must be taken, but one turned over on the draw would be voided and another dealt in its place.

Custer's first draw card was the eight of spades, much to his delight. The second, as everyone could see when it struck his hand as it was dealt, and turned face up, was the king of spades, which would have completed his flush, as became obvious to all the players as Custer began to swear and curse.

Knowing the rules, though, Custer had to be dealt another card, which he duly accepted with a glare.

As the betting continued, Custer raised aggressively, with the rest of the players assuming he was, as usual, bluffing.

Eventually, everyone called and the cards were revealed – Custer's glares turned to grins as he showed a straight flush. The card he had received instead of the king of spades had been the nine of spades.

262. THE FIRST BETTING EXCHANCE, 1822?

The text of the Old Betting Book of All Souls College 1815-73 is a privately published tome from 1912, and I managed to find one of the few copies still extant.

It contains 654 fascinating wagers struck by and between members of the Oxford establishment, meticulously logged in the original Betting Book.

Fellow and librarian of the college, C Oman, chronicled the bets over a seven-year period, discovering their outcome with painstaking thoroughness.

The very first bet recorded took place on March 26, 1815 – 'a memorable month for Napoleon had landed on the coast of Provence'. The wager: 'Cartwright bets Berens ten pounds to one that some Jurist fellow now of the College – Frank Lawley excepted – will marry before D'Oyly does.'

Oman reveals that Berens paid up on May 27, 1817 as 'D'Oyly entered into wedlock in 1820, but Paul Beilby Lawley, a Jurist and brother of Frank Lawley, was married three years before D'Oyly in 1817, thereby losing Berens the sum of £1.'

Here are some further examples of these early forerunners of the betting exchange principle:

263. BOOKIE

'Anyone who knows the interior of the Codrington Library, with its innumerable locks and keys will be lost in admiration for the agility of Edward Dawkins, who won the modest sum of half a crown from L Sneyd, by taking out every hand-catalogue in every bookcase in the Library, opening and shutting each door, upstairs and down in the space of fifteen minutes,' declared Oman of the 1815 wager.

He had to work for his winnings, as there were more than 70 catalogues, most only accessible by unlocking a door, which Dawkins had to close behind him.

264. HUNTLEY BETS BLIND

January 16, 1821 saw a remarkable challenge laid down:

'Huntley bets Cartwright a pound that setting a chair on one side of the great quadrangle, he will wheel a wheel-barrow within twenty yards of it on one side or the other, starting from the opposite side.'

Not much of a challenge, you might say. But, there was a catch – 'NB Huntley to be blinded, and running against the chains is to be counted as off the grass.'

Tension mounted, as others stepped in to take sides over this wager.

Oman noted that 'twenty yards seems a liberal limit when we consider that the whole grass-plot is only 41 yards broad. However,' he reports, 'the feat was accomplished.'

265. WEIGHT FOR IT

'Buller bets Barrington one guinea per annum for the next eight years that Barrington, now 12 stone 9lbs, gains a stone in each successive year till he is twenty stone, April 11 being the day to decide' – that was the wager struck on April 10, 1821.

A year later, Barrington had actually lost 5lb, so Buller paid up a guinea and the rest of the bet was voided.

266. TO SNUFF IT, OR NOT

'Ryder bets Peel five shillings that before Peel returns to All Souls from the East he will resume the habit of taking snuff.' This December 1859 wager, not to be sniffed at, was won by Peel.

267. ANNUAL DEBATE

An 1862 wager had echoes many years later when the debate raged over whether Millennium celebrations held on December 31, 1999 were a year premature.

Here, 'Lane bets Nutt that we are at present in the 63rd year of the 19th century and not in the 62nd year'. Oman confirmed Nutt as the winner: 'The first year of the century was 1801 not 1800, otherwise the first century AD would have had only 99 years.'

268. HEADING FOR A WINNER

On May 28, 1865, 'Malcolm bets Compton one shilling that Malcolm's head is bigger than Compton's, Stanhope to be measurer, measure to be taken just above the ears.' Big-headed Malcolm was evidently right, as Compton paid up – but promptly won his shilling back by taking a bet from Robarts that 'Robarts' dress boots are a foot long'.

269. HAIR-RAISING

A truly hair-raising bet was determined on May 23, 1869 – 'Lane bets Compton five shillings that Garnier's hair when cut off weighs more than Stanhope's.'

The subjects of the bet went through with it – and the bald truth emerged that Lane won the five bob.

270. THE LAST COLLEGE GAMBLE

On April 12, 1873, the final All Souls College wager was struck:

'Stopford bets Doyle half a crown that more of Stopford's list are married within the next five years than of Doyle's list – Nutt E; Ridley; Buller; Lane; Skene. Doyle's list – Matthew Ridley; Scott; Malcolm; Robarts; Buchanan.'

Doyle emerged triumphant with three of his list, Ridley, Scott and Malcolm, tying the knot, compared with Stopford's two, Nutt and Skene.

271. BRIGHTON EARLY

James Selby, a professional coachman, was at Ascot races in 1888 when he was wagered a bet of £1,000 to £500 that he could not drive a coach to Brighton and back in eight hours.

He set off from the White Horse Cellar, Piccadilly, punctually at 10am on July 13 – and arrived at Brighton's Old Ship tavern at 1.56pm.

Turning straight round and heading back towards London, he returned to the White Horse Cellar at 5.50pm – ten minutes within the deadline.

Selby had little time to enjoy his winnings – he was dead by the end of the year.

272. TAKE A TIP FROM ME – OR NOT!

It is an age-old scam. Dodgy tipsters convince gullible punters that they have inside information that they will impart in return for a financial consideration.

Gullible punter hands over said consideration. Dodgy tipster either runs off with said cash, providing no tip at all, or hands over a tip no better or worse than that contained in the day's newspapers.

Gullible punter has a moan and complains to media, friends, relatives and anyone else prepared to listen to the old, old story.

In June 2008 the Office of Fair Trading decided to get involved and visited Epsom racecourse on the eve of the Derby, issuing a 'new tipping scheme', which was nothing of the sort, to alert our old friends, the Gullible Punters, to the dangers of bogus tipsters.

The scheme took the form of a mock mailshot from 'Race Winners Partnership'.

The OFT estimated that punters are ripped off for at least £5 million per annum by such scams.

'These scammers are expert in one thing – parting people from their cash with empty promises of inside information, guaranteed huge profits and bogus money-back offers. It's a gamble not worth taking.'

John McCririck backed the campaign, declaring: 'The activities of bogus racing tipsters are bringing into disrepute the whole of the horseracing industry.'

No-one, though, seemed to ask a crucial question – what does our friend, Mr Gullible Punter, really expect when he signs up for such a scam?

If the answer is that he believes he will be getting details about possibly dishonest goings-on, or inside information that would be against the rules of racing if divulged, then I'm afraid there is a strong argument that they deserve all they get – or don't get.

In the event that the information they received enabled them to benefit financially from dishonesty, I don't suppose they would have any moral qualms about keeping their winnings – do you?

273. NO SUCH THING AS A WINNING SYSTEM

Malaysian gambler Koh Ah Wang listened to, and believed, a man who told him that he would teach him how to divine winning lottery numbers by invoking spirits in an anthill.

When Ah Wang failed to persuade the spirits to appear he turned on 37-year-old Azam Ramli and beat him to death with a steel bar, reported the Fortean Times magazine in 2007.

274. RIGHT CHARLIE

Charles Kennedy, former leader of the Lib Dems, won £2,000 with a bet on his own party in 1994's European elections – and it nearly cost him the future leadership.

Because Kennedy staked £50 on them to win just TWO seats – when the party was briefing that it expected to win up to TEN.

Imagine the embarrassment and headlines when the story leaked out into the press, courtesy of The Sun's chief reporter, John Kay.

Mr Kennedy had staked his bet in a William Hill branch. After party officials denied all knowledge of the wager, Kay resorted to the traditional standby of all experienced reporters – and door-stepped Mr Kennedy to obtain confirmation of his story.

When the news broke he was severely criticised within the party.

He later explained, in a Guardian interview in 1999, the year in which he actually became leader of the Lib Dems: 'I wasn't betting against the party. It was in line with what I'd publicly predicted.

'Looking back it's funny now, but it was embarrassing at the time. If I could change one walk with destiny, I wouldn't walk to the bookies on that particular occasion.'

275. WHAT NEXT, THE DOGGER?

Eyebrows were raised when the Tote introduced their latest bet in June 2008 – the Swinger! They denied that there was any sexual connotation to the wager, which involved picking two horses to finish in the first three in any order.

The Tote declared it to be the latest addition to their range of 'exotic' bets – punters of a certain sexual bent were believed to be eagerly awaiting any future innovations of a similar nature. It was unclear whether there had been any misunderstandings in betting shops when punters came in asking for details of how to join in with the Swinger.

There were no reported plans to introduce an each-way Swinger or a Lucky 69 to the Tote's portfolio of punting pleasure, or to team up with Ann Summers in any joint promotions.

276. JUMPING THROUGH HOOPS

Top basketball referee Tim Donaghy admitted in 2008 to gambling on matches he refereed and to providing coded tips to high-stakes gamblers for a $5,000 payoff.

The National Basketball Association official co-operated with investigators in an effort to secure a reduced sentence.

He faced a $500,000 fine and up to 25 years in prison, but in July 2008 was sentenced to 15 months.

The US media reported that he had begun placing bets on games in 2003 and passed information to gamblers 'including which crews would officiate games and how the various officials and players interacted'.

It was not apparently revealed, though, whether he had made calls in matches he was officiating that influenced the outcome of games and the points margins involved.

277. LONG AND SHORT OF IT

Robert Welch, one of the Great Train Robbers, was believed to be the brains behind the Rochester greyhound coup in May 1978.

'The Long and Short Stakes' was an odd contest, which involved two heats, run over a trip of 277 metres, with a final run over 901 metres.

The winners of the two sprint races were 4-1 chance Leysdown Fun, and 33-1 shot Leysdown Pleasure. Both had been bought from Ireland and had had their names changed.

The two dogs were heavily backed in a vast number of multiple bets, coupling them with every dog in a race at another track, so that all the bets naming them with the winner of that other race were win doubles.

Welch claimed that the dogs had been supported in more than 200 betting shops, and that his winnings added up to £109,000. Other estimates put the total as high as £300,000.

Many bookmakers refused to pay out once details of the coup began to emerge. There were allegations that the starting prices of the two Leysdowns had been artificially manipulated at the track. Another claim was that the perpetrators had deliberately entered sprinters in a competition designed to attract stayers – although it is difficult to see where the offence in that might be.

Frustrated punters made strenuous efforts to receive payment – the locks of hundreds of betting shops were jammed with superglue, although those involved with the coup always denied any involvement with this particular campaign.

Police spent years investigating the circumstances of the coup, eventually compiling a 200-page report. Only a few bookmakers ever paid out, with Welch claiming to have collected £20,000.

278. TWENTY GREAT GAMBLING UPSETS

The greatest sports betting upset of recent years may have been in 2004 when Greece defied all the critics and all the bookmakers' odds to sensationally win Euro 2004, beating the hosts Portugal in the final and knocking out defending champions France in the quarter-finals. William Hill had Greece at 100-1 before the tournament. Here are 19 more great turn-ups that left most punters scratching their heads and a few lucky, or psychic punters, counting their winnings.

279. COMEBACK WREXHAM

Wrexham v Arsenal – FA Cup 1992

The FA Cup has a habit of throwing up shocks and this example is one of the greatest in the competition's history. In 1992, Wrexham defeated the league champions Arsenal in the third round, Wrexham having finished bottom of the Football League the previous season. Arsenal took the lead in the game through Alan Smith but Wrexham stormed back to send the Gunners crashing at the Racecourse Ground at odds of 25-1!

280. OZ-ON LOSERS

Bangladesh v Australia – June 18, 2005

Bangladesh pulled off what may be the greatest shock ever in cricket betting with a five-wicket victory over world champions Australia in a one-day international in Cardiff in 2005. The Tigers were aided by a magnificent century from Mohammad Ashraful and surpassed Australia's 249 for 5 with four balls to spare. Ashraful was the game's top runscorer at 6-1 and the huge upset was completed when Jason Gillespie was hit for the winning runs in a victory that was priced at a massive 20-1 before the game.

281. SAINTS ALIVE

St Gallen beating Chelsea in 2000

Chelsea suffered a succession of embarrassing defeats in the UEFA Cup in the pre-Roman Abramovich era, including a home loss to Hapoel Tel Aviv. However, the biggest by far was the humiliating exit at the hands of Swiss minnows St Gallen in 2000. 1-0 up from the first leg, Chelsea were 1-100 to progress but were beaten 2-1 thanks to goals from Sascha Muller and Charles Amoah, which sent the Swiss outfit through at odds of 16-1 after the first leg.

282. STICHED UP

Richard Krajicek wins Wimbledon in 1996

In 1996, the previously little known Richard Krajicek lifted the famous Wimbledon trophy, beating the equally unrecognisable name of Mal Washington in the final. Krajicek was not fancied before the tournament and could have been backed at 66-1. He beat Michael Stich in the fourth round and then stunned the 2-1 favourite Pete Sampras in the quarter-final.

283. YANKS A LOT!

USA 1-0 England – 1950 World Cup

On June 29 1950, England were one of the superpowers in world football with a post-war record of 23 wins, four losses and three draws. The Americans had lost their last seven international matches and were supposed to be the whipping boys of a group that also contained Spain and Chile. England were 3-1 to win the World Cup with USA at 500-1! Joe Gaetjens was the goalscorer on that famous occasion in 1950 when the underdogs stunned the football world, producing one of the greatest upsets in World Cup history. A film called The Miracle Match was released in 2005 depicting the true story behind the game and capturing the circumstances leading up to this incredible result.

284. IRISH EYES SMILING

Northern Ireland 1 England 0 – September 7, 2005

On September 7, 2005, an England team managed by Sven Goran Eriksson suffered a humiliating defeat to Northern Ireland in a World Cup qualifier at Lansdowne Road. David Healy's 73rd-minute strike was enough for Lawrie Sanchez's men, giving them their first victory over England since 1972, at odds of 16-1.

Very few had fancied the Irish before the game and England had been backed heavily at odds-on; indeed, they were (laughably) only 7-1 to win the World Cup final in Germany the following year.

285. DREAM ON

Dream Team Stunned By Argentina in 2004 Olympics

The US men's basketball team, known as the Dream Team, were humbled in Athens in the 2004 Olympic semi-finals by Argentina, beaten 89-81.

Argentina had a 43-38 half-time lead and never allowed their more glamorous opponents to overtake them as the Americans tried desperately to avoid a shock defeat.

The Americans had been gold medallists in every Olympics since 1992 when NBA players started competing in the games, and were the massive favourites at 1-6 to win their fourth successive title even before the Olympics began.

286. CUPSET

Cameroon v Argentina – 1990 World Cup

Italia 90 was one of the most exciting World Cups in the last 30 years, and it threw up a classic upset in the opening game. Argentina were defending their title, won in Mexico in 1986, but were stunned by Francois Oman Biyik's header as Cameroon went on to win 1-0. Cameroon were 12-1 to win the game – the Argentinians still went on to reach the final, where they lost to West Germany.

287. KNOCKOUT UPSET

Mike Tyson loses to James Buster Douglas in 1990

When Mike Tyson took on James 'Buster' Douglas, there was almost no-one who gave Douglas a cat in hell's chance of coming out of the ring on two feet, let alone beating the invincible Tyson.

Douglas was a 42-1 outsider, while Tyson was at 1-200 to defend his title: an unbelievable price and one that cost several punters a hefty sum.

Tyson's left eye began to swell in the fifth round and in the ninth round his eye closed completely, until the final assault in the tenth round, when one of boxing's greatest shocks was completed.

288. PAR FOR THE COURSE

Ben Curtis wins the 2003 British Open

On July 20, 2003, Ben Curtis secured one of golf's greatest shocks, winning by one shot from Swede Thomas Bjorn who managed to capitulate on the final few holes.

He was the first first-time Open winner since Tom Watson in 1975 and Curtis, who was ranked 396th in the world before the tournament, beat a top-class field including world number one Tiger Woods, who finished two shots off the lead at one over par.

Curtis could have been backed at 750-1 to win at Royal St Georges and was the only man to finish under par for the tournament.

289. RUSSIAN TO THE TITLE

Miracle on Ice – 1980

In a game dubbed as the Miracle on Ice, a team of amateur and collegiate ice hockey players from the USA humiliated the dominant and heavily backed Soviet Union team.

The USA could have been backed at 33-1 just to win the match and they astonishingly went on to win the gold medal, beating Finland in the final.

290. EAST WENT WEST

USA wins Women's 4x100 metre freestyle relay – 1976 Olympics

In arguably the greatest relay victory in history, the USA 4x100m freestyle relay team shocked the world when they defeated everyone including the East German favourites who had been sweeping everyone aside and who punters had widely expected to take gold.

The US team of Kim Peyton, Wendy Boglioli, Jill Sterkel and Shirley Babashoff shocked the world, winning at odds of 20-1 and setting a world record of 3min 44.82sec.

291. NO LAUGHING MATTER

Goran Ivanisevic wins Wimbledon in 2001

Goran Ivanisevic produced an amazing display at the 2001 Wimbledon championships, winning the title at odds of 250-1!

He beat Pat Rafter in five sets in the final and became the first wild card in the history of the tournament to capture the title.

Ivanisevic had previously reached the 1992, 1994 and 1998 finals but his victory in 2001 came as a huge shock to the tennis world and only very shrewd punters would have predicted the outcome at the start of the tournament.

Ivanisevic's dour countenance on-court once persuaded bookies to take bets on whether he would ever be seen smiling on camera.

292. LEAGUES APART

Papua New Guinea 20-18 Great Britain – 1990 rugby league

In 1990 more than 11,500 fanatical Papua New Guinea fans watched their team stun Great Britain and condemn them to their one and only loss to the Kumuls. It was an historic victory and one that was not backed before the game despite an amazing price of 20-1. Papua New Guinea were even given a +28 point handicap!

293. CUE SHOCK RESULT

Shaun Murphy – World Snooker Championships 2005

In 2005, Shaun Murphy became the first qualifier to win the World Snooker Championship at The Crucible since Terry Griffiths in 1979. Murphy was a 150-1 shot at the beginning of the championship but defied all the odds, beating a host of stars including John Higgins and Peter Ebdon before overcoming Matthew Stevens by 18 frames to 16 in the final.

294. ALL BLACKS STUNNED

France beat New Zealand 43-31 – World Cup 1999

Although France are one of rugby's superpowers, they were heavily unfancied at the 1999 World Cup and produced an upset that some have described as the greatest shock in World Cup history when beating the mighty New Zealand in the semi-final.

Jonah Lomu scored two tries but even he could not prevent France marching on to the final, where they were beaten by Australia.

France were 8-1 to win the game and had a massive +25 point handicap!

295. PAPA'S THE DADDY

Senegal 1 France 0 – 2002 World Cup

In a story that virtually mirrored Italia 90, the defending champions were beaten in the opening game by an African team making their first appearance at the World Cup finals (Cameroon were making their second appearance when they beat Argentina).

Papa Bouba Diop, later of Fulham, scored the only goal of the game to stun the footballing world at odds of 10-1.

Punters steamed into France in every game in Group A, assuming that a change in fortune was round the corner, but it never came and France limped out of the World Cup at the group stage with one point and no goals scored.

296. LLOSER

Lleyton Hewitt loses to Ivo Karlovic – Wimbledon 1999

Lleyton Hewitt was defending his Wimbledon title in 1999 when he was sent tumbling out in the first round by Ivo Karlovic, in the worst performance ever by a defending champion – he was the first champion to crash in the first round since tennis became professional in 1968. Karlovic was ranked number 203 in the world and nobody had seen this result coming – indeed, he could have been backed at 12-1 to beat the Australian!

Karlovic was beaten in the third round by Max Mirnyi.

297. FOINOHOPE TRIUMPHS

Foinavon wins the 1967 Grand National

The 1967 Grand National has become part of horseracing and betting folklore and gives once-a-year punters reason for hope. Foinavon was priced as a 100-1 outsider in the 1967 Grand National and coming to the 23rd fence the bookmakers' judgement looked spot-on, as the bottom weight was tailed off. But a loose horse caused a pile-up at Aintree's smallest fence and no-hoper Foinavon eluded the melee to go clear of his field; he eventually won by 15 lengths. A friend of mine, who knew a bit about racing, took a bet from a pal of his on Foinavon to win this race. Aware that it had no chance on the book he stuck the 2/6d (12.5p) bet – well, we were 16 at the time and still at school – in his pocket and forgot all about it. He couldn't afford to pay the £12.50 and it was some while before the pair were reconciled.

298. WOULD YOU LIKE CASH, SIR ?

Patrick Lummis briefly feared that his business was bust when a punter entered his Classic Racing betting shop in February 1993 and handed over a slip boasting a £5 accumulator showing seven winners, which totted up to the small matter of £1,000,000,000 in winnings.

Taking a closer look, Lummis spotted that the seven winners detailed did not appear to tally with those appearing on his copy of the slip.

'I told him we would not be paying as it was not an authentic slip, but he insisted it was genuine and demanded payment,' recalled Lummis, who decided to let the constabulary adjudicate.

The punter was eventually let off with a caution, but no cash.

299. PISSING AWAY QUARTER OF A MILLION

Nick The Greek and Joe Bernstein, two of the biggest gamblers of their generation, were facing each other in a winner-take-all $150,000 buy-in Five Card Stud showdown at the Flamingo Hotel in Las Vegas in 1947.

Bernstein had a pet superstition – maybe for well-founded personal safety reasons – that he would never sit down in a game unless he could do so with his back against the wall. Possibly so that no-one could pass behind him to catch a glimpse of his cards, possibly because he was well aware of the fact that when Wild Bill Hickok forgot that identical trait it ended with him being shot from behind.

Nick The Greek – of whom we will read more later – seemed to harbour no such concerns and alongside him was a beautiful showgirl, his date, named Marie, who was happy to sit and watch Nick playing his cards.

The game was an hour old and it was going Bernstein's way – he was $25,000 to the good, meaning his stash of chips was now worth $175,000 while Nick was reduced to $125,000.

The current hand was building nicely – there was $90,000 in the pot when the pair received their last upcard. Nick drew an ace; Bernstein was showing a pair of twos.

Nick looked at his hole card. Marie looked, too. Nick 'tapped out' for his remaining $80,000. He shoved his entire stash into the middle of the table. As he did so, Marie pushed her chair back, stood up and announced she was heading to the ladies room.

Nick made a comment to Bernstein – encouraging him to match the 80 grand if he dared. If he did the hand would be worth a cool quarter of a million dollars to the winner.

Bernstein stared at Nick's ace, jack, six and five, comparing them with his own visible pair of twos. Knowing that his own hole card did not improve his hand, Bernstein had to deduce whether the Greek had a hidden card to match any of the visible four – if he did so then Bernstein knew he could not win.

He thought some more before, slowly, he called the $80,000 bet.

The Greek immediately threw in his hand, commenting: 'You win, Joe. Marie blew the pot for me – you read her actions.'

He was spot-on. Bernstein confirmed, as Nick had feared, that he had deduced that Marie would have refrained from leaving the room had she believed that her boyfriend had a hand good enough to beat Bernstein.

Bernstein was relieved that Marie had decided to relieve herself. The Greek was left pissed off.

300. GAMBLING GHOSTS

Jane Whitaker, manager of a William Hill betting shop in Launceston, Cornwall, was spooked when a photo was taken in her branch – 'when it was developed there was a ghostly apparition in the background'.

Alan French, manager of a betting shop in Merton, London, was left wondering when one of his fruit machines stopped working at precisely the same time that it later emerged a regular user of it had died.

George Wallis played a jackpot fruit machine at the Plume & Feathers pub in Weedon, Northampton in the autumn of 1997, and landed the big payout – which was marginally unusual, as George had died 80 years earlier.

Known as a ladies' man and a snappy dresser, George put in an appearance at the pub when cleaner Jackie Cook-Walker was working alone – 'He was playing the fruit machine and there was a shadow over it. I was out like a shot, it was terrifying.'

When Jackie told locals of her experience they told her about the pub's resident spectre, about whom landlord Paul Breese commented: 'He does seem to be addicted and it may be time to call in Ghostly Gamblers Anonymous.'

301. MUST HAVE BEEN FED UP

Francine Hodges from Southend placed a £50 bet with me at odds of 25-1 that she could lose six stone from her 16st 13lb frame in six months.

Standing to collect £1,250 in winnings, she confessed to me that she was a clairvoyant, and therefore 'knew' she would win. She put weight on.

302. EYE'VE WON

Robert Alois won £45,000 at the roulette table in Monte Carlo in July 1996, without even placing a bet. The money was paid to him as compensation after the steel ball flew off the roulette table and struck the Frenchman in the eye.

303. WINNING VIRTUALLY EIGHTY GRAND

Virtual racing is heavily criticised in certain quarters. However, the computer-generated betting opportunity broadcast regularly in the betting shops accounts for a significant volume of turnover and, in May 2008, a Belfast man landed the biggest ever winning bet of its type.

Well known in the city as a popular cab driver, the punter picked the four selections in his Lucky 15 bet on the Steepledowns 'virtual' meeting in his local shop, watched the first three win at odds of 5-1, 25-1 and 16-1, and then went off to pick up a fare.

At this point the cabbie was already set to pick up a handy £3,401, but he returned later to check the result of the last 'runner' at 6.22 and 'whooped' his way around the betting office when the staff told him his last selection had also won at 20-1. Including William Hill's ten per cent 'tip' (a bonus for all correct Lucky 15 winners) his virtual winnings totalled a breathtakingly real £82,327.30

304. BLAZING ROW

Tens of thousands of partisan supporters flocked to London's Lillie Bridge stadium, then Britain's premier athletics venue, in September 1887 to see the sprint showdown between Londoner, Harry Hutches, and Geordie, Harry Gent.

Dubbed 'the Race of the Century', hundreds of thousands of pounds had been staked in bets with the bookies thronging the arena.

Unbeknown to the spectators, the managers of the two runners had agreed to fix the result to enable them to land a betting coup.

But when their runners learned of the scam they wanted nothing to do with it – and left the stadium.

Word began to spread and the crowd became a rampaging mob that began to riot – eventually burning down and destroying the stadium.

305. THE GAMBLER WHO DIED OF 'COMPASSION'

As he celebrated his 50th birthday in 1858, professional gambler John Powell, a poker expert, could claim to have built up a fortune of half a million dollars through his shrewd but honest play.

He was a real rarity – contemporary estimates calculated that of some 2,000 riverboat gamblers operating on the Mississippi waters aboard the flourishing steamboats, just a fraction were honest folk. One writer suggested that he knew of just four above-board operators.

Not long after his half-century celebrations, Powell had taken part in a poker game aboard the steamer, Atlantic, in which he played for three days and nights, running up his share of the $791.50 bar bill among the four players, but also winning $50,000. He then became involved in a game with a young English traveller, winning his entire fortune of $8,000, together with his luggage.

The Englishman, showing typical stiff upper lip control, accepted his loss and retired to his cabin for the night.

Next morning he appeared in the dining saloon for breakfast. He shook hands with fellow passengers before shooting himself dead.

Powell was so distraught that he discovered where the young man lived and sent the $8,000 and the luggage back to his family. He also gave up gambling for a year as a form of penance.

Returning to the profession, Powell discovered that he had lost the element of ruthlessness from his game and very soon began to become a regular loser.

Eventually his decline contributed to his death. One unimpressed writer said: 'He died broke – an example to his colleagues of the dangers of compassion.'

306. PROOF OF THE PUNTING

Colin McLean, a proof-reader at the Sporting Life newspaper, came up with what seemed to him to be a foolproof system to ensure his dog bets were winners in May 1966.

He simply altered the results from out-of-London tracks while he was checking the proofs of the paper, to make sure that they corresponded with bets he had placed.

Of course, this was just too blatant a fraud to survive for any length of time and he was inevitably rumbled and fined £100 for trying to obtain money by false pretences – almost certainly less than the amount by which he had profited.

307. CRADLEY CONMAN

A mystery man turned up at a Birmingham news agency that was responsible for distributing results from Cradley Heath dog track to the media in 1974, telling them that he was a representative from the Sporting Life newspaper.

The man then arrived at the dog track when racing was going on, and persuaded the agency man that he did not need to send through the result of the last race to the Life as he would phone it through for him.

Unbeknown to the agency man, though, the self-styled Life representative was no such thing, but a conman who had already placed a number of hefty wagers on the outcome of the last race being four to beat five.

Although that was not the actual outcome he nonetheless rang it through to the Life, purporting to be from the agency, and it was the result that duly appeared in the paper next morning, complete with forecast payment of £5.27.

The conman was paid out on one of his bets at a Putney, London betting shop the next day – but he was unable to collect the rest of his £10 units, each of which might have gained him £527, because he had not realised that the size of his bets would lead to the small bookies with whom he had placed them 'hedging' them on to larger firms, to lay off their potential payouts.

The larger firms had had representatives at Cradley Heath who quickly pointed out the bogus result supplied to the Life and notified betting shops.

However, the conman made off with the £527 he had managed to be paid and was never caught, leaving Archie Newhouse, greyhound editor of the Life, wondering whether it might have been an inside job – 'He must have been quite a conman, he even had what appeared to be *Sporting Life* notepaper!'

308. NOT SO WISE

Nigel Wise, 23, was jailed for two years, and Paul Miell, 22, for nine months, in June 1975 after admitting conspiring to defraud Ladbrokes.

The pair planned to intercept and delay the Exchange Telegraph commentary on a greyhound race. While Wise operated the equipment, Miell would go into the betting shop and place a bet.

Miell stole the key to a shop next door to Ladbrokes in Reading, and Wise climbed a telegraph pole to redirect wires from the betting shop into the empty premises.

But when they arrived to carry out the coup, police were waiting for them.

309. WAT'S IT ALL ABOUT?

Watford greyhound track, which shared the football club's Vicarage Road ground, inspired a man called Heinz Kuhl to come up with what he believed to be a cunning plan to beat the bookies in 1976.

Kuhl stationed himself at the track, in a position where he was able to signal the outcome of the race just run to his accomplice, Maria Lawrence, the moment the dogs passed the finish line. Her job was to rush into the betting shop and slap down her bet before the 'off-time' of the race would have been notified.

They rehearsed, then went for it for real. Kuhl watched the race, signalled to Lawrence, who dashed into the shop, selecting the appropriate pre-prepared betting slip. It was accepted. A doddle. Or was it? When the result came through to the shop she'd backed a loser. Kuhl had signalled the wrong number.

D'oh!

They tried again. This time someone had shopped the would-be Bonnie and Clyde criminal masterminds and the bungling pair from Shepherds Bush were nabbed and sent to court, where they were fined for conspiracy to defraud.

Then, a year later, four members of a gang based in the Watford area were convicted of using walkie-talkie radios to swindle bookies out of £250.

Prosecuting, Michael Wilkinson explained how the fraud, based on races at the Watford track, had worked: 'As the race finished, the gang member would shin over the fence and would shout the name of the winner to another man in a nearby phone box. He would phone the result to yet another member in a phone box near a bookmaker's shop in or around London. That man would be using a walkie-talkie radio and he could pass the message to a fourth gang member already inside a betting shop. He would have a walkie-talkie radio hidden under his clothes, with an earpiece hidden by a woolly hat. As soon as he got the winning greyhound he would fill in his betting slip, make his bet and collect his winnings. The whole operation, from race-track to betting shop could be completed within a minute of the race finishing.'

Police filmed the operation taking place to, er, trap those involved in the plot, which relied on late notification of 'off' times or lax staff, who assumed that those placing the bets could not possibly be aware of the result.

It must have been difficult to find an empty phone box in Watford in those days!

310. RITZ CRACKERS

A mysterious Hungarian woman was dubbed the 'mistressmind' behind a million-pound casino sting that prompted a nine-month police investigation in 2004, before the perpetrators were allowed to keep their winnings.

Three people – including the 'chic and beautiful' 32-year-old who, according to sources in Budapest, had been banned from casinos in her home capital, together with her accomplices, two 'elegant' Serbian men aged 33 and 38 – turned up at London's Ritz Casino in March 2004.

It would later transpire that the trio had introduced into the casino, via a mobile phone, a laser scanner linked to a microcomputer.

The scanner apparently detected the speed of the roulette ball as it left the croupier's hand, identified where it dropped, and measured the declining orbit of the wheel.

These factors enabled the computer to predict the seven number section of the wheel in which the ball would come to rest.

The numbers to back were signalled as the wheel completed its third spin, just leaving time to 'get on'. With the random odds of success reduced from 36-1 to 6-1, the scammers were in a position to win big, courtesy of the law of averages.

Not the sort of betting strategy welcomed by casino bosses, as a general rule.

The three won a reported £100,000 on their first stint, then, next day, landed a £1.2m windfall. They cashed in their chips, taking £300,000 and a £900,000 cheque. Security experts, alerted by this mega-win, examined close-circuit footage of the three in action and called the police, who arrested them on suspicion of obtaining their winnings by deception.

In December 2004, Scotland Yard announced: 'The case has been stamped 'no further action'.'

The Ritz declined to comment.

311. LITTLE WHITE LIE?

It was reported in 1988 that when 17-year-old David White decided to stop playing once he had won $100 from his mother, Lemira, during a poker game in Chicago, she became so angry that she pulled out a gun and shot her son dead.

Lemira later told police – 'He was cheating, anyway.'

312. PUNTER WHO GAVE HIS WINNINGS BACK

William Hill were staggered to receive a letter dated April 11, 1990, from a punter telling them he didn't want his winnings.

Signing himself just 'Mr M', the correspondent wrote: 'I won £475 in a bet with your company four years ago, involving two horses, but I now do not want the money and I am therefore returning it to you. An extra £25 has been added for the trouble to which this letter/money puts you, ie book-keeping and money transfer.'

The letter contained £500 of postal orders. When we failed to identify the punter we handed the money over to a racing charity.

313. A MESS OF BETS

I own a unique volume, which catalogues – without comment or, indeed explanation, other than the outcome of the various matters therein gambled upon – the wagers and bets of the 2nd Battalion (78th) Seaforth Highlanders between 1822 and 1908.

Originally 'privately printed for the Officers' Mess' in 1909, the book records a sequence of fascinatingly eccentric wagers between said officers, beginning with a bet struck on October 4, 1822, when 'Capt Cameron bets Adjt Cooper that the Regt will not leave Kilkenny [where they were at the time based] before March 1, 1823, one bottle Prt wine'.

The outcome? The arbiter records: 'Lost by Adjt Cooper.'

The following stories record more admirably unorthodox punts:

314. OH, WHAT LARKS

The second bet listed would not be well received in today's politically correct climate.

On November 19, 1822, Lieutenant Mitchell bet that 'he shoots 12 larks in one day'.

Lt Hemmans opposed the wager for one bottle of port, gambling that Mitchell's shooting prowess was not up to it.

Hemmans was spot-on – but it was no real solace for the local lark population, as Hemmans himself showed how it should be done, cleaning up by shooting a dozen larks himself to collect a bottle of port from the appropriately named Ensign Gore.

315. GORE, BLIMEY

Ensign Gore attempted to win his port back on March 2, 1823, by staking another bottle against Capt Lardy's assertion that 'one of the crystal dessert dishes now on the table holds a bottle of wine'.

Sure enough, the wine remained in the dish without slopping over the sides and Gore lost again.

316. GORE OFF THE MARK
Ensign Gore finally won for the first time on March 14, 1823, when he bet Lardy 'that the Grenadiers will beat the other Companies at Foot Ball'.

317. XMAS ACTION
On Christmas Day, 1824, another bottle of port was riding on the outcome of a novel contest in which Mr Cooper bet Mr Wilson that he 'drinks with a spoon a bottle of beer, while Mr W is eating a penny roll. Mr W is not to take anything with the bread and is to whistle afterwards to show that his mouth is empty'.

Who would you have backed? The book reveals that Wilson lost.

318. HORSING ABOUT
On March 8, 1828, Major Mill collected 'one dozen wine' from Mr Montgomery, who failed to 'carry 4 shillings over a four foot wall, one between each foot and stirrup and one between each knee and saddle'. One presumes Montgomery was atop a horse at the time.

319. HAMMERED
Egged on by his accomplices at Armagh on February 21, 1837, Mr McIntyre made a winning bet of a bottle of champagne that 'Mr Pattison will not break an egg in an empty dirty clothes bag, provided he does not use an iron sledge hammer of greater weight than 15lb'.

This wager was subsequently offered and taken up on several occasions – but never achieved, even when six hours was allowed.

320. HOPPORTUNITY SEEMS TO NEED FINISHING OFF
Colonel Douglas did not stand on ceremony on September 4, 1839 in Edinburgh when more booze was at stake, but both Mr Horrocks and Mr Fletcher failed in their task to 'hop as far as the sentry box at the new barracks'.

321. HANGING AROUND
While at Shorncliffe on March 16, 1863, Ensign Smith bet Ensign Colin McKenzie one bottle of champagne 'that he will tomorrow after parade hang by his toe from the iron

bar that runs across the roof of the anteroom'.

As if that were not spectacular enough, Smith then embellished the wager by betting Lt Richardson a further bottle of bubbly that having completed the above feat 'he will hang by one heel for twenty seconds from the same bar'.

Smith duly completed the first part to win against McKenzie – but failed in the second stage, handing the booze straight on to Richardson.

322. SICK BET

'Lieut Carstairs bets Capt Sir A Mackenzie five shillings that he – Capt Sir A Mck – is seasick crossing over from Dublin to Glasgow this evening, Jan 16, 1864.'

Mac managed to avoid throwing up.

323. BODY OF EVIDENCE

A morbid wager was struck on October 16, 1885 at Lucknow when Lt Colin Mackenzie wagered Capt Mackenzie a magnum of champagne that 'any living man will weigh lighter in the scales than the same man dead'.

The bet went unsettled.

324. SMASHING BET

In 1899 Capt Holland bet Major Arbuthnot a bottle of port that he 'will break a soda water bottle by throwing it on the floor'.

Notes the book, deadpan – 'Capt Holland broke a lamp – but not the bottle.'

325. WEIGHED IN

On April 3, 1899, at Fort George, Major K R Mackenzie bet both Capt and Adjt G R Elliot 'that a criminal condemned to death is not officially weighed from the time that he is condemned to death until the time that he is hanged'.

The bet, for one bottle of champagne, was never settled. The book remarked, matter of factly – 'Bet off; Major Mackenzie killed S Africa.'

That comment no doubt explains why men with such a potential future fate awaiting them should be anxious to indulge in somewhat frivolous behaviour that might keep reality at bay.

326. PUTT UPON

Captain P G Anstruther gambled six bottles of best port against Capt C Macfie on September 8, 1906.

The bet was riding on whether Lieutenant N O Orr, playing with a putter only, would beat said Capt Macfie, playing with all his clubs on the Bruntsfield golf course.

Somewhat surprisingly, to an admittedly non-golfer like me, Macfie was beaten by Orr and left feeling a little under par as a result.

327. CARR SUNK

The final bet in the book was struck at Aldershot on August 13, 1908 in which '2nd Lieut Carr bets 2nd Lieut Sir John Fowler that he will beat him in a race from Edinburgh Castle to Blackness – Lt Carr to drive his motor car from Croall's Garage; Lt Fowler his motor boat from Granton Harbour; Lt Carr is allowed 75 min start. This bet is for one bottle of champagne.'

Carr drove hard but finished 40 minutes after Fowler's boat – resulting in the very last battalion bet leaving the loser with a sinking feeling.

328. BATTEN DOWN THE HATCHES

Derby day punters on the 'Hill' at Epsom racecourse in 1997 were tempted by the odds on offer for the big race by bookie John Batten.

Those who were fortunate enough to back the winner discovered that their luck was short-lived when they returned to collect their winnings.

Batten had gone, disappeared, vanished, done a runner.

Despite photographs of him appearing in the media, Batten was never identified and his reported takings of up to £40,000 were never recovered.

329. A BRIDGE TOO FAR

In December 1807, a sporting man called Mr Arnold, who resided at Pentonville, London, made what was described at the time as 'a cruel wager', when he bet Mr Mawbey of the Fulham Road 20 guineas that the former – Arnold – would produce a dog 'which should be thrown over Westminster Bridge at dark, and find its way home again in six hours'.

Arnold obtained a spaniel bitch, belonging to a groom from the Tottenham Court

Road. The dog was 'thrown over from the centre of the bridge'.

Arnold was the easy winner when 'the dog arrived at the house of her master in two hours'.

330. WINNING NAP

A bet on when Napoleon would die eventually ended up in a court case.

John Ashton, in his 1899 book, A History of Gambling in England, explained: 'In the early part of this [19th] century, sporting men were fond of betting on the duration of the lives of celebrities.

'Napoleon I was specially the subject of these wagers. It is related that, at a dinner party, in 1809, Sir Mark Sykes offered to pay anyone who would give him a hundred guineas down, a guinea a day so long as Napoleon lived.

'The offer was taken by a clergyman present; and for three years Sir Mark Sykes paid him three hundred and sixty five guineas per annum. He then thought he had thrown away enough money, and disputed further payment.

'The recipient, who was not at all disposed to lose his comfortable annuity, brought an action, which, after lengthy litigation, was decided in favour of the baronet.'

331. BLAKE'S WATERTIGHT WAGER

Writer Horace Walpole's correspondence revealed details of a bizarre, almost certainly criminal wager. He wrote on July 10, 1774 that a man named Blake had wagered £1,500 that a man could live 12 hours under water; hired a desperate fellow, sunk him in a ship, by way of experiment, and both ship and man have not appeared since.

'Another man and ship are to be tried for their lives – instead of Mr Blake, the assassin.'

332. WHEN THE PRIME MINISTER
BET HE WAS RIGHT – AND LOST

During a House of Commons debate, the prime minister, Sir Robert Walpole, who came to office in 1721, was charged with misquoting Horace by fellow member, Mr Pulteney.

The prime minister responded by offering to bet that he had not done so.

The wager was accepted, and the clerk of the house called upon to determine who was correct. He declared that Pulteney was in the right – whereupon Sir Robert hurled a guinea across the house to be picked up by his opponent, remarking that it was 'the first public money he had touched for some time'.

333. A GRAND ON GRANNY

In the 18th century Adventures of Ferdinand Count Fathom, by Smollett, a unique gambling tale was related. It happened, we are told, in a club where gambling was commonplace:

'In one corner of the room might be heard a pair of lordlings running their grandmothers against each other, that is, betting sums on the longest liver; in another, the success of the wager depended upon the sex of the landlady's next child.

'One of the waiters happening to drop down in an apoplectic fit, a certain noble peer exclaimed, "Dead, for a thousand pounds".

'The challenge was immediately accepted; and when the master of the house sent for a surgeon to attempt the cure, the nobleman, who set the price upon the patient's head, insisted upon his being left to the efforts of nature alone, otherwise the wager should be void; nay, when the landlord harped upon the loss he should sustain by the death of a trusty servant, his lordship obviated the objection by desiring that the fellow might be charged in the bill.'

334. CRACKPOT GAMBLE

In 1709, recorded a book snappily entitled Malcolm's Anecdotes of the Manners and Customs of London During the Eighteenth Century, 'Mrs Crackenthorpe, the Female Tatler, tells us that four worthy Senators lately threw their hats into a river, laid a crown each whose hat should first swim to the mill, and ran hallooing after them; and he that won the prize, was in greater rapture than if he had carried the most dangerous point in parliament'.

335. UNHAPPY LOSSES

The Morning Post newspaper reported to agog readers in April 1805 that: 'The sum lately lost at play by a lady of high rank is variously stated. Some say it does not amount to more than £200,000 (oh, that's all right, then! – GS), while others assert that it is little short of £700,000.'

The article continued with one of the great understatements of all time – 'Her Lord is very unhappy on the occasion, and is still undecided with respect to the best mode to be adopted in the unfortunate predicament.'

336. THAT'S MINE

An Englishman, Alfred William 'Fairlie' Cox, sat down in an Australian pub in the late 19th century to play the gambling game, euchre.

Also at the table was George McCulloch, owner of a significant share in the Broken Hill Mines.

The pair had a showdown over one hand during the game with Cox staking his life savings of £200 against the eighth share in the mines owned by McCulloch.

Cox won and was rewarded when, shortly after, the mine revealed one of the world's largest deposits of lead, zinc and silver.

Cox received dividends of £1, 260,000 over the next few years, of which he spent much buying racehorses, including 1910 Derby winner Lemberg.

337. BOOKIES TRODDEN INTO TURF

In 1898 cunning punting plotters invented a complete race meeting at a mythical racecourse – Trodmore.

They persuaded the leading racing papers of the day, including The Sportsman, to print the card – and then, having placed bets with a large number of bookmakers, who assumed that as the card was in the papers it must be legitimate, they supplied results for the entirely fictitious meeting, which the papers also printed.

The bookies paid out and it was only when someone noticed a slight discrepancy between the results in different papers that questions were asked and the hoax revealed.

The perpetrators were never unmasked.

338. GREATEST BETTING DAYS NEVER

It was the greatest non-event in betting history – the day the 1993 Grand National was declared void after chaos at the off resulted in a false start and a non-race.

Bookies bemoaned the loss of millions in turnover – although, of course, no-one could have predicted whether it would have been a losing or winning race.

Then, in 1997 there was almost another disastrous non-race – Grand National day was disrupted when a bomb warning was received, leading to a course evacuation.

Eventually, though, the race was rescheduled for two days later on the Monday.

This time, the betting public responded enthusiastically to the reprieve and gambled record amounts before 14-1 shot Lord Gyllene came home the winner.

339. CARPET CLEANER

During the mid to late years of the 18th century, the clubs of London – White's, Boodle's, Brooks's among them – hosted great aristocratic gambling games of whist and faro, to which the 'Lords Selwyn, Carlisle, Robert Spencer and other great whigs' were reportedly addicted to such an extent that social historian Stella Margetson records that 'it was nothing for a gentleman to lose £30,000 or £40,000 in a single evening'.

Shrewder, and perhaps less well-off people were also able to profit from the gambling, without necessarily playing at the tables – 'Raggett, the proprietor of White's, used to sit up with the gamblers all through the night, sending his servants to bed, so that he could sweep the carpets himself in the early hours of the morning to retrieve the gold carelessly scattered on the floor.'

Some gamblers, too, were better prepared than others – 'The Duke of Portland's father-in-law, General Scott, by dining off boiled chicken, toast and water, kept a clear head and a cool judgement over his opponents at the whist table and succeeded in winning the enormous sum of £200,000' from his too frequently 'fuddled with wine and sick with fatigue' opponents.

340. BOB'S LAST BOB

Captain Rees Howell Gronow was a celebrated Regency dandy. He was a renowned gambler, debtor, a duellist and Waterloo veteran, whose memoirs were a fascinating mix of scandal and social history of London in those days.

St James's Street, SW1, came into existence during the reign of Henry VIII. Sir Christopher Wren once lived there, as did Alexander Pope, Horace Walpole and Lord Byron. Around the 1720s the street's famous gentlemen's clubs sprang up, among them, White's and Brooks's.

White's was the grandest of them, located at No. 37–38. It became an infamous gambling den, with a gaming room known as 'Hell'. Gronow wrote: 'Play was carried on to an extent which made many ravages in large fortunes. General Scott was known to have won at White's £200,000 [£10 million today].'

Brooks's Club was founded in 1764 by William Almack, proprietor of the Assembly Rooms in Pall Mall. By 1778 the club had relocated to 60 St James's Street, where, under William Brooks, it gained a reputation for excessive gambling: 'At Brooks's,' wrote Gronow, 'for nearly half a century, the play was of a more gambling nature than at White's. Faro and macao were indulged in to an extent, which enabled a man to win or lose a considerable fortune in one night. On one occasion, Lord Robert Spencer contrived to lose the last shilling of his considerable fortune, given him by his brother, the Duke of Marlborough.'

341. OLYMPIC ODDS

These days the International Olympic Committee goes out of its way to have nothing to do with gambling, but a report from the 1908 Games in London suggests that times were different then.

A silver medal winner in the 100 metres, American sprinter James Rector later remembered: 'The bands were furiously playing national airs, while the bookmakers were calling their bets and the whole stadium seemed to be disordered.'

342. GUILTY?

A juror in the dramatic 1995 O J Simpson double murder trial in the US was dismissed by Judge Lance Ito, following allegations that he had been investigated for offering to bet a co-worker a week's salary that the former American football star would be acquitted over the murders of Nicole Brown Simpson and Ronald Goodman.

Known just as Juror 620, he was replaced by a 38-year-old woman.

343. ARCHIE EDUCATES PROS

What may well have indeed been what top gambling writer Frank Scoblete called 'one of the greatest runs in Vegas history' saw Greek immigrant Archie Karas turn a $10,000 debt into a $17 million asset at the poker tables during 1992-3.

Karas (real name Anargyros Karabourniotis), an immigrant to America at the age of 17, started his working life as a waiter in Los Angeles where he began hustling for money at pool. He also learned poker and cost himself his job by cleaning out the restaurant owner.

As his gambling increased he won and lost huge sums and by December 1992 reckoned that he had managed to get through $2m in high-stakes card games, and was left with just 50 bucks in his pocket when he drove into Vegas.

Making for the Mirage, he talked a fellow gambler into loaning him $10,000 to 'take a shot at the biggest action in the card room' in a high-staked Razz (a Seven Card Stud variation) game. He quickly won $20,000 and paid off his debt.

From there Karas took on a big-shot hotel executive at pool for $10,000 and more per game – beating him out of between $1m and $2m.

Now the pool gave way to poker, at which Mr X was rated highly – not highly enough, though and in early 1993 after a week of heads-up Archie beat him for $1m. He then put out an all-comers invitation to high-rolling poker players to take him on.

Chip Reese was the first to take the bait, and they met in April 1993 at Binion's Horseshoe where the games of choice were Razz and Seven Card Stud. In a fortnight Karas was a reported $2,022,000 ahead of the game.

Finding it difficult to get the poker action he wanted – 'Nobody would play poker with me for that much', Karas turned to the craps tables, winning and losing seven-figure sums, and at one time had all of the Horseshoe's $5,000 chocolate-coloured chips in his possession – until at last another poker challenger turned up in Stu Ungar.

Karas again came out on top, winning a reported $900,000 in a six-hour showdown, at which point those who had been bank-rolling 'The Kid' cried enough. 'The nearly $1m loss hurt more than Stuey's pride. It made those people who had still been willing to back him gunshy,' wrote Ungar's biographers, Nolan Dalla and Peter Alson.

Doyle Brunson came and had a go at Karas. They broke even, but Karas claimed 'he didn't want to play high enough'.

Puggy Pearson and Johnny Chan took him on – Chan managed to beat him once out of four attempts.

At the end of what became known as 'The Run', Karas was said to have 'busted'

15 of the world's top players and at the peak of the winning streak been $17m ahead of the game.

'I've gambled more money than anyone in the history of the planet. I don't think anyone will ever gamble more than I have. I'm the biggest ever,' boasted Karas, who is still around today playing the tournament circuit.

And few argued. But how much of that $17m – some reports suggested it was even more than that – remained in his possession for how long is another question. One source declared that 'the only thing he bought out of that money was a car. He lost it all in poker games'.

344. TON-UP ALEC

Alec Holden celebrated his 90th birthday by placing a bet that he would survive to be 100. The Epsom man snapped up Hill's offer of 250-1 with a £100 stake – and on April 24, 2007, collected £25,000.

'I've been very careful about what I've been doing in recent months. If I saw any hooded groups from William Hill standing in the street, I avoided them,' he said, which is actually a very good joke for a 100-year-old.

345. HEATHER'S LEGENDARY BET

After reporting the above story, Sky News' website reported: 'Heather Mills was so confident her false leg would not fall off during her time on US TV show Dancing With The Stars that she bet money on it. Bookies were taking wagers on the fake limb flying off.'

Appearing on the show, Mills said she had strapped her leg on so tightly there was no chance of it coming off. 'I've bet a few hundred dollars it's not going to come off – so I'll win some money. Everyone's betting on it.'

There were no reports that Paul McCartney had joined the gamble. Please notice that I was at pains not to make any puns about not having a leg to stand on.

346. CROC-ED

Irishman Sean Treacy attended his sister's June 2008 wedding in Cancun, Mexico and bet a fellow guest £10 that he would swim across the nearby crocodile-infested Nichupte lagoon. He lost.

The 23-year-old dived in, but was soon grabbed by a two-metre-long croc which attacked him, taking a sizeable chunk out of his arm and puncturing his lung with a huge bite. Treacy's 37-year-old brother, Billy, finally managed to pull him clear – even though the croc again tried to take up the attack.

Treacy was taken to hospital and survived to tell the tale.

347. NEVISON'S BLOODY GOOD

Professional gambler Dave Nevison scored a surprise hit with his autobiography, *A Bloody Good Winner*, which topped the Amazon.co.uk racing bestseller charts for weeks before Christmas 2007 – and I should know as he kept this tome's companion volume, Racing's 500 Strangest Stories, stuck at number two for a frustratingly long while!

In the book, Nevison claimed that: 'Within about four years of becoming a professional punter I was making about £50,000 a year – a grand a week, in cash, tax free,' and also boasted: 'I've won £10,000 a lot of times.'

He told how he was a five-time winner of the Scoop6, entering with permutations costing up to £10,000 – but even when he had two winning tickets for a £1,322,000 pool 'our profit after a lot of toil and tension, was a few hundred pounds'. He did rather better on the Tote Jackpot, winning £268,643 at Haydock in August 2004.

Nevison concludes in the book: 'I doubt if I am financially better off now than I was before I became a professional punter, but every day I am doing what I want to do.'

348. £3M TAKES FLIGHT FROM BOOKIES

Aussie bookies were happy to keep taking cash for popular choice Even Stevens to win the 1962 Caulfield Cup and Melbourne Cup double.

After all, they knew just what the trip from the horse's native New Zealand over the sea to Australia took out of a highly strung thoroughbred, and they also knew full well that with the Caulfield Cup just days away, Even Stevens had not yet set off from his Kiwi stable.

Still the mugs kept pouring their cash on the horse, who had been allotted a very lenient weight in both races and whose odds had plummeted from an opening 1,000-1.

However, bookmaker complacency was replaced with something akin to panic when the horse suddenly appeared in Australia – he had been flown over on the first flight for horses ever laid on by Qantas.

Now the bookies were in real trouble, and Even Stevens promptly won the Caulfield Cup. The layers faced an estimated £3m payout if Sir James Wattie's horse could also win the Melbourne Cup.

He went off 3-1 favourite, and won comfortably.

349. FROM THE HORSE'S MOUTH

Mr Ed was a talking horse – but even that equine worthy was not a gambling horse.

However, it is recorded that in or around 1670 a gambling cheat of the day, Joe Haynes, was imprisoned and thrown into the army, being made to march from London to Dover. Unimpressed by this, and claiming illness, he demanded that his captain furnish him with a horse for the trip.

The captain reluctantly agreed, but declared: 'If you must ride you shall have one horse and you shall throw dice with him, and if you win the horse shall have no victuals, but if the horse wins you shall go without pay.'

The captain had a horse brought out, whereupon, recorded writer Theophilus Lucas, 'a pair of dice was put betwixt the horse's lips, which falling from thence six, Joe Haynes takes 'em up and throws 8; whereupon the captain cried out "You cheat the horse, for that was not a fair cast".'

Haynes replied – 'I vow it was very fair – ask the horse, else!'

350. BALL, BAT, BET

Although today baseball has an almost pathological hatred, fear even, of gambling besmirching it, it was not always thus.

'A ball, a bat and a bet. Baseball was all three from the beginnings of its history,' wrote Eliot Asinof in Baseball As America, explaining that 'hardly had the National League been formed in 1876 when the leading Louisville club took a dive down the stretch, and four star players were banned for taking bribes'.

Indeed, earlier, in 1872, the New York Times wrote that the purpose of baseball was to 'employ professional players to perspire in public for the benefit of gamblers'.

The growing influence of those gamblers was always in evidence. Asinof explained: 'An outfielder, settling under a crucial fly ball, would mind himself stoned by a nearby spectator, who might win a few hundred dollars if the ball was dropped. On one occasion a gambler actually ran out on the field and tackled a ball-player. On another, a marksman prevented a fielder from chasing a long hit by peppering the ground around his feet with bullets.'

The 1919 World Series was fixed for betting purposes – 'Say it ain't so, Joe,' was a possibly apocryphal comment from a youngster to legendary player Shoeless Joe Jackson, who was banned for his alleged role in the match-fixing scandal.

Later, one of the all-time greats of the game, Pete Rose, who starred in the game from 1963-86, was banned for betting – albeit not against his own team, and never in a fixed game. He was kept out of the Hall of Fame even while one player convicted of drug charges and another who had admitted to cheating were allowed in.

351. I BET YOU A CIGAR, A HAT AND A DINNER

New York lumberman William D Cox, 34, took over the Philadelphia 'Phillies' baseball team in 1942, but within a year he had been thrown out of the game – for gambling.

The bets he was alleged to have placed – up to 20 of them, with stakes of $25 to $100 – were hardly massive.

And they were on the Phillies, a particularly poor side at the time – to win!

At first Cox denied the 'offence', then he claimed he hadn't known it was against the rules to bet on his own team – and finally he declared that he had only made 'small, sentimental wagers involving cigars, hats and dinners'.

352. WHEN BASEBALL WAS STRUCK OUT BY GAMBLING

The ludicrous lengths to which baseball was prepared to go to avoid any association with gambling was demonstrated vividly when, in 1979, Hall of Fame player Willie Mays was publicly divorced from the game he had graced.

Mays, then no longer playing baseball, was offered a job as assistant to the president of Atlantic City casino, Park Place.

His role was to play on his celebrity status by welcoming high-rollers visiting the casino. A stipulation of the job was that he must not gamble in the casino.

Mays was also working for the New York Mets at the time, as a part-time coach.

The commissioner of the sport, Bowie Kuhn, was alarmed at what he perceived as a link between Mays, gambling and baseball.

He wanted it stopped. He issued Mays with the ultimatum – betting or baseball? 'If Mayes were free to associate with and entertain the big gamblers in Atlantic City, how was I to keep our personnel away from gambling types?'

Mays opted for the casino and was duly expelled from the sport – although the sport's followers were not happy and even Frank Sinatra weighed into the row: 'Mr Kuhn told Mays to get out of baseball. I would like to offer the same advice to Mr Kuhn.'

Twice Mays applied for reinstatement. Twice he was turned down.

At around the same time, another baseball hero, New York Yankee Hall of Famer Mickey Mantle, was also offered a job with a casino.

He accepted – and he, too, was threatened with a baseball ban. 'Some threat – what would I be banned from?' he hit back.

In 1985 Kuhn himself was out of baseball, replaced by new commissioner Peter Uberroth, one of whose first actions was to invite Mays and Mantle back into the bosom of the game – it was one of the first occasions in which a new incumbent had reversed a decision by a former commissioner.

353. SUITS YOU, SIR, AGAIN

Eddie 'The Fireman' Birchley, who set about burning Australia's bookies after spending 17 years working for the fire brigade, staked such enormous amounts that he had his suits made with specially roomy extra pockets to keep his punting cash in.

When he became well known for his habit of betting up to $208,000 a time on odds-on certs like Caboul – who started at 1-6 at Flemington in November 1974 – on his way to a profit during that year of $200,000 from a betting bank of $1,000,000, he realised the habit might attract the attentions of unsavoury racecourse elements and began to replace the cash with blank cheques.

When his luck turned in December 1974 – when he lost $105,000 on beaten 1-4 chance Danish Dancer – he claimed that bookies and jockeys had instigated a signalling system to ensure the defeats of hot favourites he had backed.

With a system that saw him happy to take long odds-on 'as long as I think the correct price is 1-100' he was bound to lose eventually.

He vanished from the course, only reappearing in a sad postscript in 1980 when he was fined $225 for shoplifting a packet of sausages, a packet of peas and a packet of bacon. Well, he HAD lost a packet!

354. WHEELING AND DEALING

Probably the most successful roulette player ever to frequent the Monte Carlo casino was not the fellow who was immortalised in song for being 'the man who broke the bank at Monte Carlo', of whom more later, but William Darnborough, an American who settled in England.

Between 1904 and 1911 he won a total of £83,000. How did he do it? Well, he never revealed his secret. Some said he was just a publicity stunt by the casino to make people believe they could win; others thought he worked with an accomplice who could predict where the ball would fall.

'His play was on numbers, but seemed to vary, often skipping from one side of the wheel to the other. No-one could understand what he was doing,' wrote gambling correspondent C N Williamson in 1913.

355. JAGGERS TAKING THE MICK?

If Darnborough's secret proved elusive there was no doubt about how Yorkshire mechanic William Jaggers managed to take Monte Carlo for £80,000 – once being £140,000 ahead of the game – at the turn of the 19th/20th century.

He employed six assistants to do nothing but check the numbers that came up at different tables for a month.

Having analysed the results, Jaggers then played on the tables where he had detected slight, but distinct evidence of a bias towards certain groups of numbers.

Alarmed by his success, the casino eventually had the wheels Jaggers identified replaced.

Jaggers was no fool and once his profits began to dwindle, called a halt and departed, content with his haul.

356. BUT DID HE REALLY BREAK THE BANK?

Charles Deville Wells must have had a great PR man because he was the chap who took the credit for being The Man Who Broke The Bank At Monte Carlo in the hit song of the day, sung by Charles Coborn.

Yet, really, the low-level conman, who sold worthless rights to worthless inventions, did no such thing.

With investigators on his case in England, Wells headed for sunnier climes in the 1880s, pitching up in Monte Carlo, where he attacked the casino with a system that involved backing the number five in virtually any way permitted.

He struck lucky within three days, playing up his initial bank of £400 to £40,000. At the time, if someone won £4,500 at a given table, the casino would shut it down to make sure nothing strange was going on.

Self-publicity brought Wells to public attention before he returned to London to live the high life there – until his past caught up with him and he was forced back to Monte Carlo where, in a few days in November 1891, he again hit the jackpot.

But on his third trip in January 1892 it all went wrong and Wells and his followers began to lose everything – while the Fraud Squad closed in on him. In March 1893 he was convicted of obtaining £50,000 by false pretences – albeit not at the casino – and he was sentenced to eight years' penal servitude, eventually dying a poor man.

357. THE WILMSLOW GIRL CLEANS UP

A woman from Wilmslow who said she got fed up with being left at home on her own when her partner and their son went off to football matches without her, decided to show them that she knew as much about football as they did by placing an accumulator bet – which won her almost a quarter of a million pounds, the biggest winning football accumulator ever placed by a woman.

Angela Kennedy studied soccer statistics and placed an accumulator bet on nine footballing eventualities, all of which came up to turn her stake of £2,000 into £242,391.66 in May 2006.

She placed the bet on March 31 over the telephone, and her selections were: Manchester United to finish second in the Premiership at 1-10; Sheffield United to finish second in the Championship at 3-10; Southend to win League One at 3-10; Carlisle to win League Two at 3-10; St Mirren to win Scottish Division One at 1-100; Cowdenbeath to win Scottish Division Three at 4-1; Liverpool to win the FA Cup at 9-4; Hearts to win the Scottish Cup at 5-6 – and her final selection was Grays Athletic to win the FA Trophy at odds of 4-6, which they duly did.

358. BETTING BLIND

Professional poker player Hal Lubarsky was very pleased with his top 200 finish in the 2008 World Series of Poker, the biggest event in the game's calendar.

And with good reason – as the 26 year old from Brooklyn is blind. Sighted when he first began to play, Lubarsky initially gave up the game and became a victim of depression when a genetic disorder caused his loss of sight.

However, he began to play again with a helper when online poker came along and then began to play in casinos, also with a sighted helper.

Initially refused permission to contest the WSOP, the 'world championship' of the game, Lubarsky told them: 'I could probably make more money suing you than playing in the tournament.'

They let him in.

359. BROLLY GOOD IDEA

The casino at Homburg in Germany flourished from its inception in 1843 for the best part of 30 years under the stern, watchful eye of its French owner, Monsieur Blanc.

He saw gamblers come and go and was well aware that early success was almost inevitably followed by ultimate failure at the tables.

Happily married, he decided one year that an attractive parasol would make a fine present for his wife's birthday.

However, he baulked at the 20-mark price and asked the shop assistant to put it aside for him.

Having seen how frequently and easily gamblers would win small amounts he decided to break the habit of a lifetime – he had never played roulette – in order to win the 20 marks to pay for the parasol.

'Walking up to the table and unobtrusively stationing himself behind a group of players, Blanc furtively slipped 20 marks on red – black won,' recorded a contemporary account.

'Forty marks on the red – black again won.

'Eighty marks on the black – red won.

'He now became excited and the money in his pocket being exhausted, instructed an astonished chef de partie to whom he was well known to place 160 marks on red.' Red lost.

By now Blanc was openly playing against his own casino and other players stopped what they were doing to watch.

He played his losses up to 20,000 marks – at which point he seemed suddenly to come to his senses 'and rushed out of the rooms'.

He was, though, cured of gambling forever, and later commented: 'That was the dearest parasol I ever bought in my life.'

360. TIPSTER'S TOM IS A LOSER

The RSPCA took an inordinate interest when famous Australian tipster Fred Coghlan (1916-1974) successfully tipped 6-1 winner Black Cat in his racing paper, The Newsletter.

Anxious to remind punters and would-be subscribers of his great success, Coghlan thought it would be great publicity to buy a black cat – which he then set up in the paper's office window on a thick carpet with all the milk and sardines a punting puss could wish for.

The public responded favourably to the stunt, the RSPCA not so favourably – they came and took the cat away.

361. TAKING THEIR OWN ADVICE

A female business consultant took her own advice – and in September 2007 made a profit of £226,834.36 from an investment of just £1,000 in the space of 24 hours.

For 33-year-old German-born Kathrin Rotmann, who lives in Central London, placed a £1,000 bet with William Hill on the outcome of eight Champions League matches played on Tuesday and Wednesday, and successfully predicted the outcome of all eight. Her winning teams were Arsenal, Manchester United, Rangers, Slavia Prague, Barcelona, Roma, Fenerbahce and PSV.

★ Financial adviser Ken Brown, 34, discovered a way of turning £50 into £10,000 in just eight years. The part-time rugby coach invested £54.50 on a hunch in 1999 – betting that amount with William Hill at odds of 200-1 that the teenager playing for his local club, Aldwynians, would go on to play for England. And when Dean Schofield, by then a Sale player, took the field for England in their game against South Africa in May 2007, Ken, from Manchester, was £10,900 better off.

362. LIQUIDITY

In 1814 a bet was struck in a London tavern, which was later thought worthy of recording by gambling historian Ralph Nevill.

Two gentlemen undertook to drink against one another – one to drink wine, and the other water – glass for glass, until one cried enough.

How would you bet?

Nevill recalled: 'The wine-drinker was triumphant – the unfortunate water drinker was afterwards taken ill, being confined to his bed with an attack of gout.'

363. BAYERN BLOW

Clive Palmer, a William Hill customer from Surrey who is married with three children, scooped a record win in May 2006 of £375,375 after his pre-season accumulator came up trumps. Palmer placed the £2,000 accumulator on August 6, 2005 and included Chelsea, Lyon and Gretna to win their leagues and for Millwall, West Brom and Rushden & Diamonds to be relegated. The lucky/unlucky punter also wanted to include Bayern Munich in the accumulator but they had already played a match the night before so were left out of the bet – if he had placed the bet 24 hours earlier his win would have been in excess of half a million pounds (£563,063).

364. THE WINNER LOOKED A PICTURE

When Hialeah racecourse in Florida opened for business in 1925 it devised a smart way of getting round the inconvenient fact gambling was illegal.

It sold picture postcards of the runners in each race – then purchased back the pictures of the winners at an appropriate premium.

365. OLD STOCK

Mr H Blechman of Christchurch, Dorset, just needs to sit and wait until his 100th birthday comes round, in 2031, to collect the £20,000 winnings from his 1,000-1 bet with me that he will make it to that landmark.

If he makes it he will be able to put himself up for sale in his own antique shop.

366. A NEAT EXTRACTION

London dentist Sydney Lewis spotted a profitable loophole in pools rules in February

1970. Thirty games were postponed because of inclement weather, not quite enough to call into action the 'Pools Panel' of experts, who were used when 31 or more games were off.

Lewis realised that he could now make a full cover entry for all the remaining matches, guaranteeing first dividend payouts.

By notifying a pools agent in time to place his bet and supplying him with a blank cheque to fill in when instructed, Lewis outwitted the rules, confident that hundreds of thousands of lines involving postponed games had no chance of winning.

With 24 matches left on the Vernons coupon he required an outlay of £1,600 to cover every possible combination – and he duly landed nine first dividends and numerous smaller ones, picking up £50,000.

The rules were rapidly changed.

367. FATAL FAILURE

The money was definitely down when trainer George Brown's horse Risley was backed from 14-1 to 4-1 to win a race at Doomben in Australia in 1984.

Some heavy-duty punters had invested big time on the horse and were thought to be extremely unhappy when it finished second-last in a field of 13 runners.

Two days later former hurdles jockey-turned-trainer Brown's mutilated body was found in his burnt-out car.

A port-mortem revealed that both of his legs had been broken above the knees, his upper right arm was smashed, and his left arm twisted up behind his back until it had snapped. He had been clubbed to death and his car had been doused with petrol and set alight.

Risley's jockey, Maurice Logue, took an anonymous call threatening that he 'would be next' – and he immediately gave up riding.

Brown's murderer(s) never came to light.

368. LAUGHING HIS HEAD OFF

Council worker John Font was so pleased when he was dealt a winning poker hand that he almost literally laughed his head off, it was reported in 1994.

The 32-year-old Merseysider was so excited when he saw the full house he'd been given that he threw back his head to roar with delight – and the pressure split open an old fracture in his skull, which had been left from a fall when he was just six years old.

John's worried workmates called an ambulance and he was rushed into hospital, where surgeons had to glue his skull back together, and put dozens of stitches into the wound on his scalp, to hold it together.

John, whose winnings only came to a few pounds, later vowed to keep a poker face next time he played the game.

369. SHOCK RESULT

The betting plunge, from 33-1 to 7-2, on Thundering Legion to win a race at Adelaide, Australia in 1955, alerted suspicious stewards who discovered that the horse's jockey, Bill Attrill, was equipped with a battery powered whip, designed to administer an electric shock to the horse at a crucial moment of the race.

Attrill was taken away for interrogation, but a substitute jockey was allowed to partner Thundering Legion – who stormed to a legitimate victory, thus landing all the crooked bets!

Attrill was later disqualified for ten years and trainer N Conway for life.

370. CABBIE ON GAMBLING

A cabbie whose gambling debts landed him in the bankruptcy court blamed his nagging wife for driving him to temptation.

'My wife Joyce nagged me non-stop,' 47-year-old taxi driver Hymie Goldberg explained in May 1986. 'Every day there were arguments. In the end I stopped going home and started to gamble.

'I spent whole days and nights in the clubs. I would lose more than £150 per week,' added Hymie, whose debts reached £13,612.

371. INNER CLEANLINESS

Lloyd Cragg, 26, won a £10 bet at The Crown pub, Horsted Keynes, Sussex, in May 1993 – by the simple expedient of eating four blue toilet disinfectant cubes.

I've no idea whether they had been used.

372. BOHNING UP ON A WINNER

Llanelli factory worker Kevin Bohn noticed a 14-year-old lad playing snooker in a local working men's club and thought he had the potential to be a top player.

Kevin contacted Coral and staked that week's wages of £140 at odds of 300-1 on the teenager becoming world champion in or before 2000 – and in that very year, Mark Williams won the title for himself and £42,000 for Kevin.

373. JOCKEY JIGGERY POKERY?

Tom Stenner was a man involved in sport in various capacities, who wrote his autobiography, *Sport For The Million*, published in 1959, in which he highlighted an allegation that there was a 'jockeys' ring ' involved in race fixing, shortly after the Second World War.

Stenner was publicist for the Greyhound Racing Association for more than 16 years and was also involved in promoting ice hockey. He was also a prolific writer and racecourse tipster.

He was a confirmed racing man with many contacts, and wrote that 'when racing was resumed on a big scale after the war remarkable stories of a so-called "jockeys" ring' went the rounds. A number of riders, it was said, banded together and by arranging what should win and financially supporting the same, made a pretty penny for themselves.

'There was no proof of this and as far as I am aware no investigation by authority. But there was an odd sequel. I told the friend who passed on the story that I didn't believe it. Somewhat nettled he retorted by offering to give me the names of the horses before they ran. 'As a joke I had half a crown (12.5p) on the first, which duly obliged and placed my winnings on the next to run. It is incredible but I had 13 winners in a row, one of which was practically left in a five furlong sprint yet got up to win.

'Starting prices ranged from two to six to one so with playing up my winnings I netted a considerable sum.'

374. BENNY AND THE RINGER

Benny O'Hanlon was the unsung hero of a plot that deprived bookies of more than a quarter of a million pounds.

Former trainee Jesuit priest, trainer, owner and punter Barney Curley was its architect, and Yellow Sam was its perpetrator. Not to mention the telephone box.

On Wednesday, June 25, 1975, Curley was contemplating an uncertain future – 'I badly need to pull off a touch,' he told friend and trainer Liam Brennan.

They decided to entrust moderate hurdler Yellow Sam with the responsibility of winning the race they targeted – the Mount Hanover Handicap Hurdle for amateur riders over two and a half miles at Bellewstown.

'In all honesty he was one of the worst horses I've ever owned,' reckoned Curley later on, but he would be up against some pretty poor opposition, and the plotters felt he just might be up to defeating them. 'We had the horse. We had the race. Now the crucial, but most difficult part was getting the money on in sufficient quantities at suitably rewarding odds.'

Curley had selected Bellewstown as the venue for the plot 'because I knew that the rarely used, remote course only had one public telephone, which was the only means the on-course bookmakers had of receiving intelligence of market moves.'

Curley knew that the racecourse odds, set by bookies at the track, would be used to settle betting shop wagers throughout the country – 150 of which Barney's team would be using to place their money.

All the bets would be for modest amounts, placed just before the race, minimising suspicions. Curley had recruited a dozen 'generals' who he entrusted to take on their own 'soldiers' to help get the money down. Each general had £1,200 to stake.

To ensure that word did not get out of or into the racecourse to influence the starting price, Barney recruited Benny O'Hanlon, a tough-looking former betting shop worker, whose job was to monopolise the racecourse telephone 'without drawing attention to the fact'.

Nine runners lined up for the race, in which Curley had managed to stake a total of £15,300 on the horse, who was trading at 20-1 on course.

'The betting offices were happy to accept the bets, thinking they'd have no trouble laying them off. All they would have to do was pick up the phone and have it backed on course.'

At this point, younger readers should be reminded that this all happened during the pre-mobile phone era.

O'Hanlon had been instructed to enter the phone box 25 minutes before the race – and to stay there for at least half an hour.

'He got talking to some non-existent hospital, where he had an aunt who was dying. Every few minutes Benny would announce his relative's state of health. Never has a patient gone through so much recovery and relapse in half an hour.'

Jockey Michael Furlong had been told nothing other than 'you'll win' – and he duly did so, Yellow Sam coming home two and a half lengths to the good.

Curley watched after the race as 'all hell broke loose. All the shops were now getting through on the phone that Benny had vacated. I thought it was an appropriate moment to make a diplomatic departure.'

It took the best part of a week to collect the winnings – 'about £300,000 – equivalent to around £1.4 million nowadays,' said Barney in 1998.

375. TIGER'S ACE WIN

According to a story in The Sun in April 2006, Tiger Woods is not only an ace on the golf course.

'Tiger Woods has been boasting to pals that he won more than £282,000 playing blackjack in Las Vegas,' the paper reported – adding that the amount was greater than the £178,000 he had won for finishing third in the US Masters just a week or so before.

376. £100,000 WINNINGS FOR LOSING BET

Three football punters, who had staked treble bets with bookies Coral and Betfred at the start of the 2005-06 season, coined in a hundred grand each – despite the fact that their bets turned out to be losers.

Alan Reid, 50; Hash Mistry, 43, and Arthur Wills, 55, all from Kent, had picked out 11-4 shots Reading to win the Championship; Colchester to win League One at 50-1, and Carlisle to finish top of League Two at 33-1.

They each placed £77 trebles with Coral, and £47.40 trebles with Betfred. Reading won the Championship; Carlisle won League One – leaving Carlisle one win from the League Two title – and needing to beat Yeovil to do it, clinching the trebles and winning each punter £500,000 from Coral and around half of that each from Betfred.

Not over-confident that Colchester would do it, the punters approached Coral and Betfred and asked if they would settle the bets there and then.

Coral offered them £80,000 each, Betfred £20,000 each.

The three settled for the £100,000 payouts and were delighted when Colchester could only draw with Yeovil, leaving Southend to take the title – and leaving them quids in.

377. BIG MAC LOVING IT

John McCririck became a celebrity because of gambling. A failed bookie-turned-investigative journalist on racing and gambling matters for the Sporting Life, Mac found himself on TV explaining the mysteries of betting to viewers and soon established himself as a colourful eccentric – he is to gambling what Screaming Lord Sutch was to politics, Rolf Harris to art and David Bellamy to natural history.

He has transcended his natural milieu with appearances on Celebrity Big Brother, Wife Swap and other 'tabloid TV' shows but at heart he remains a betting man.

'A smart gambler never bets more when losing, but does when winning,' is an example of his advice to punters. 'Take full advantage of a successful streak and contain losses while things aren't going well. Never quit on a winning run, but bail out early otherwise.'

Mac also relishes making comparisons between gambling and sex. 'The experience of gambling closely resembles that of love-making – a great deal of anticipation for a few moments of fleeting pleasure. Each finish is a separate orgasm.

'For me, the thrill of gambling on horses and a thousand other weird and wonderful possibilities is the most riveting human activity of all, excluding sex of course.'

Mac has also launched himself into the world of celebrity poker tournaments – with mixed results, and has admitted: 'If you want to win money at poker, play with a mug like me.'

378. TO BE FRANK, HE LOVED A BET

Sir Frank Duval was a Kerry Packer-size gambler in Australia before Packer came along. 'A reckless punter who, once charged with champagne, would bet wildly in race after race. He wagered in telephone numbers,' wrote Aussie gambling scribe David Hickie of the failed gold prospector-turned-accountant, air-force Major and scrap-metal tycoon whose first bets were placed on frog races.

He loved to back his own horses and first came to prominence when he lost £75,000 at Canterbury racecourse in 1963, when he was 54.

On November 3, 1966, he launched his fiercest assault on the bookies at Flemington, backing his On Par to win $62,000 in the second race; following this up on even-money winner Legal Boy in the next.

Some $102,000 up, he staked $50,000 on 2-5 shot Yootha, who won in a photo-finish.

Now he was ready to back his filly What Fun in the VRC Oaks. He asked top bookie Bill Waterhouse for $20,000 at 5-1. Waterhouse took it and went 9-2, after which What Fun shortened up to 4-1, and Duval went for a drink.

When he came back the 4-1 was still on offer so he handed Waterhouse a further $25,000.

Duval's potential winnings – and Waterhouse's losses – were $290,000.

What Fun ran second to Farmer's Daughter, despite jockey Rod Dawkins going flat out and earning a two-month whip ban. Undeterred, Duval bet $10,000 on Pharaon, beaten a head in the next, before staking an amazing $80,000 on Bastille in the last. The horse completed a hat-trick of runners-up for him, going down by a head.

Duval was $3,000 down on the day.

Six months later Duval flew to the Wagga Gold Cup meeting – and lost $193,000 on day one. On day two he won $197,000 – as What Fun won the big race.

He donated the $4,000 he had won in total towards prize-money for the Gold Cup next year.

That was a shrewd move – as What Fun won it again in 1968.

In September 1970 at Randwick he lost $100,000. By this time Perce Galea, at that time regarded as the country's biggest gambler, declared: 'This man makes my blood run cold. He must be the greatest punter ever known.'

In 1974 he won a reported £200,000 when he backed Go Fun from 40-1 to 16-1 before it won the Stradbrooke Handicap in Brisbane.

He was knighted in 1977 – but went bankrupt in 1980 when several of his companies collapsed. He died of a heart attack in 1981, aged 72.

379. I BET WE CAN SAVE YOUR JOBS

Jim Bendrodt, a racehorse owner, was running a nightclub in Sydney known as the Palais Royal in 1931 when the business fell on hard times and he could barely afford to pay the staff's wages.

He called them together for a meeting and told them he had £1,200 left. This was approximately the amount owed to the staff in wages, but if he handed it over it would have to be their last pay-packet.

However, he said, if they agreed to let him stake the lot on his horse Firecracker, he may win enough to keep the business going.

The staff agreed and Bendrodt took several of his heftier employees, the bouncers, along to Menangle racecourse to ensure that they were able to invest their cash at the best odds available. Their gamble forced the odds down from 10-1 to 6-5.

'Firecracker won by a length and the Palais Royal stayed open,' records Jack Pollard in Australian Horse Racing.

380. RUSSIAN AROUND LOOKING FOR A WINNER

When *Racing Ahead* writer Colin Phillips visited Bath races during 2008 he was intrigued to see a woman looking at racehorses in the paddock at very close quarters.

He was even more intrigued when told by an acquaintance who works for professional Chinese gamblers that the young lady he had seen using her binoculars from very close range was 'looking into the horses' eyes, and that she worked for a group of Russian backers'.

381. PARKINSON PUNTERS

Sufferers of Parkinson's disease were warned that a drug developed to combat the illness could turn them into 'sex-mad gamblers'.

Drugs company Pfizer, makers of Cabaser, had written to British GPs after studies revealed that the drug may have the side effect of causing 'pathological gambling' and 'increased libido, including hypersexuality' according to an 'exclusive' report by reporter John Coles in *The Sun* newspaper on April 21, 2007.

It was also reported that in the US up to a dozen patients were suing the drug firm for the money they had allegedly lost gambling.

382. WET BET

Competing in a poker event in September 2007, at the Club Med Hotel in the Turks & Caicos islands, Matt Giannetti soaked another player by accepting his bet of $15,000 for him to spend 12 hours continuously – starting at midnight, ending at noon – in the hotel swimming pool.

'Giannetti won the bet, climbing out of the pool to applause, shortly after noon,' reported a watching player, B J Nemeth.

383. LUCAN AFTER NUMBER ONE

Lord Lucan has been the subject of speculation and conjecture ever since he disappeared after a fatal attack on his family's nanny.

He was a close friend of late racing writer and fellow Old Etonian Charles Benson, then The Scout of the *Daily Express* who, in 1999, while being interviewed in Aspinall's casino, recalled: 'I remember blowing £7,000 in here the night Lucky's [Lucan's inappropriate nickname] son was born. Lucky lost about five times as much. That was his idea of celebrating.'

It has been reported that should Lucan's whereabouts ever be discovered, he will be entitled to receive some unpaid Premium Bond winnings.

384. STUNNING PLOT

Ile de Chypre, backed from 6-1 into 4-1 to win the 1988 King George V Handicap at Royal Ascot, looked like doing so under Greville Starkey as they hit the front and went clear – only to 'swerve badly left and unseat rider inside the final furlong' according to Ruff's Guide to the Turf.

That the horse may have been deliberately targeted as part of a system 'to undermine the fabric of racecourse betting' wasn't even hinted at until, in October 1989, a certain James Laming went on trial in a case involving a multi-million-pound cocaine chain, and claimed that he and another man had come up with the gambling scheme.

Sensationally, he declared he had invented a set of binoculars capable of emitting sound waves inaudible to humans, but which when aimed at a horse could cause it to swerve or act in an erratic manner.

Laming further claimed that these 'bins' had been used on Ile de Chypre.

Starkey even took part in a re-enactment of the race and some respected observers of the scene announced their belief in the 'stun-gun' scam, although others regarded it as an inventive smokescreen to deflect attention from the real point of the cocaine trial – in which Laming was ultimately convicted.

385. CHILLED OUT

Austrian international skier Rainer Schoenfelder lost a bet in October 2007, and paid for it by skiing nude down the Lauberhorn in Switzerland.

The 29-year-old, who hurt his neck and back in a crash the previous week, lost a bet with his physiotherapist, who had been treating his injuries. Schoenfelder had vowed to ski naked if his pains had lessened within a couple of days.

Schoenfelder skied wearing only yellow boots and an orange helmet and gloves, and a photographer snapped a shot of the skier that was circulated on the internet.

'Somehow I didn't notice the photographer,' Schoenfelder said. 'It was an internal bet and of course the whole thing wasn't planned for the public.

'I am happy, though, that the pains have eased up and that it was not cold when I honoured my debt.'

386. THIRTY-SEVEN HOURS FOR THIRTY-ONE GRAND

One of the earliest reports of a private high-stakes poker game concerns a lengthy showdown, which took place in 1840, and is recorded in an 1891 title, Poker: How To Play It.

'One of the best American citizens, and a man whose name can be found on all the fences within a radius of a hundred or more miles of Cincinnati, in the nature of advertising a specific medicine [please let me know if you can identify the 'citizen' – GS], told a friend that in 1840 he tackled a game of poker, and played for two nights and one day.

'After sitting it out for thirty-six hours he won $69,000. He broke those playing against him, and went home to take a much-needed rest.

'The second day afterwards he tackled the same party, and in less than an hour he lost $38,000.

'He then quit and came up the river with the rest of his wealth.'

387. UNLUCKY, ED

Edward Hodson was undoubtedly the unluckiest of winning punters. The Wolverhampton man landed the bet of a lifetime on February 11, 1984 when his 5p yankee, total stake 55p, produced four winners, whose accumulative odds totalled 3,956,748-1. Or would have done, had his bookie not put in place a maximum £3,000 payout rule.

388. JUMBO CATCH

'Jumbo' Howard cashed in on the betting shop boom of the early 1960s – they became legal in May 1961 – by opening his in perhaps the most unusual ever location – his Lowestoft-based North Sea fishing trawler. He must have taken plenty of plaice bets.

389. HOT STUFF

Poker player Erick Lindgren was challenged to a $340,000 bet. To win he had to play four consecutive rounds of golf in 100 degree Las Vegas heat, scoring under 100 in each round, carrying his own clubs and playing from the 'pro' tees.

He did it in the summer of 2007 – and won the cash

390. GOOD ADVICE THIS ONE IS IN ELSEWHERE

Financial adviser Ken Brown, 34, discovered a way of turning £50 into £10,000 in just eight years. The part time rugby coach invested £50 in a hunch in 1999 – betting that amount with bookies William Hill at odds of 200/1 – that the teenager playing for his local club, Aldwynians, would go on to play for England.

And in May 2007 when Dean Schofield, a Sale player, took the field for England in their game against S Africa, Ken, from Manchester, was £10,000 better off.

391. UNLUCKY – OR DISLOYAL?

A Manchester United fan would have won £795,000 for a £10 bet in March 2008 – had he not changed his mind and crossed out his 'own' team for his match accumulator bet and replaced them with their deadly rivals, Arsenal.

Of his 14 selections, 13 won. Manchester United won their game but Arsenal could only draw, meaning that instead of celebrating winning more than three-quarters of a million, Paul Greenwood, from Barnsley, was left bemoaning the loss of his £10 stake.

392. DEBBIE DOES BOOKIES

A woman from Newcastle-under-Lyme who began 2001 weighing 31 stone was celebrating a weight loss of 12 stone by the end of the year, winning herself £1,000 from William Hill after she gambled on shedding 168lb during the year.

Deborah Dale, 40, landed her bet of £50 at 20-1, when she weighed in on January 1, 2002 at under 19 stone.

393. ROOFER ON TOP OF WORLD

A Staffordshire man won £500,000 from William Hill in May 2001 for a mere 30p stake after landing world record odds of 1,666,666-1.

Roofer Mick Gibbs, who was in his 50s, staked his 30p, 15-event wager in a Hill's branch in Lichfield in August.

He then watched and waited as, one by one, his selections proved to be winners – he tipped Manchester United, Fulham, Millwall, Brighton and Rushden & Diamonds to win their English Divisional titles; Partick, Livingston and Hamilton to do likewise in Scotland; Arsenal, Hibs and Falkirk to win individual league games; Surrey to win cricket's County Championship; Gloucester the NatWest Trophy; and Leicester the rugby union Premiership.

Gibbs, a longstanding Manchester United fan, had previously won £157,000 from a similar bet – for a stake of £2.50 – when United won the 1999 Champions League final.

394. TEACHING BOOKIES A LESSON

Passing three A levels with A-grade passes in 2001 not only secured Yan Li Kathy Lee from Croydon a place at London's Kings College – but also landed a winning bet of £1,200 from William Hill.

For Yan Li's mother Alice, and her aunt, Wai Fong Lee, from Hornchurch in Essex had teamed up to place a bet on her achieving three A-grade passes and were so confident that they staked £1,200 at odds of even money.

Yan Li passed Maths, Law and Economics and planned to study Law.

'This was the largest bet we've ever taken on exam results,' I told the media at the time. 'It was clear from Yan Li's report and mock results that she is very talented so we were cautious with our odds – but not cautious enough!'

395. TAKEN FOR A DUNCE

In 1989 Dr David Wright placed the first bet ever on the results of a child's exams – staking £50 at 20-1 on his son Andrew passing his ten O levels with a perfect sweep of A grades.

Having laid the bet, I pretty much knew we would be paying up £1,000 when Andrew's headmaster at Hummersknott School in Darlington contacted me – and also backed him 'for school funds'.

✴ A teacher of Spanish, Mr Discenza, who struck a £15 wager with me in 2001 at 20-1 that a third or more of his students from Cheltenham Kingsmead School would pass their Spanish GCSE with A-C grades, won his star pupils a £300 payout!

396. GAY RIGHTS

Wherever and whenever betting men of a certain age gather, the talk will eventually turn to the Gay Future affair.

Gamblers will claim it was the perfect coup and the perpetrators should have been paid in full; racegoers will ask just how they could have had a chance of backing the winner of the race had they tried to do so, and bookies will remain convinced that it was a deceitful piece of skulduggery, aimed against them.

It happened on August Bank Holiday Monday, 1974, at Cartmel.

Troon permit-holder Anthony Collins had four horses due to run – Gay Future and Racionzer at Cartmel; Opera Cloak at Southwell and Ankerwyke at Plumpton.

That morning an estimated £30,000 worth of doubles, all involving Gay Future with another of Collins' intended runners, were placed in £5, £10 and £15 units.

Shortly after midday, despite the way in which the bets had been placed, bookies became suspicious and declined to accept any more.

Collins was at Plumpton, ostensibly to look after Ankerwyke, while his wife was at Cartmel with Gay Future, and to place on-course bets on his Racionzer, in the same race, to give the impression that this was the better of the stable's two.

The unknown amateur declared as Gay Future's rider was then suddenly replaced by leading Irish amateur Mr T A Jones, who had won on him in Ireland.

Bookies were surprised to learn that Collins' Opera Cloak and Ankerwyke had both been scratched from their races – all doubles on them coupled with Gay Future now became singles.

Gay Future drifted to 10-1 on course, possibly because he seemed to be sweating up badly – although this may have been due to being lathered with soap flakes!

Gay Future won by 15 lengths.

With huge liabilities on the horse, the bookies were relieved when the Betting Office Licencees Association advised members to withhold payment, pending the outcome of enquiries.

Scotland Yard was called in to investigate, and decided to prosecute Collins and an acquaintance with conspiracy to defraud bookmakers.

After a seven-day trial both were found guilty, with the judge commenting: 'The degree of dishonesty is in my assessment, although a conspiracy to defraud, very much at the bottom end of the scale.'

BOLA advised members to hand back stakes on Gay Future's race – but to pay none of the estimated £300,000 winnings.

The prosecution had alleged that neither Opera Cloak nor Ankerwyke had ever been intended to run in their races, and there was much discussion about whether Gay Future had actually been in the care of Collins in England for long enough to be qualified to race.

There was no ultimate happy ending for either the perpetrators, or Gay Future himself – killed in a fall at Wetherby three weeks before the trial began.

397. DON'T PANIC

Captain Mainwaring won the 4.20 race at Chepstow on Tuesday, May 27, 2008.

Yet in a William Hill shop a customer came to the counter to claim his winnings, despite having quite clearly, according to his betting slip, backed a beaten runner, lo.

When the counter clerk pointed this out, the punter declared: 'No, that doesn't say lo, it says 10, the number ten [Captain Mainwaring's racecard number] – that's the horse I meant.'

He didn't get paid, but bookies throughout the country were probably left wondering how an owner could be allowed to name his horse in such a potentially confusing way.

398. JERRY-MANDERING

Villainous Yorkshire crook and conman Robert Ridsdale bribed jockey Harry Edwards to stop Jerry, a hot fancy for the 1824 St Leger. He then accepted huge bets for the horse, safe in the knowledge that it could not win.

On the eve of the race, Jerry's trainer got wind of the plot. Next afternoon, just as Edwards appeared clad in his racing colours and ready for the race, the trainer informed him his services were no longer required, and substituted him with trustworthy jockey Ben Smith, who went out and rode the 9-1 shot to victory.

In 1832 Ridsdale's St Giles won the Derby, landing him a fortune in bets – but the rumours that the horse was a four-year-old and that all but four of the jockeys in the race had been 'squared' were probably true.

As befits such a gambling scoundrel, when he was found dead in 1836 in a Newmarket hayloft, his total wealth amounted to three half-pennies.

399. DOG GONE

The Daily Mirror reported in August 1978 that a group of London greyhound followers had hit on a smart scheme – enter all the dogs in an open race up north, then clean up by backing the one they knew was best prepared for the coup.

They duly entered five greyhounds for a race at Askern Stadium, near Doncaster, and five carloads of them drove up to pull off the plot – only to discover when they arrived that it wasn't a five-dog race as they had believed, but there was a sixth entry, local runner Reggie.

With Reggie badly drawn the Londoners went ahead with their betting plunge, only for 'sod's law' to strike as Reggie romped home by seven lengths.

Graham Searson, spokesman for the track, laughed: 'As soon as they entered their five dogs we warned the bookies, but two were still prepared to take bets. All the locals thought it was a great laugh when Reggie won – the Cockneys certainly went home with their tails between their legs.'

400. BUCK OFF

Thomas 'Buck' Whaley was born in 1766, the son of a wealthy Irish protestant landowner.

He loved a bet and once accepted a wager from a fellow member of the Dublin Hell-Fire Club that he could not ride an Arab stallion while jumping out of the drawing room of his father's house on Stephen's Green to the street some 30 feet below.

Whaley accepted the bet.

'He won his bet,' reported a contemporary source.

'But killed the horse.'

When Whaley later moved to the Isle of Man he made a bet that he could also live on Irish soil and imported a considerable amount of Irish earth, to form the 6ft deep foundations of the new house in which he lived, thus winning the bet.

401. HAIR-RAISING REG

Sonny Liston in his 1960s prime was one of the most fearsome world heavyweight champions ever, but veteran boxing commentator Reg Gutteridge once brought a smile from him.

At a press conference Liston had declared that 'black men have fewer leg hairs than white men'. But Gutteridge challenged him: 'Bet you ten bucks you've got more hair than me'– then rolled up his trouser leg to reveal his false leg.

Liston roared with laughter.

402. FISHY STORY

An angler claiming £30,000 winnings turned up at his betting shop without his betting slips – and told staff that he had been so delighted to win the competition he had backed himself in that he had jumped in the water in triumph at the end, ruining the slips.

Marc Jones, 42, had beaten hundreds of other anglers to win the 2005 Fish O Mania Trophy and the Wakefield man had backed himself at odds of 25-1 down to 9-1 to give himself a potential payout of £30,000.

'It is traditional for the winner to be thrown in the water. I decided to beat them to the punch and jumped in – but forgot I had the betting slips in my pocket,' said Jones. Bookies Totesport, who had taken his wagers, were able to verify his claim and paid him out.

403. NUMBER IS UP

A Buddhist monk in Thailand was warned to stop predicting winning numbers for the national lottery or he would be dismissed, reported *The Times*, admittedly on April 1, 1998!

Unghonwet had successfully predicted winning numbers on 15 occasions before the Religious Affairs Department in Bangkok allegedly announced he would be banished from his temple if he did not desist after thousands flocked there looking for guidance.

404. SHORT ODDS

Photographer Keith Shillitoe won £600 by wearing shorts for an entire year up to July 1998 – once even attending a black-tie dinner thus clad.

405. GUNNER BE A WINNER

Royal marine Carl Ford won £2,000 when his Viking armoured car was hit by a rocket grenade in Afghanistan's Helmand Province.

Gunner Ford, 26, was one of 40 commandos who staked £50 each with the winnings going to the first to be hit but not hurt while in action.

'The money will come in handy as I'm getting married,' said Carl, from Plymouth, in June 2007. 'But my fiancée Susan doesn't like to think about how I won it.'

406. KING OF THE PUNTERS?

Alex King gatecrashed a movie world premiere at London's Leicester Square Odeon, and joined a line-up of celebrities waiting to meet Prince Charles and Camilla.

In the process he claimed to have won a bet of £100,000 with wealthy friend Lord Edward Davenport. King, a 30-year-old property developer, told The Sun in October 2006: 'Eddie was a guest and bet me £100,000 I couldn't gatecrash my way in. I said not only would I get in, but I would also shake hands with both Charles and Camilla.'

He did so, telling Charles he should be in a James Bond movie and was mingling with stars like Stephen Fry, Frances de la Tour and Richard Griffiths until Sun royal photographer Arthur Edwards unmasked him as an imposter.

'*The Sun* watched at Lord Davenport's plush London home as he whipped out

£100,000 in cash and in a grand gesture flashily handed it to Alex on a silver salver,' reported the paper.

'I jumped over the barrier and walked in. I just acted like I imagined a celebrity would act,' said King.

407. POT LUCK

When Dougie Whithead was trounced by a12-year-old snooker player in 1995 he decided the lad had great potential – so he backed him at 1000-1 to grow up to win the world title.

And in 2005 he cashed in his betting slip for £10,000 when Shaun Murphy won the title, aged 22.

Former boxer Dougie, from Northamptonshire, met Shaun when his dad asked him to help with his training: 'I just knew he was going to be great,' said the delighted 74-year-old.

408. FILIPINO YOUR BOOTS

What was believed to be the first single bet of 100,000 Aussie dollars on a horse to win was struck on May 1, 1968 when mega-punter Felipe Ysmael, from one of the wealthiest families in the Philippines, staked that amount on Silver Strike in a two-year-old maiden, worth $350, at Newcastle.

Bookie Bill Waterhouse accepted the bet at even money. The horse started at 4-7 and romped home.

Bookies had plenty of subsequent chances to take Ysmael on as he bet in massive amounts, with Waterhouse recalling in 1984: 'Ysmael was daddy of them all. He put a million dollars on a horse with me once. He wasn't betting with anyone else, and I took him on and beat him.'

409. MY STRANGEST EVER BET REQUEST

In February 2005 I was asked to accept a bet that my correspondent could name a murderer.

Outlining a high-profile, longstanding homicide case unfolding in America, the emailer told me: 'I have solved the most baffling and mysterious serial killings in the United States. I will bet that the person I name will be the mysterious murderer. Give me sufficient odds and I will provide you the name and complete date of birth of the murderer, who will confess within 30 days of the date the bet is placed.'

The bet request, to which I did not accede, was signed 'The Mystic'.

410. IMAGINE THAT

Schoolteacher Michael O'Lara won a high-stakes card game against Beatle John Lennon at a London hotel in 1961.

'I beat him. But when I asked for the money he owed me, he said he didn't have it,' recalled O'Lara in 1999. 'Then he walked to the back of the hotel and came back a couple of minutes later and threw two suits at me.'

In 1999 O'Lara auctioned one of the suits for £5,000 to raise cash for a charity donating cash to footballers in East Timor.

411. WHITE OUT

In January 2006, six-times world snooker title runner-up Jimmy White outlined his gambling exploits in an interview with the late Elkan Allan, telling him: 'I earned six million quid and lost a million buying and selling horses, half a million on blackjack, and squandered the rest on women, racing and poker.'

412. SICK AS A PARROTT

John Parrott told fellow snooker star Willie Thorne that his favourite cue had been stolen on the eve of his forthcoming match against Ken Doherty in the 1996 Regal Masters tournament in Motherwell, Scotland.

Keen punter Thorne was convinced this was his key to riches. 'No snooker player can play without his own individual cue,' he said.

Thorne started to back Doherty, getting a total £38,000 stake on with various bookies. He also 'tipped off everybody I owed money to, asking them to put on a grand for them and for me'.

Doherty's odds shrank from 6-5 to 4-7 favourite.

Thorne was doing the TV commentary for the game as Doherty went 2-0 up, and then Parrott hit back to go 5-2 ahead, before Doherty rallied.

'The final frame was the hardest I ever commentated on. Against all the odds, Parrott won the match. My friends weren't too pleased – about half a million quid had been lost by people I tipped off.'

I am well aware of Willie's penchant for a punt. We were both on a TV programme once when the interviewer asked him how much he had gambled – and he turned and pointed at me, saying: 'Ask him, he'll tell you.'

In an interview with Inside Edge magazine in December 2005 Thorne estimated that he had lost £3.5m gambling.

413. MESSIAH

'What odds would you offer on the Church of Scotland proclaiming myself to be the messiah?' asked the letter I received in March 2005 from a gentleman living in Bonnyrigg, Scotland.

I offered him 1,000-1 that the church would officially accept that the messiah was alive, within a year of his bet being staked.

414. WAS IT A BOOKIE?

Waterford public library had never seen such a scramble to borrow their books as the one that broke out in June 2007 when the word spread that a mystery benefactor had spent £20,000 hiding scratchcards between the pages of various volumes.

With 70,000 books in the place, regular readers and those who could barely read stormed into the library desperate to get their hands on the books, some of which contained no scratchcards, some just one and others up to ten.

The majority seemed to have been hidden in biographies.

Lucky finders won up to £200 – one assistant librarian landed a £100 win.

'It was like a flock of locusts descending on us. They were shaking books, flicking through them, and the library is now in an absolute mess. We have no idea who has done this,' said chief librarian Richard Fennessy.

415. FIND THE LADY – MONEY OR YOUR WIFE

Is it gambling's great urban myth – or do poker players and other gamblers really resort to using their wives as stake money when they run out of cash in high-rolling hands?

During 1987 German police reported that a Cologne poker player staked his other half to cover his bet.

When he lost he had to bring the winner home with him to collect, only for the unenthusiastic spouse to grab the baby and flee.

He wasn't charged, 'but he had a lot of explaining to do,' the police spokesman was quoted.

Then in May 1989, Rio de Janeiro police were reportedly called in when Brazilian poker player Pedro Becone, 31, lost his wife, Maria, while the pair were on honeymoon.

In February 2000 Mexican gambler Alberto Flores, 22, was said to have staked 16-year-old wife Patricia to cover his £3 bet on a cock fight – and lost.

Moving on, in January 2007 I read that Andrei Karpov from Murmansk ran out of money in his poker match and offered up Tatiana instead to opponent Sergey Brodov. When Tatiana found out she taught hubby a lesson by starting a relationship with Brodov.

Such stories have been doing the rounds for hundreds of years, I discovered. In his 19th century work *Gambling: Its Votaries and Victims*, Andrew Steinmetz wrote: 'This staking of wives by gamblers is a curious subject. The practice my be said to have been universal, having furnished cases among civilised as well as barabarous nations.'

I don't know – is this sort of stuff really going on, or is there a smart freelance journalist out there writing up variations on this theme every couple of years and coining in a fee every time he manages to con another gullible editor with a gap in his paper to fill?

416. WOODS YOU BELIEVE IT?

When Alan Woods died, aged 62, in January 2008, worth an estimated 670 million Aussie dollars, he was described by David Ashforth of the *Racing Post* as 'perhaps the most successful gambler in the world'.

Yet few people had heard of him.

Woods, born in Australia, was a talented mathematician, who used that ability to help him make a living after being fired from his job as an investment analyst for a merchant bank.

He learned how to 'card count' at blackjack and, after cleaning up in Tasmania, moved to haunt the Vegas casinos, earning an estimated $4,000 a week but having to use a variety of disguises to stay ahead of the game.

He then started to bet on horseracing in New Zealand, followed by Hong Kong in 1984 – where he and a partner, Bill Benter, joined forces to develop computerised betting systems, which cut a swathe through the tote system there. 'Our whole theory was based on taking a contrarian approach to whatever the public were doing,' he said.

After the pair split in 1987 Woods flourished, winning almost £250,000 in 1988; and double that in 1989, eventually graduating to an annual profit of almost £1.5m.

Eventually his operation accounted for up to two per cent of Hong Kong's annual betting turnover.

John Schreck, former chief steward for the Australian Jockey Club and later for the Hong Kong Jockey Club, said of Woods: 'He had in his employ dozens of Filipinos running around carrying mobile phones and hundreds of thousands of dollars in cash waiting for his instructions on how and what to bet.'

In 2005 he laid out £328,000 to make a profit of £271,000 but he was so relaxed about the process that he fell asleep while racing was going on.

He also gambled on the stock exchange where he also did well, apart from one occasion when he found himself, briefly, US$100m down on a trade.

In his latter years, he claimed the money made him happy: 'Probably less so now than in years gone by. There's a cliche that says getting there is much more fun than arriving.'

And after Woods departed this world, the word was that his successor as the biggest punter out there was reclusive Australian-based Zeljko Ranogajec – whose turnover, said to be more than Woods', is invested on racing and sports gambling.

Born In Hobart in 1961, the son of Croatian immigrants, he began as a card counter but in 2007 he was reported by website PuntingAce.com to be wagering A$500m on Aussie racing per year – nearly five per cent of tote turnover across the country.

417. BIGGS' BET

Ronnie Biggs, the Great Train Robber and career criminal, dabbled in bookmaking.

In a November 1988 interview he said: 'I was always the prison bookmaker. When

Never Say Die won the 1954 Derby it was the biggest loss I ever took.

'From underneath my work-bench I paid out 66 ounces of tobacco in winning bets.'

418. GONE FOR A BURTON

Superstar actor Richard Burton was buried dressed in red – to win a bet from beyond the grave.

Burton had once bet fellow actors Peter O'Toole and Stanley Baker that they would never catch him not wearing at least one item of red – national colour of his beloved Wales. Every day for years, Burton wore red to maintain the bet, and when he was buried in August 1984 he was wearing a red jacket, red trousers, red polo neck and red socks.

Burton's brother, Verdun, said: 'I can see him up there now, laughing his head off after so decisively winning the bet.'

419. DOWN WENT BROWN

Mourners gathered to bury racing fan Bill Brown in November 1988 when the Reverend Bob White told them that Bill wanted them all to back a horse for him – Grey General, running that afternoon in the 2.30 at Wolverhampton.

They had a whip-round and backed the horse, who went in at 4-1. Bill's brother, Jak, from Southend, said: 'He just wanted to make his friends happy for the last time.'

420. BOOKIE

Jeff Ehrhardt, quarter back for the Murray State US Football side, ended up facing misdemeanour charges 'after pushing a campus police officer and taking his ticket book to win a $20 bet,' reported website dailycamera.com in May 2008.

421. LE GRAND STING!

The most audacious attempted gambling coup on the French turf took place in 1973, when nine outsiders were suddenly heavily backed for the Tierce – a 1st, 2nd and 3rd forecast bet – in the Prix Bride Abbatue at Auteuil.

So unexpected was the betting pattern that the authorities were alerted, and were watching closely as the race began.

After less than a quarter of a mile, the field of 24 split into two, with the nine backed horses heading the rest. Eventually, the first three to pass the post were all among the nine, resulting in a 13,500 franc dividend to a three-franc stake.

The authorities froze all payouts and launched an investigation – which took five years to complete – after which 14 jockeys and 40 punters were arrested for conspiracy to defraud the public.

422. MAJOR GAMBLER?

The fact that former prime minister John Major called an election for a date within days of one of the greatest topical tips of all time, Party Politics, wining the Grand National, may have been related to the Tory leader's revelation when appearing on Desert Island Discs that he had flirted with a career in bookmaking as a youngster – 'From time to time neighbours would dispatch me to place bets with an illicit bookie who plied his trade in the environs of Loughborough Junction Station.'

423. POKER'S 17-YEAR GAME

I have to admit it sounds a bit unlikely, but I got it from LJ Ludovici, a pretty sober-looking guy who served in the RAF during World War II, reaching the rank of Squadron Leader.

Well, if you can't believe a Squadron Leader – particularly one who went on to write the biography of Sir Alexander Fleming, the inventor of penicillin, then who can you believe, I wonder?

LJ wrote a book called *The Itch For Play*, which was published in 1962, at which point, to judge from the photograph on the inside back cover, he was approximately 109 years old. If that is an accurate estimate then he would have been born about the time – June 15, 1853 – at which, so he tells us in his book, a certain Major Danielson and another Texan, known as 'Old Man' Morgan, sat down to play poker in Austin, Texas. LJ pins the precise start time down to 'eight in the evening'.

By dawn the next day, he explains, 'they had agreed to abolish any limit to the stakes'. The game, reports Ludovici, 'progressed'.

Just how it progressed, I will let our flying ace inform you in his own words: 'It continued week after week, month after month and, as it turned out, year after year.

'The two men rose only to eat, snatch some sleep, answer nature, or change some part of their property into cash so they could play on.

'Texans flocked to watch them bent solemnly over their cards,' LJ tells us – well, perhaps there wasn't much else to do in Texas in those days.

'The railways were built and reached Austin, hotels sprang up everywhere, the Civil War was fought and reconstruction commenced. These events flowed right over the heads of Major Danielson and 'Old Man' Morgan.' Yes, I know it sounds pretty unlikely, but LJ looks like a man of his word and I for one am prepared to allow him the benefit of the doubt, so read on:

'In 1870, seventeen years after they first sat down, they were still at it.' Stretching credulity, I accept.

'In 1872 both died at one and the same moment.' Mm, it does seem likely that LJ is testing our gullibility ever so slightly.

'In their wills they instructed their sons to carry on where they had left off. Their sons obeyed. After the sons had played for another five years ...' – hold on, that makes it, er, 17 years, two more, um, five extra – that makes it 1877, by my calculation.

'... one was killed by a railway train and the other went off his head. The families became impoverished.

'Today,' – don't forget that LJ's today meant 1962, the year in which his book was published – 'the cards with which Major [do you think it was that exalted rank which impressed our Squadron Leader enough to accept this tale at face value?] Danielson and 'Old Man' Morgan started their family card-marathon are said to lie, soiled, torn, curling at the ends and yellowing in the safe deposit of a bank at Austin.'

See: there it is all you sceptics who think this could be an ever so slightly apocryphal yarn – all you have to do is get on the internet and check out all the banks in Austin. One of them will undoubtedly confirm the story – or my name's not LJ Ludovici.

Which, of course, it isn't.

424. TOTE-AL JOY

Four Tote workers at Glasgow's Shawfield greyhound stadium thought they would hit the jackpot with their 1980 scheme – they printed winning tickets for themselves after races were over.

However, they were rumbled when it was noticed that the number of tickets sold did not balance up with the figures recorded by the stadium's computer, and the four were exposed.

In November of that year they were each fined up to £50.

425. RE-MARK-ABLE WINNER

On November 14, 1973, Princess Anne wed Captain Mark Phillips – and bookies were almost cleaned out by coincidence backers as Windsor's Royal Wedding Handicap Chase on that very afternoon was won by Royal Mark.

426. BLONDIE MOB

An ingenious racing scam was pulled in the 1960s by a group of women known as the 'Blondie Mob' who were operating at a time when racing results were only released from the track to the outside world after the last race had been run.

The mob was operating in Hollywood and gambling expert John Scarne was called in when a bookmaker who had lost $100,000 to one fair-haired female client in just four weeks became suspicious. The bookie worked out of a room on the top floor of a building.

He told Scarne: 'It's air conditioned, soundproof and has no windows. What's more, my players must arrive before post time. After post time, no-one is allowed in the elevator at this floor until after the last race. The bettors are not permitted to make or receive phone calls while they are here, and the phone number is not listed.'

Scarne, who often acted as a troubleshooter for gambling bosses, spent an afternoon watching Blondie at work. 'I could see at once she didn't have a radio-receiving gimmick on her – the low-necked dress she wore was a tight fit and no room to spare.'

By the end of the afternoon she had won $2,000 – but Scarne was on to her. He told the bookie: 'She's been past-posting you, and the guy who's been tipping her off is … you!'

Scarne revealed that Blondie's confederate must be whoever had phoned through a bet on Snow Shoes in the eighth race at Hialeah.

'That was May – another blonde,' said the bookie.

Scarne explained: 'May is operating from a room that has a direct line from one of the wire services. She gets the result of the race a minute after it's over. As soon as she knew High Noon had won the third she phoned and gave you a bet of 50, 20 and 10 (win, place, show)| on Snow Shoes in the 8th and asked you to repeat it, which you did. Blondie heard you say 'You bet me 50, 20 and 10 on Snow Shoes in the 8th at Hialeah' and simply added the first digits of the amount of the bet, got an answer of 8 and knew that the horse listed as number 8 on the scratch sheet had won the third.'

427. MRS MOLLY

Elizabeth Dawson, 13, back from evacuation in the country, had returned to London at the end of the First World War only to discover that 'Mother had embarked on a new career as, of all things, a Turf Commission Agent – to put it bluntly, she was now a lady bookie'.

Molly, her mum, had discarded a drunken husband, cashed in her savings and opened up a newsagents, before starting a lucrative sideline, suggested by local bookmaker John Swain, who had asked if 'she might like to earn a little extra on the side by taking bets over the counter'. Soon, she had entered a profession in which there were few – if any – other female participants.

When the betting income overtook the newsagent earnings, Molly opted for the former full-time and opened a betting office in Hackney, advertising herself as 'London's Only Lady Bookmaker' and collecting bets from punters on the street and over the telephone.

Her activities were later collected for posterity by Elizabeth, who wrote a book about her – 'With a bookmaker for a mother, life couldn't possibly be dull … Pol Roger, Mumm or the 'Widow' generally flowed pretty freely whenever a rank outsider turned up for the book. The toast was always the same – 'Here's to the punters – bless their little cotton socks'.'

With business flourishing, a new office was opened in London's Bishopsgate. She was now dealing with more upmarket clients, but had her own standards to which she adhered: 'None was allowed more than two weeks' credit. If they didn't pay up at the first polite demand, she would cut her losses and cross them off the books forthwith.'

She had no time for those who bet beyond their means, and would lecture them piously on 'the evils of gambling'.

At first her new business flourished, but as it was so dependent on personal contact to keep the wagers rolling in it became very time consuming and she soon sold it on, after 'a lucrative offer from a firm of West End bookmakers'.

As results went against her she found it difficult to survive on the Hackney earnings, which would not support her preferred diet – 'fresh herrings and frozen cod would replace oysters and Scotch salmon,' remembered her daughter.

But, 'fortunately these eras of retrenchment and self-denial seldom lasted for long. The racing luck would turn in our favour, rank outsiders would romp home again, punters would plunge to no avail and our finances would be out of the red.'

One of the chief reasons for the improvement in her fortunes was that Molly was now embracing street, telephone and postal betting.

Street betting was, though, still illegal, and occasionally clamped down on. 'She had one or two narrow squeaks when runners [people bringing the bets to her] were almost caught trying to sneak in betting slips. She employed about twenty of them, working on a 10% commission, and doing very well, since each one of them might bring in as many as twenty or thirty pounds on a normal day, and considerably more on big race days.

'As their turn came round at intervals, one of the runners would be picked up by the police, hauled in front of the local magistrates and fined under the Betting and Gaming Acts. Mother paid their fines.'

A little personal acquaintance with local bobbies saved Molly much hassle as profits boomed: 'Mother's daily winnings could amount to quite fantastic sums, and they often ran into several hundreds of pounds. No wonder she used to refer to the telephone business as 'bread and butter'. The more humble tanner (2.5p) each-way punters supplied a liberal spreading of jam.'

Into the 1930s business slowed as the country's financial health showed signs of recession and, to make matters worse, Molly fell foul of the taxman.

Nor was it easy to shrug off increasing health problems and she contracted jaundice with complications.

Molly died in October 1938, the day before her 50th birthday. 'I'll wager it wasn't long before she was organising a Pearly Gates Handicap and laying odds against the angel with the shortest wings,' wrote her daughter, Elizabeth.

428. SEEING TRIPLE

Olive Harris, together with her sisters Mrs June Muggleston and Mrs Dorothy Harrison, must have made punters do a double – no, triple – take, and also made a little bookmaking history, when they made a book at Uttoxeter's evening meeting on June 15, 1967. Not that the three, daughters of trainer Arthur Birch, were exactly novices – they already owned eight betting shops.

429. ODD SORT OF FAVOUR

Judy Higby became a strong contender for the unenviable title of World's Unluckiest Punter after she walked into her local betting shop in St Albans on the morning of April 3, 1993 and asked for a price that that afternoon's Grand National would NOT take place.

Proprietor Richard Halling, believing he was doing her a favour and not wanting to take money under what he believed to be false pretences, declined to offer odds. 'It should have been at least 1,000-1,' he later confessed.

That afternoon Ms Higby watched in stunned silence as the Non-National unfolded in front of her eyes, courtesy of Captain Keith 'Cock-Up' Brown.

430. LUCKY LAZENBY

Marie Lazenby won £22 when she backed Miinnehoma to land the 1994 Grand National but, as a consequence, she wound up in hospital.

For, as the horse crossed the line, she jumped for joy, and cheered, so upsetting her pet golden retriever that the dog jumped up – and bit her on her left nipple.

Marie, 27, was rushed to hospital in Middlesbrough where the doctor treating her said: 'I have to ask – it WAS your dog, and not your boyfriend?'

431. BLANK LOOKS

Joy (a totally inappropriate name, it would emerge) Monteith, the chief librarian at Greenock in Scotland, admitted in 1985 that her staff were blacking out the racing pages of newspapers provided in the libraries with an ink pad and roller in a bizarre form of censorship that had apparently been going on for many years. Finally ending the practice, Ms Monteith confessed: 'I'm mortified. The practice seems to have been carried on unthinkingly.'

Local readers had got used, said one, to 'holding the papers up to the light and reading through the ink'.

432. IN THE STARS?

Mystic Meg, the Sun's ace fortune-teller, was reported in 1996 as saying: 'I have occasionally used my crystal ball to 'see' results of races. Or asked the runes to spell out a winning name. But I don't think this is very sporting. So I only do it when I truly need to win.' Yes, we believe you, but thousands may not.

It is probably apocryphal, but I have been told a number of times that Mystic Meg once went racing to see one of her horses run, only to miss out because she arrived late, due to, er, unforeseen circumstances.

In 1988 the Sunday Sport racing pundit, psychic Doris Balwark, gave readers tips she claimed were supplied 'from the other side' by long dead former champion jockey Fred Archer.

433. NIGHTMARE DREAM

Edwina Lees, 42, from Bristol kept dreaming about a racehorse during early1992, but could never remember the animal's name when she awoke. Until, one afternoon she heard Peter O'Sullevan running through the names of the runners for a race – and as soon as he said 'Docklands Express' she just knew that was the one haunting her dreams. She persuaded doubtful boyfriend Peter Bateman to stick £100 on the horse. See what she did there? Her profit if it won, his loss if it didn't!

Anyway, Docklands Express ran out a 5-1 winner.

Happy ending, then? Well, yes, except that Bateman then became so convinced that Docklands Express would win the Grand National that he stuck £1,000 on it to do so – twice as much as the original dream bet had won. This time there was a nightmare outcome as the horse was beaten.

434. RIGHT CHARLIE

Prince Charles won a reported 50 quid in 1997 when he bet Camilla that amount that she would fail to give up smoking. He was right.

435. FEEL FREE TO ARREST ME, BISMARCK BARRY TELLS COPS

'Come and nick me,' invited a defiant Barry Dennis after learning that he had been reported to police for allegedly placing a bet on an event whose outcome was already known to him.

The high profile racecourse bookie, a regular on Channel 4 Racing and its Morning Line programme, known for his efforts to advise viewers of well fancied horses NOT to back – his 'Bismarcks', Dennis had related in his weekly *Sun* newspaper column how he had won a substantial amount by placing a bet on the outcome of a stewards inquiry at Aintree, having already discovered the result.

'I wrote the column about two years ago, while the incident was five years ago,' an unrepentant Dennis told the *Racing Post* in July 2008. He added: 'There was a stewards inquiry and when the winning jockey came out with his thumbs up I made a few grand backing Le Duc on the Betfair market which was still open.'

Invited the layer: 'They – the police – know where I am. Come and nick me if you think I have done something wrong.' At time of writing, the police had not taken any reported action.

436. WINNING BET LAID ON FOR THE POPE

When the Pope caused Randwick racecourse in Sydney to be shut down for ten weeks to accommodate his July 2008 visit to Australia, local trainers had to move 300 racehorses as a result.

One very prominent Aussie trainer, Bart Cummings was outspoken against the situation: 'The Pope's all right in his place, but Randwick isn't his place.'

However, the 400,000 'pilgrims' who visited the track to hear Benedict XVI's address clearly did not agree with his views. So, Cummings decided to lay on a winner for the pontiff and duly entered his horse, Xavier, named after a Jesuit priest, in a race at Rosehill Gardens the day before the mass, telling visitors to his website that this was an 'omen tip'. Sure enough, Xavier bolted up, to Cummings' – and possibly the Pope's – delight: 'I thought the Pope was going to have a bet. I waited till the right day to send him out to win – I worked on it for months'.

I'm sure Cummings will eventually get his reward in Heaven!

437. A PLAGUE ON YOU, SIR

During the plague year of 1665 an extraordinary gambling tale unfolded, to be recorded for posterity by publication of the day, Ainsworth's 'Old Saint Paul's'.

It concerned a Captain Disbrowe of the King's bodyguard, who lost 'a large sum of money' to a 'notorious debauchee, a gambler and bully named Sir Paul Parravicin.'

Parravicin had apparently made 'an offensive allusion' to Disbrowe's wife after winning his money, picking up the dice box with which he had cleaned out the other and suggesting: 'Although you have lost your money, you still have a valuable stake left.'

He continued, 'I have won from you two hundred pounds. You are a ruined man. I give you a last chance. I will stake all my winnings – nay, double the amount – against your wife.'

'You have robbed me of my money and would rob me of my honour,' said Disbrowe, who had no option but to take on the gamble – 'If I lose, I will not survive my shame.'

They played a single main of dice – and Disbrowe lost again. He resorted to his sword, but was swiftly disarmed by Parravicin, who took from him the key to his house.

Parravicin gained admittance to the captain's house and found his way to the chamber of his wife, who was then in bed. 'Declaring himself, he belied her husband, stating that he was false to her, and had surrendered her to him.'

Mrs Disbrowe screamed and fainted. Parravicin brought a light towards her – when he looked closely at her he noticed a mark on her neck which shocked him and made him rush out of the house – where he encountered the returning husband, who vowed 'you shall not escape my vengeance.'

'You are already avenged' cried Parravicin, 'Your wife has the plague.'

Disbrowe rushed indoors where he told his now recovered wife 'I was compelled to yield up the key of my house.'

She said, 'It is plain you value me less than play.'

Then she asked why Parravicin had fled.

'Your preserver was the plague,' he replied.

Shocked, she then demanded that he kill Parravicin to 'wipe out the wrong he has done me'. Disbrowe set out to do so, seeking out the other man and challenging him, eliciting the response, 'I will have your life first and your wife afterwards.' The pair duly arranged to fight a duel in Hyde Park, which Parravicin won, running Disbrowe through, fatally.

Parravicin returned to the Disbrowe home, where he was in time to see 'a body, wrapped in a shroud, brought out.'

It was Mrs Disbrowe. 'She died of grief,' the man removing the body told Parravicin, 'Her husband was killed this morning, but as she had the plague it must be put down to that. There is no money to pay for coffins, they must go to the grave without them.'

This evident morality tale now closes with a big ending: 'As the body of his victim also was brought forth, Parravicin fell against the wall in a state of stupefaction. At this moment, Solomon Eagle, the weird plague-prophet, with his burning brazier on his head, suddenly turned the corner of the street, and stationing himself before the dead-cart cried in a voice of thunder: 'Woe to the libertine! Woe to the homicide! For he shall perish in everlasting fire! Woe! Woe!'

I think we can assume that henceforth, Parravicin became a reformed character!

438. FIRST OF MANY

Melvyn Eddison, 47, was the first millionaire to win a million on the National Lottery. The Manchester businessman did it in 1995.

439. DUMBER AND DUMBRELL

Matthew Dumbrell was the first – but far from the last – punter to bet on the end of the world. He wagered £1 at 1,000,000-1 that it would coincide with the August 1999 eclipse and when asked how he would collect his winnings, told me: 'I suspect there will be bookmakers in heaven.'

I told him that if there were, no doubt punters would always back winners – thus making it a living (?) Hell for the resident layers.

Matthew was left a little shamefaced when the world failed to end, as he had sold virtually everything he had in order to move from London to Lewes for a better view of both the eclipse and the apocalypse.

But he contacted me again to predict 'that the end of time will not be later than midnight on Saturday, December 31, 2000AD'.

When that tip failed to materialise he showed no hard feelings and said to me:

'Whenever the Chief Bookmaker in the sky opens the seventh and final seal, may your name also be in the Book of Life.' Amen to that.

440. SAINTLY DECISION

Legendary former Liverpool star Ian St John confessed in his 2005 autobiography The Saint to being part of a Motherwell side ready to accept £100 each – in the days when the average weekly wage was £10 – to lose a home match with Third Lanark to help land a coup on the fixed-odds football coupons.

'We got the £100 plus the chance to bet at long odds on two 'certain' results,' wrote Saint, explaining that they were to be told in advance of another rigged game.

When the players explained what was going on to their keeper, Hastie Weir, he 'went berserk' and stormed off to tell the manager, Bobby Ancell, who shot the idea down in flames.

'Everybody knew that the great betting coup was dead in the water.'

Motherwell went on to win the game, scoring seven times with St John hitting a hat-trick.

441. MAKING MINCEMEAT OF BOOKIES

'Mincemeat' Joe Griffin acquired his nickname when, just after the Second World War, he made a healthy profit by purchasing a shipload of dried fruit from the Greek government and using it to create mince pies which he sold on to British grocers.

His company, the Redbreast Preserving Company was soon turning over up to £2m a year and Griffin indulged his love of horseracing by buying chaser Early Mist to run in the 1953 Grand National, trained by Vincent O'Brien.

Early Mist won at 20/1 and the flamboyant Griffin not only danced a jig in the unsaddling enclosure – but also won a massive £100,000 in total from bookies Wilf Sherman and Jack Swift – the latter of whom had a copy of his cheque framed and hung in his office.

Griffin had Royal Tan running for him in 1954 – and he won again as 8/1 joint second favourite. But although he backed his winner again, financial problems with his business had begun to dilute the Griffin family fortunes and he had to turn down the chance of buying Quare Times for a mere £2,500 – only to miss out on an incredible hat trick when that horse won the 1955 National.

Griffin was declared bankrupt and his fantastic but brief racing career was over as his horses were sold off – Early Mist for 2,000gns; Royal Tan for 3,900gns and Teapot II, for which he had paid £10,000, for just 40gns

442. HOW TO LOSE TO YOUR OWN MONEY

What may have been a unique occurrence took place at a poker event in France at a venue called the ACF.

According to eye witness Tony Rafter, who passed the story on to the magazine *Poker Europa*, two gamblers took a comfort break and when they returned to the table, inadvertently sat in each other's seat – 'both these guys were so absent-minded that neither one realised their mistake and play continued with both players playing each other's stack instead of their own.' This despite the fact that one of them had had some 15,000 more chips than the other.

But now came what Rafter described pretty accurately as "the insanity'.

'The two players got involved in a big pot and the guy who accidentally sat down behind the larger stack busted the guy with the smaller stack. That meant the guy got knocked out by his own stack! Absurd.'

443. BURGER ALL

Poker player Howard Lederer, a confirmed vegetarian, discovered that a bet could overshadow his principles whe he accepted, and won, a $10,000 wager from fellow player David Grey – by eating a cheesburger.

444. JUBILATION FOR ERNIE

Ernest Benzon was one of the best known gamblers of the late 19th century. He became known as the Jubilee Plunger ('a name I hate, although I am now accustomed to it') after he won a reported £16,000 when Bendigo won the 1889 Jubilee Stakes at Kempton.

But it wasn't success all the way, and his autobiography, *How I Lost £250,000 In Two Years* – probably equivalent to around £10million today – explained how card playing led to his ultimate financial downfal. 'I may say card-playing is, bar none, the worst game that was ever invented. Not only is it bad for the pocket, but it is most injurious to one's health.'

445. JUST KEEP BREATHING

Paul Khanna has taken odds of 10,000,000-1 that he will become the longest lived human by reaching the age of 127 alive – in the year 2100. The North Londoner has staked £1.

446. BLAIR NECESSITY

George Elliott, a Sedgefield cabbie, liked the cut of the jib of the young local parliamentary candidate who'd just been in his taxi, so he staked a tenner at odds of 500-1 with a local bookie on the lad becoming prime minister. He collected £5,000 in 1997 when Tony Blair got the job.

447. NICK'S NESSIE PLUNGE

Nicholas Witchell, BBC TV's royal commentator, has placed a bet with me that the Loch Ness monster exists.

448. WHO CARES ABOUT WINNING?

Kim Ward from Bristol selected 49 different love-making positions from the Kama Sutra, then she and boyfriend Neil Filer used the first six they tried out each week to make up their National Lottery numbers.

449. MAD MAGGIE

Margaret Francis and ten colleagues at Roundway Psychiatric Hospital became the first million pound-plus pools winners after letting their patients pick the winning numbers in 1986.

450. A ROYAL RINGER?

Henry VIII lost the 'Jesus' bells of St Paul's in a dice game with Sir Miles Partridge who put up £100 as his stake. Partridge won – but lost when he was later hanged!s

451. WE WUZ ROBBIED

Robbie Williams lost £1,000 when he bet on himself to be Christmas number one in 2003.

452. HAVE YOU EVER SEEN THEM IN THE SAME ROOM AT THE SAME TIME?

Simon Timmins has taken odds of 500-1 that Michael and La Toya Jackson will be proved to be one and the same person.

453. PUNTING ON PASSIONATE PERDITA

Actress Mary Darby Robinson had already enflamed the passions of the Prince of Wales before moving on to his friend, Lord Malden, a keen gambler with whom the prince would often stake large and absurd bets – they would reportedly gamble on geese and turkey races.

But in 1782, Malden, confident that Robinson, who had taken the thespian world by storm when portraying Perdita in Shakespeare's A Winter's Tale, was fully committed to him, gambled 1,000 guineas with army officer Banastre Tarleton that the military man would fail in an attempt to seduce the actress.

Several weeks later Tarleton had won both Perdita and Malden's money, although she was not best pleased when she discovered the truth.

Tarleton's sea-trader father had left him £5,000 on his death in 1773 when Banastre was 19 years old. Very soon he had lost it, mainly through ill-advised gambling at the Cocoa Tree gambling den in London. Gambling was Tarleton's Achilles heel ('he squandered his brilliant reputation through his compulsive gambling and stormy relationship with Perdita,' wrote Janie B Cheaney) and his family, unhappy with his relationship, offered to settle his debts only on condition that he leave for the continent alone.

On his return, unrepentant Tarleton opened his own gambling club in an effort to make his fortune from other gamblers, and became friendly with noted rake Charles James Fox, who is also believed to have had a relationship with Ms Robinson.

Fox was another dissolute gambler. At the age of just 14 he was apparently taken from Eton to the continent where 'for four months he was introduced to gambling' according to a 'Regency Personalities' website, which also averred that 'the habit caught with him and on his return he turned Eton into a small gambling den'.

There was probably something in that, because in 1774, when he was 25, his father, Lord Holland, paid off his betting debts of £140,000 – and 20 years later his political friends (Fox was by then a notable Whig) had to make a similar gesture. In return, Fox apparently gave up horseracing and gambling.

Perhaps gambling was in the Fox genes. His grandmother, Sarah Cadogan, was just 13 when she was married to Charles Fox, later the second Duke of Richmond – to settle a gambling debt between their fathers!

454. IVES WON TEN GRAND

Michael Whitelock sold his house to Samuel Ives in 1995.

Whitelock's valuation of the St Johns Wood, London, property was £635,000 – Ives's best offer was £625,000.

No problem – to break the deadlock they agreed that they would each pick a runner in York's Magnet Cup. Ives won the day and saved himself £10,000 when his selection Yoush finished third, with Whitelock's tip Quango plodding home 14th.

455. WHO ATE ALL THE PIES?

A hungry farmer cashed in when he was offered a tasty wager. *The Word* newspaper informed readers on May 4, 1787, that 'At The Wheel at Hackington Fen, on Wednesday, se'en night, a fen farmer laid a wager he could eat two dozen of penny mutton pies, and drink a gallon of ale in half an hour.'

The amount at stake is not recorded, but the trencherman farmer 'performed with ease, in half the time'.

456. A RUM DO

The first ever race meeting in Melbourne, Australia, took place in March 1838 – and proved to be the last for one successful gambler.

Aussie racing historian Maurice Cavanough recorded how 'what the first race meeting lacked in refinements it made up for in enthusiasm. Bets were laid and paid in bottles of rum, with the unfortunate sequel that one successful punter imbibed so freely of his winnings that he blundered into the River Yarra and was drowned. Nonetheless, the meeting was voted a huge success.'

457. THE FIRST POKER CHEAT

Joe Cowell, a touring actor from England, found himself on board a steamboat chugging along from Louisville en route to Kentucky in December 1829. Cowell observed a game taking place which he recognised as a derivative of the popular gambling game brag, and soon identified as having the name poker.

His account of one of the hands of the game he watched is the earliest report of cheating in a poker game.

Cowell records that on what was a foggy night, the boat ran aground, causing most of the travellers to dash around checking on what happened. He noted one man, wearing distinctive green spectacles and a diamond 'stickpin', who had remained calmly seated, shuffling his pack of cards, and who then got the game under way once more:

'It was his turn to deal and when he ended, he did not lift his cards, but sat watching quietly the countenances of the others. The man on his left had bet ten dollars; a young lawyer, son to the then Mayor of Pittsburgh, who little dreamed of what his boy was about, who had hardly recovered from his shock, bet ten more; at that time, fortunately for him, he was unconscious of the real value of his hand, and consequently did not betray by his manner, as greenhorns mostly do, his certainty of winning.'

What had actually happened, it was by now obvious to 'Green Spectacles', was that his intention to deal himself a pre-ordained winning hand had resulted in the hand going to another player, leaving him with a guaranteed loser in his own hand.

Now, one player matched the ten dollars, then raised a massive $500.

'"I must see that," said Green Spectacles, who now took up his hand with "I am sure to win", trembling at his fingers' ends; for you couldn't see his eyes through his glasses; he paused for a moment in disappointed astonishment, and sighed, "I pass" and threw his cards upon the table. The left-hand man bet "that $500 and $1,000 better!"

'The young lawyer had had time to calculate the power of his hand – four kings with an ace – it could not be beat! But still he hesitated at the impossibility, as if he thought it could – looked at the money staked and then put his wallet on the table and called. The left-hand man had four queens with an ace; and Washington, the four jacks and an ace.

'"Did you ever see the like on 't?" said he, good humouredly, as he pushed the money towards the lawyer, who very agreeably astonished, pocketed his $2,023 clear!'

Green Spectacles, noted Cowell, had discarded a hand of four tens with an ace. He added, deadpan: 'In that pursuit, as in all others, even among the players, some black-sheep and black-legs will creep in, as in the present instance.'

Yes, and green specs, too.

458. GAMBLING ON A ZOO

John Aspinall was one of the most flamboyant figures on the London gambling scene in the 1960s, when his Clermont Club became enormously popular with a certain circle of society, among whom was one Lord Lucan.

Aspinall sold the club in 1972, in order to 'spend the rest of his life with animals', according to his biography. He founded an extraordinary zoo at Howletts, a grand but decaying house in Kent, but was forced backed into the gambling world to raise money as the costs of his animal antics increased.

But it was poker that had first brought him into the world of gambling. When he was at Oxford University from 1947, he met up with a friend from the Marines, Desmond Dunphy, who organised poker sessions at his rooms.

Aspinall watched closely – he 'witnessed ten whole games with careful attention before he decided he would attempt to play, and from that moment, with the cards in his hand, he knew that he had found his metier.' So wrote Brian Masters in The Passion of John Aspinall.

Aspinall began to clean out the low-stake games at Oxford, and engineered himself an invitation to a rather richer affair, organised by Ian Maxwell-Scott, great-great-grandson of Sir Walter Scott.

Maxwell-Scott played poker for the 'almost sensual pleasure' in placing bets, but Aspinall was more pragmatic and he preyed on the game, which 'was distinguished by very high stakes and very poor players'.

Aspinall raised his sights again and became involved in a regular game, which attracted artists and wealthy hangers-on. 'Aspers' soon dominated this game, too. 'He seemed possessed of a unique microscope to look into the soul of his opponent and understand his psychology. He knew what card a man would play before he had decided to play it, because he knew his temperament and character.'

His style included a love of drawing to an inside straight and an instinctive understanding of when and how to bluff, which 'earned him a glamorous reputation'.

He also, declared Masters admiringly, 'used his will in order to win'.

Such was his personal charm, though, that many of his victims felt positively grateful to be able to lose to him!

By this time, though, Aspinall was partial to gambling in other ways, too – it was 'poker in the morning, the races in the afternoon, dog racing in the evening and perhaps another card game until late at night'.

Once out of Oxford, Aspinall had to begin to make his way in the real world and the poker became less important to him, although in 1954 he ran a poker game at the world famous Ritz Hotel. Not that the Ritz either knew or permitted it. He and Maxwell-Scott managed to stay at the hotel for seven months in room 505 in which 'they ran a small game of husband and wife poker, the takings from which enabled them to pay their bills'. They pulled the same stroke at the Park Lane Hotel.

As the room became an early, illegal betting shop, also being used for the placing of horseracing wagers, so the management of the Ritz eventually cottoned on to what was going on and demanded full settlement of their bill, which was beyond them, despite almost landing a betting coup on a horse – which won the race only to be disqualified.

Aspinall by now had realised that it was more profitable being a bookie than a punter and played less and less himself as the casinos he ran became more lavish and profitable.

Aspinall died in the year 2000 after a lengthy battle against cancer, and his biographer believes – not, in my opinion, completely accurately – that 'in years to come, no-one will remember Aspinall the gambler – his renown as a visionary zoo-keeper will be assured'.

459. WAUGH TIME WINNER

Aussie cricket star Mark Waugh confessed to deliberately getting himself out so that he could find out how a horse he had backed would get on.

'I was playing grade cricket for Bankstown, and we were winning easily. It was coming up for race time for the 1992 Cox Plate. I had backed my favourite horse, Super Impose, so I hit one in the air.

'It is the only time I have ever done that, but I have no regrets. We won the game, Super Impose won the race, and I had a good win.'

460. EVERYTHING'S BIGGER IN TEXAS

During the course of the 1992 US presidential election campaign, I received a call from a man claiming to be a Texan who wished to place 'a small bet' on Bill Clinton winning.

'Just how small is this bet?' I asked.

'Three million dollars,' he drawled.

'I'm sorry – that's a bit too big for our book, I'm afraid. Anyway, you should be grateful to have that sort of money, let alone be looking to gamble it all.'

'Hell, no, man, it ain't all mine – there's THREE of us in this together!'

461. ADD IT TO MY (GER) BILL

Pub customers were revolted when a fellow regular accepted a bet – then won it by grabbing the landlady's son's pet gerbil from his cage and eating it.

'It was awful,' said Gaynor Ford, landlady of the Greyhound Hotel, Midsomer Norton, Avon. 'There were bits of fur and blood everywhere – and he just laughed.'

A local, who witnessed the incident in August 1993, commented: 'The man was very drunk, and ate the gerbil for a bet – he was sick everywhere afterwards.'

462. DO YOU KNOW OF A RASHER BET?

Even today pig races are few and far between – although it was reported in May 2008 that a Russian breeder was trying to create a type with longer legs to improve their sprinting abilities – but one well-documented example took place during the 19th century for a £1,000 stake.

Gentleman owner Dr Hutton had his horses with trainer Harry Barnes of Ilkley in Yorkshire.

Hutton was very proud of Barnes's ability and boasted to friends: 'I'd back that man to train anything.'

Two of Hutton's friends, Walter Long from Christ Church College, Oxford, and Lamont Rose of Brasenose, took him up on the boast – and Long challenged: 'There's one thing I'll wager he can't do – train a pig to jump hurdles.'

Hutton refused to back down and the £1,000 wager was struck, Long and Rose going halves against him.

To win the bet, Barnes had to train eight porcine specimens to clear a course of eight flights of hurdles 2ft 6ins high.

Barnes devised a plan. He laid out a course of fixed hurdles, with others alongside to prevent the grunters from running out.

He starved his pigs during the day, then stood lads with food pails at the end of the course – and slowly taught the porkers that it was a case of jump or starve.

After several weeks Barnes declared he was ready.

The whole village turned out to watch as the pigs, which had been left hungry all day, were lined up. Barnes set off, jumping the hurdles himself while carrying a steaming food pail.

At the same time the lads at the end of the course banged and rattled their grub buckets. Away went the pigs in pursuit of Barnes, snorting, stumbling, jumping, squealing and grunting as they went. The whole field eventually made it around the course and Hutton collected his £1,000.

463. GRACE AND FAVOUR

Legendary cricketer WG Grace was the subject of a sovereign wager between racehorse owner and gambler Bob Sievier and his friend Archie McLaren.

The two men, both well aware of Grace's fondness for the odd tipple, decided to bet on whether he could be rendered 'unsteady on his legs' during a session.

Sievier believed he could; McLaren took the opposite view.

Grace was duly invited to a cricketing house party at Sievier's home, where 'the choicest wines and liqueurs were placed before the Doctor in great goblets and gargantuan measures'.

Grace knocked them back before sampling champagne laced with brandy, which he consumed while playing cricket during the afternoon.

After the game there was dinner 'when more champagne, port and old brandy was poured down that mighty throat'.

Grace played a completely straight bat and Sievier feared he would lose the wager – until the great man leant against a piano to listen to a lady guest playing.

She asked him to hand her a sheet of music, but as he reached for it 'he over-balanced, stumbled and slid to the floor.

'McLaren, with a show of ceremony, solemnly handed Sievier the sovereign across the doctor's prostrate body.'

464. HAVING A BALL AT THE DOGS

A football suddenly landed on the track at Crayford dog track as the runners rounded the final two bends in the 11.37am race there on May 24, 2008.

Opinions as to whether this was a race-wrecking attempt by punters endeavouring to save their money on a botched coup of some kind were mixed.

Stewards allowed the winner, 4-1 shot Misterin Ash, to keep the race, but voided other finishing positions as one of the other runners appeared to have been distracted by the incident.

'The ball came from the car park area and our track staff went there immediately after the race, where there was just a man and a boy, but they denied they had kicked a ball over the wall,' said racing manager Danny Rayment.

The skill level needed to ensure the accurate kicking of a ball on to the track from that distance might suggest that it would be a less than reliable race-rigging tactic.

Rayment added: 'If it was a race-wrecking attempt we managed to foil it by getting a part-result from the race.'

465. MAUDE THE LEVIATHAN

Known as 'the mysterious Madame X' when she launched her financial assault on bookmakers in the early 1920s, Australia's 'first leviathan female punter' was later revealed to be Mrs Maude Vandenberg, whose bookie husband had collapsed and died in 1920.

She decided to continue going racing and began to bet on a large scale, thinking little of betting from £3,000 to £5,000 a time.

She was closely associated with the success of Amounis, bred in 1922, and winner of 33 races from 79 starts and at the time the country's top winner of prize-money.

When Amounis contested the Cantala Stakes at Flemington in 1929, Maude approached the biggest bookie of the day, Jim Hackett, and asked for £2,000 at 7-2.

'You can have it again if you like,' offered Hackett.

She did, and went one better – 'Yes, I'll have it – and bet another £7,000 to £2,000.'

Amounis won, and Maude collected £21,000 profit.

In another race that year in Sydney she collected on a £10,000 to £1,000 bet on Amounis and the next year backed him for £20,000 in the Caulfield Cup.

The latter wager was a small part of a bookie-busting gamble master-minded by Vandenberg and another high-rolling backer, Eric Connolly. The pair teamed up when flamboyant bookie Andy – the Coogee Bunny – Kerr attempted to stimulate his turnover by offering 50-1 for Amounis and Phar Lap to win the Caulfield – Melbourne Cup double.

Not only did the two get on themselves, they quietly funded other punters to get even more on for them.

When the six-figure gamble on the double was landed Kerr was temporarily broken.

When she finally quit Vandenberg was estimated to have removed a massive £150,000 from the betting ring.

466. LET'S HAVE A WHIP FOR THE FINE

In 1190 King Richard of England and King Richard of France agreed – perhaps the last time the rulers of those countries did – that they needed to make a joint decree to restrict the spread of gambling.

So they ruled that only noblemen could gamble for money – and even then for a maximum of 20 shillings per day. If anyone were to be found exceeding that limit they would be fined, stripped naked and whipped. Can't help but wonder how many who might not otherwise have been, then became gamblers!

467. NOT GOOD ENOUGH FOR GOODENOW

The news for Christine Goodenow was mixed in November 2005.

Yes, her lottery ticket had won the Oregon woman $1 million in the state lottery.

But police had discovered that she paid for it with a stolen credit card.

468. BLINDING BET

Colin Montgomerie revealed that he was given an incentive to win the European Order of Merit towards the end of the 2005 season when a supporter told him he had backed him to the tune of £30 at 100-1 in order to fund an eye operation for his mother.

'Blimey, that makes you think, doesn't it?' *Racing Post* golf writer Jeremy Chapman reported him as saying. 'It was nice to receive a letter from him recently saying the operation had been a success.'

469. GERRARD ON SONG

The *Daily Mirror*'s Jan Disley reported in an 'exclusive' on January 10, 2006 that England and Liverpool footballer Steven Gerrard 'has won £5,000 from England international pal and clubmate Peter Crouch by singing at a gay club'.

Apparently, in order to win the wager Gerrard took the mike at Liverpool club Garlands, and sang Herd and Fitz's 'Just Can't Get Enough'.

470. REF ROB RED-CARDED

Robert Hoyzer, the 26-year-old German referee accused of taking money to fix the outcome of heavily gambled-on matches, was jailed for two years five months in November 2005.

Hoyzer was convicted of fraud and admitted to receiving £45,000 and a flat-screen TV from a betting syndicate run from a Berlin café by three Croatian brothers, one of whom, Ante Sapina, also received a jail sentence of two years 11 months.

Hoyzer was shocked by the sentence as it was believed that a plea-bargain of a suspended sentence in return for appearing as a witness had been agreed by the prosecution.

In one German Cup game Hoyzer wrongly awarded two penalties to help Paderborn win 4-2, after trailing Hamburg 0-2.

Hoyzer claimed he had been drunk when he first agreed to fix games and that his first attempt had gone wrong when he had awarded a penalty that wasn't, only to be over-ruled by his linesman, but admitted that eventually he fixed a minimum of 11 games.

In another game he twice disallowed perfectly good goals in a regional league game to land a 560,000-euro win for those paying him.

Players and other officials were also implicated during the trial.

The scam was believed to have netted the perpetrators at least £1.2 million in gambling winnings.

There was an ironic incident during the trial when Austrian-based bookies Intertops began betting on the outcome – offering 100-1 that charges would be dropped.

471. HITLER'S GAMBLE

A report given some credibility at the time declared that Adolf Hitler had not died during the war but that in January 1946 was working as a croupier in a casino in Evian, France.

472. CRICKET MATCH

Hong Kong police reported smashing an illegal insect-fighting ring in September 2004 after arresting 43 people who had been betting on cricket fights.

The men, aged from 48 to 73, were held in a swoop on a building in Kowloon, where 115 had been charged for the same offence only a month before.

473. YOU BET HE'S GONE

Shoemaker James Burne Worson of Leamington Spa was definitely inebriated when on September 3, 1873, he made a bet with a friend that he could run to the nearby town of Coventry and back – a distance of some 40 miles.

Nonetheless, accompanied by three friends, who hired a wagon to travel with him, Worson, still in his cups, began the attempt.

A contemporary report explains what happened after he had gone several miles but was still in full sight of his friends. 'He seemed to stumble, pitched headlong forward, uttered a terrible cry and vanished! He did not fall to the earth: he vanished before touching it.

'No trace of him was ever discovered.'

474. MAKE HAY WHILE THE CARDS SHINE

The Guardian Hay Festival, one of the major literary events of the year, was launched in 1988 by young actor Peter Florence – who funded it via the winnings from a poker game.

475. NO KIDDING STEVE, YOU'RE A LOSER

Steve McQueen lost perhaps the most famous poker hand ever – in the 1965 film *The Cincinnati Kid*, based on the 1963 book by Richard Jessup, and ever since arguments have raged among poker purists as to the authenticity of the hand, and the way in which it was played out.

Writer and poker player David Spanier called the showdown 'a somewhat incredible hand of five card stud, illustrating the interaction between courage and restraint'.

And the way Spanier read the eventual defeat for The Kid, was that he 'allowed his calculation of the chances to be overridden midway through the hand by overconfidence'.

Fellow author Anthony Holden said 'the film blows itself away with a climax still laughed to scorn in card rooms the world over' – yet despite that it cemented McQueen's thespian reputation to the extent that in 2005 he topped an internet survey designed to reveal the 'Favourite Poker Playing Character', beating Paul Newman – for his roles in *The Sting* and *Cool Hand Luke* – into second.

McQueen, playing 'The Kid', comes up against Lancey 'The Man' Howard, played by Edward G Robinson. In the movie, The Kid draws a full house of aces and tens (queens and tens in the book) against The Man's queen (jack in the book) high straight diamond (hearts in the book) flush. Holden, perhaps overlooking the fact that it is supposed to be entertainment, protests: 'The chances that both of these hands will appear in one deal of two-handed five-card stud have been calculated at a laughable 332,220,508,619 – 1.'

In fact, so outlandish is the nature of this showdown that many critics argue that any player beaten in such a manner would immediately be suspicious. As Poker Player newspaper writer Michael Weisenberg wondered: 'Why didn't The Kid start screaming foul. If YOU got beat like that, would you just walk away shaking your head, muttering to yourself, 'Well, them's the breaks?' I doubt it.'

However, others point to the fact that to arrange a fix of this nature would be just too blatant and surely anyone organising such a scam would make it less obvious – perhaps letting one player have a slightly higher but not outrageous hand; 'By all means enjoy the movie,' adds Weisenberg, 'So long as you pretend it's three sevens being beaten by three nines.'

Holden believed the showdown would have been improved had The Man won by bluffing The Kid into folding a superior hand. Writer Phil Gordon just thinks The Kid was the victim of 'the greatest bad beat in the history of poker cinema'.

But not everyone is so critical. Rustin Thompson of moviemaker.com believes 'the tension-wracked final hand is worth watching again and again for a crash course in how to bluff and when to bet. When Robinson is scolded for making what appears to be a reckless raise, he sums up the game's timeless, intractable appeal: "It gets down to what it's all about – making the wrong move at the right time."'

Long-time pro Roy Cooke summed the arguments up well: 'If you put any of the world's top players in either The Kid's chair or The Man's, they might play this hand under these rules and these circumstances just this way. I'm not saying they would, but they might. I wouldn't – but that might be why I'm not The Man!'

By the way, if you reckon a poker fan is kidding when they tell you they have read The Cincinnati Kid, win yourself a few bob by asking them what The Kid's Christian name is – they will be hard pressed to come up with the correct answer, which is ... Eric.

476. RIOTOUS RESULT

A double-bluff scheme involving the ringer that wasn't caused a riot in New South Wales, Australia in the 1820s. A Captain Lane owned a champion racer called Hector, entered at the Regentville track.

The captain had been strongly suspected of using Hector as a ringer in other races, and the word was that the horse running as Hector would in fact be the inferior Cripple, made to look like Hector and that the captain's cash would be on Bennelong.

In fact, Hector was running as Hector, and the captain was going to be backing him for substantial sums.

To confuse other racegoers the captain ensured that Hector performed badly in the heats, before scraping into the final run-off for the prize. Everyone was convinced Bennelong was a certainty and it was backed accordingly – until, just before the off, there was a flurry of support for Hector, whose odds plummeted to joint-favourite.

Hector won – and the result sparked a genuine riot between the deluded punters and the captain and his accomplices. Soldiers were called in to split up the warring factions and calm matters down, by which time the captain had fled down the road – on Hector.

477. BOYCIE DIVED IN

At The Races presenter Sean Boyce dived in to take the best value bet of his punting career when he discovered that bookies were way out of line with their odds for Channel 4 reality show The Games.

Actress Terri Dwyer, from the Hollyoaks show, had been installed as 6-4 favourite to win the swimming event.

But Boyce had spoken to top British swimmer Mark Foster, who had four Olympics to his credit with another one on the way and who had been coaching Ms Dwyer.

'Could any of the others catch her?' Boyce asked Foster: 'Sure – but only if they start swimming now.'

Boyce took the hint – 'It's tough to get much on these novelty markets, but that didn't diminish the enjoyment I got from watching Dwyer nearly lap her rivals inside two lengths of the pool, and 6-4 about a 1-50 shot has to be the best bet I've had in terms of prices.'

478. CUNNING PUNTS

My two favourite examples of punters trying to pull a fast one concern very high-profile sporting events, and both took place in 1989.

Ian Moo Young, a 45-year-old born in Jamaica of Chinese parents, but with an English passport, told me he had taken up tennis a month ago and was so convinced of his ability he wanted to back himself to win Wimbledon.

It was clearly impossible but as it might make a fun media story – 'Is This The Next British Wimbledon Winner?' – I laid him £20 at 50,000-1, giving him potential winnings of £1 million.

I even arranged an exhibition match against top British player Nick Brown and invited the media to meet him.

As Wimbledon approached I began to receive calls from the media asking whether Moo's bets were still on as he seemed to have a great chance of winning.

'Why?' I asked. 'Because, if you look closely at the betting slips he wrote out you'll see that he has backed himself to win the tiny Wimbledon Club Tournament held down the road from the All England Club – whose championships are what you thought he was betting on!'

Gulp! They were right. Panic all round. Until Moo managed to get knocked out in the quarter-finals of the Wimbledon Club Tournament – to my great relief.

Then in August of 1989 a 38-year-old man visited my office to tell me that he wanted to bet that he could play in the First Division (no Premiership in those days) next season.

He'd be up front with me, he once was a promising youngster with a professional club, but injury had curtailed his career.

Now, though, his wife was promoting a book she'd written about willpower, self-belief and a revolutionary diet, and he wanted to support her and make a bet that would help publicise the book. To make it newsworthy it would need to have a huge potential payout, perhaps in the millions of pounds.

I told him he was a 10,000-1 chance at least to make the top grade at his time of life, so why not place a bet that he could make it at a lower, more realistic level.

No, only the First Division would do.

Wondering whether he might have contacts with a top club in some way, I told him I'd get back to him with a quote very shortly.

Within days the Sun newspaper ran an exclusive story revealing that wealthy businessman Michael Knighton was about to purchase Manchester United in a £20 million takeover deal.

The same Michael Knighton who had sat in my office days before asking for the bet.

The phone rang. 'Hello, it's Michael Knighton – I suppose that bet is out of the question now? You had a narrow escape. I would have insisted on being registered as a player and coming on as a sub in the last seconds of a game.'

479. WEIGHTING FOR THE RIGHT OPPORTUNITY

Sydney owner-trainer James Kingsley came up with an audacious plot to win a fortune with a supposed no-hoper.

He devised a scam that allowed him to run Gentleman Jim, due to carry 10st 9lbs in a valuable sprint handicap at Newcastle in April 1903, with an actual weight of 8st 8lbs on his back.

Waiting until just before the off, Kingsley managed to place £1,000 at 20-1 on his 'good thing', who promptly trotted up.

When Kingsley accompanied the jockey to the weigh-in a puzzled official said that he hadn't made the weight.

'Nonsense!' shouted Kingsley, stamping his foot and demanding 'he must be right, weigh him again'.

This time the weight was spot on and the correct weight flag was unfurled.

Kingsley dashed off to collect his winnings – worth about £500,000 today.

Meanwhile, a baffled clerk of the scales began to check his scales, and discovered a wire running through a hole in the floor.

Lifting the floorboards, the clerk and the stewards he had now called in traced the wire back to a 29lb lump of lead, and a young boy concealed in a small hole, where he had been placed the night before with provisions and instructions that when he heard Kingsley stamp his foot he should attach the weight to the wire – thus ensuring that the jockey 'weighed' his allocated burden.

The game was up.

480. SHEIL BE A WINNER

A mystery woman (is there any other kind?) landed Australia's biggest ever bet on a greyhound when she turned up in December 1989 at Wentworth Park in Sydney to put A$202,000 on 1-2 favourite True Blue Tah.

Described as 'bespectacled, short, slightly built and in her mid 40s,' the woman struck the bet with bookie John Stollery after having lost A$87,000 by backing the first three favourites on the card.

She watched as the dog led all the way to win by seven lengths, then left the track.

She was believed to operate a system whereby she backed favourites until she was $14,000 up and would then quit.

She kept her stake money in an armoured security van and was accompanied to the track by a bodyguard.

481. RICH PICKINGS

Unusually for an active American trainer, Richard Dutrow is up front about the fact that 'we're a betting stable' and demonstrated his willingness to back up his stable stars with hard cash when staking a reported $160,000 on his 2005 Breeders' Cup Classic winner Saint Liam, making a profit of $384,000, having earlier in the season left $34,000 behind on the same horse, beaten in the Santa Anita Handicap.

He hit the jackpot though when his Big Brown won the 2008 Kentucky Derby – 'He'll be favourite on Derby day, I can guarantee that. We'll make sure he's favourite. I know he's the best horse, so I might as well bet.'

Dutrow was right on both counts as Big Brown, the favourite, stormed to victory.

482. GETTING THE BIRD

Goldie, an African Golden Eagle, captured the imagination of a nation when he twice made a break for freedom from London Zoo in 1965.

After going missing for 12 days on his first attempt in February, he flapped off again shortly before Christmas – and Ladbrokes' canny PR man, Ron Pollard, spotted an opportunity to bet on when the bird, sitting impassively in Regent's Park trees regarding his would-be captors with disdain, would be recaptured.He offered 12-1 that Goldie would stay free until Christmas Day. A gamble developed and Pollard faced a £14,000 payout as December 25 approached.

'Then, after 12 days and with the weather worsening,' recalled Pollard, 'his keeper had the last word. He left an overweight rabbit out overnight as bait – and Goldie just could not resist. Down he fluttered to be recaptured hours before our midnight deadline.' When Pollard retired in 1989 he was given a solid silver eagle.

483. HILL TOP

Graham Hill, 26, from Oxford, became Britain's biggest betting shop winner in March 1995 when he landed a win of £814,257 after laying out £90 on accumulators involving three-balls in golf's Doral-Ryder Open event.

Shrewdly, to avoid exceeding payout limits, the test engineer for Oxford Magnet Technology had placed similar bets with Coral – from whom he collected £267,724.22; Hills, who paid him £274,903; and Ladbrokes, who handed over £271,630.

But for one of his selections, Billy Mayfair, dead-heating in his three-ball, Hill would have doubled his payout.

484. EAR, EAR

After cheating his fellow players out of their cash during a card game in October, 1777, a Norwich tradesman was sentenced to 'standing on the pillory for one hour, with his ears nailed to the same'.

485. TAPPED UP

A Scottish punter shocked the racing world in March 1991 when he claimed he had made almost a quarter of a million pounds by betting on information he had obtained by tapping into conversations on mobile phones used by trainers, jockeys, bookies and punters.

The *Racing Post* told how the anonymous punter had contacted them, wanting to sell his bugging equipment, as well as tapes of conversations between racing people, discussing horses.

The mystery man, who called himself Philip, told reporter Tim Richards that he had a small piece of machinery resembling a portable phone, which could be programmed to intercept the airways used by mobile phones.

'My brother and I have been driving into racecourse parks and listening to the conversations of the racing people and marking off the relevant horses. I would say I have made more than £200,000 over the last nine months.'

'Philip' played Richards a tape 'of a person closely connected with a big stable putting £150 on a horse for himself and £150 for the stable jockey'.

The horse they backed won – albeit at 4-9 – reported the Post.

'Philip' then offered to meet Richards at Carlisle racecourse and to sell his equipment for 'in the region of £200,000'. He told Richards: 'Come to Carlisle and we will make some money together. But I don't want to be messed about so you must bring payment in readies. You can have everything and I don't want anything else to do with it.' He claimed to have set up a legitimate business on his profits from the bets he had made and that he was going to settle in America.

Was it genuine, or a scam? Frustratingly, Richards said: 'The meeting did not take place.'

486. PHAR OUT

In May 1930, Aussie equine superstar Phar Lap was matched against a moderate opponent, Fruition, in a warm-up race in Adelaide.

The race was a formality – some bookies were actually offering 1,000-1 against Fruition; others were 1-500 Phar Lap.

However, a group of cunning punters managed to pull off a considerable coup in one of the first ever tote-rigging cases on record.

They placed bets at tote odds on Phar Lap with unsuspecting starting-price bookies – many of them strictly illegal. Then, just before the 'off' time they plunged £100 on the course totalisator.

With virtually no money being staked on Phar Lap because of the restrictive odds being anticipated, Fruition's odds came tumbling down, with the result that Phar Lap was actually returned at 1-3 – remarkable odds for a 1-500 shot!

Phar Lap sauntered home by five lengths and the conned Aussie bookies were battered.

487. OGGIE, OGGIE, OGGIE – DID HE START IT ALL?

Conclusive proof is highly unlikely ever to emerge to confirm that in 1790 or 1795, depending on which account one accepts, at Newmarket racecourse a 'leg', as bookmakers were then known, stood and caused a sensation by offering specific odds about every horse taking part in the race about to be run.

Up until this time betting consisted either of setting odds for each of the horses in a match race, or quoting odds for one selected runner in contests of three or more participants and setting a blanket price for all the others, known as 'betting between one and the field'.

The quantum leap, which at a stroke enabled interested parties to bet on the one particular horse they wanted to support, is widely credited to the Lancastrian bookie who went by the name of William Ogden.

The leading racing and betting authority of the 19th century, The Druid, named along with Ogden Messrs Davis, Holland, Dearden, Kettle, Bickam and Watts as the leading, most honest, reliable and influential bookmakers at a time when the reputation in general of such 'sharps' or (black) 'legs' was not high. As the author of *Better Betting With A Decent Feller*, Carl Chinn, put it in 2004, they 'were the architects of the final stage in the development of professional betting into bookmaking'.

488. HOW 'JAMES BOND' LEARNED
AN EXPENSIVE POKER LESSON

Ian Fleming won worldwide fame as the creator of the immortal, archetypal cold-war spy, James '007' Bond. Bond was a frequent visitor to casinos, where he would gamble confidently.

Fleming, as befits the author of *Casino Royale*, also enjoyed a gamble, but after 1957 he was always very wary of playing poker.

That was the year in which he penned the piece that would become the introduction to the critically acclaimed 1958 book by Herbert Yardley, *The Education of a Poker Player*.

Fleming began his article by complaining that playing poker for money – 'a legal game over half the world' – was illegal, and pointing out that a London club, The Hamilton, had been fined £500 in a 1945 show trial on the grounds that poker was not a game of skill. A decision with which Fleming did not agree – calling it 'hypocritical balderdash'.

Fleming then praised the book, which he said he had bought when it was originally published in America and then tried to persuade his publisher, Jonathan Cape, to bring it out in Britain. The publisher declined – until Fleming offered to write a preface.

'I am not a good poker player,' confessed Fleming. 'Poker is a cold-hearted, deadly game that breaks and bankrupts men.'

Then he revealed: 'The last time I played poker I lost more than I could afford in rich brassy company in a house at Sunningdale.'

His fellow players introduced variations of the game that Fleming was 'mocked' for not understanding. Finally, 'numb with martinis and false bonhomie' he pretended that he could play a poker variation called Minnie Everley. 'I remember the name but not the variation.'

In his confusion and embarrassment Fleming 'played a ragged, brash game that cost me dear. I was fleeced and deserved to be'.

Fleming bemoaned the fact that had he at that time read Yardley's book he might not have been taken in so easily. 'Very few fine card players are the sort of people you and I would like to play with,' he warned his readers before saying that 'not as a poker player, but as a writer of thrillers, I can recommend this book to every consenting adult card player in Great Britain.'

489. 0 ... 0 ... 17?

James Bond actor Sean Connery is reputed to have won over £10,000 in 1963, by backing the number 17 on three consecutive spins of the roulette wheel at the St Vincent Casino in Italy, defying odds of 50,652-1 in the process.

490. WINNER UNDER OATH

Newlyweds Jamie Wilde and Sarah Green made their vows in Ross on Wye in June 1999 – and then walked to their marquee reception to be greeted with a massive cheer and the news that Jamie's sister Louise's wedding present of a £50 each-way bet on Derby hope Oath had paid off big-time – landing the happy couple more than £500.

✶ Earlier in the year, all 50 of the guests at Bobby and Jo Everitt's Lincolnshire wedding had taken the topical tip and backed that day's 10-1 Grand National winner, Bobbyjo. But no-one had thought to ask the newlyweds whether they would like to back their equine namesake!

491. BROUGHT TO HIS KNEES

The Duke of Cumberland was so convinced that hot favourite Jack Broughton would win his 1750 English title boxing match against unfancied Jack Slack that he staked the largest wager ever gambled at the time on a big fight.

The duke accepted odds of 1-10 for his £10,000 stake – giving him potential winnings of £1,000.

He watched, stunned, as a wild punch by Slack found its target, virtually blinding Broughton, who was defeated ten minutes later.

492. POKER TOWN

Great film director John Huston was born in 1906 in a small town called Nevada in Missouri – which he always claimed his grandfather had won, lock, stock and barrel, in a poker game.

Huston himself became a great gambler, allegedly once losing $50,000 in a three-hour Reno casino session, and he featured the game of poker in his Judge Roy Bean movie.

He died in 1987.

493. GAMBLING'S MOST QUIZZICAL MOMENT

James Daly was a theatre owner in Dublin in 1791 – or, perhaps in 1780, depending on which version of this tale you prefer to accept.

He made a bet, although it does not appear to be clear just how much or just who with, mind you – passage of time, and all that, maybe.

The bet was that Daly could introduce a new word – a nonsense word with no particular meaning, at that – into the language of the day within 24 hours (some say

48). No mean feat in the days before TV, radio, internet, that type of thing.

The word Daly had in mind, apparently, was 'quiz'.

Whether he knew what he thought it meant or what he wanted it to mean is another matter, a bit of a quiz, in fact.

Anyway, in order to get the word put about and to win his bet, Daly is said to have hired what is usually referred to as a bunch of street urchins who he paid to print up the word all over the city, on walls, doors and other available surfaces. Probably the first orchestrated graffiti attack.

How these street urchins learned to write or read in those days is not explained by folklore, either.

Nonetheless, the job was done, people began to talk about the word they had seen displayed all over the place and they assumed that as they didn't know what it meant its meaning must be to symbolise some sort of test or question or, even, quiz!

Daly's unknown opponent in the bet apparently accepted that he had lost, and paid up.

'Unfortunately,' admits one of the sources for this tale, 'there is absolutely no evidence to support it.'

Worse, the word was apparently around before 1791 – being first attested to in the Oxford English Dictionary in 1782, when it meant some kind of odd person. This is perhaps why some sources now place this story in 1780.

But even if that is the case then the use of the word by one Fanny Burney in her June 24, 1752 diary entry– 'He's a droll quiz and I rather like him' – presents another problem.

Still, the Daly bet account of the word's derivation was first quoted in 1836, and it convinced almost contemporary writer FT Porter, who gave an account of the story in his 1875 book, *Gleanings And Reminiscences*.

And further support for the belief that Daly created the word comes from the fact that most dictionaries are hard pressed to account for the derivation of its current day meaning.

494. GLOVELY DAY AT RACES

Shanghai staged British-organised racing festivals in the late 1850s and early 1860s. Fashionable etiquette of the day precluded ladies from wagering with anything as vulgar as cash.

As a result 'they started wagering gloves instead' recorded author Austin Coates in his book about those times, China Races, 'and by 1860 they were wagering all kinds of things – bonnets, hats, cigar boxes, fans, even umbrellas. At the spring meeting of 1861 a husband was overheard restricting his wife to wagers of ten dozen gloves.'

495. YOUNG NICK

On June 8, 1991, the *Spectator* magazine published a letter from RA2703 Nicholas Young, HM Prison, Ford, West Sussex, in which the inmate wrote: 'I was horrified to read in Portrait of the Week (May 25) that I 'stole up to £36 million from investors and bet it on horses'. According to calculations made by learned experts, the figure most widely quoted has been about £5million.'

Oh, well, that's alright then.

496. HEAVY DUTY

Aussie bookie Barney Allen strongly fancied his horse, The Idler, for the 1903 Caulfield Cup, but was a little concerned that his jockey, Teddy Turner, might be got at. So he decided to get at him himself first, and promised the rider a £3,000 sweetener if he won.

The Idler could only manage second and a distraught Allen demanded an explanation from Turner, who told him that the three grand had weighed so heavily on his mind that it had adversely affected his concentration during the race.

497. LIFE OF STUPIDITY

Twenty three year old Scott Henry decided that rather than face the music for the crime he had committed, he would flee the country to play poker.

The Torquay man admitted to stealing a safe containing £6,000 and was duly sentenced to a community order.

Instead, he flew off to gamble in Las Vegas where he had been given a place in a major poker tournament. On his return he was handed a three month jail sentence by Recorder, Frank Abbott, who told him in August 2008: 'If there was a sentence for stupidity you would be serving life imprisonment.'

498. THE LEVIATHAN LAYER

William Davis – also referred to as Davies in contemporary reports – was one of the biggest, and most honest, of 19th century bookmakers, who was willing to lay the odds for up to 'half a plum' – or the small matter of £50,000. His financial bravery, or foolhardiness, saw him acquire the nickname 'Leviathan'.

He began betting in 1840, having worked as a carpenter/joiner engaged in the building of the Subscription Rooms at Newmarket, where he 'had some small success as a backer in trifling sums, which encouraged him to start laying odds in half-crowns among his fellow workmen,' wrote Ralph Nevill in The Sport of Kings in 1926.

This venture into bookmaking coincided with winning himself £100 by backing the unfancied Atilla for the Derby. 'That was the turning point in his career for, on finding himself possessed of so much wealth, he cast aside his joiner's tools and resolved to become a bookmaker,' explained WAC Blew in 1900.

He branched out, and soon created a name for himself by 'laying generally a point or two more than were attainable inside the public betting rooms,' according to a contemporary report. He opened a betting list – effectively an early betting shop – at the Durham Arms in Serle Street, the Strand in London.

He soon found himself in the midst of high-rollers. 'His first heavy hit is said to be for £12,000 over The Cur (5-1 in 1848) for the Cesarewitch. Hotspur's not winning the Derby (1849) made a difference to him of some £50,000 and Barbarian's failure (1852) of nearly twice that sum. The Londoners also backed Voltigeur (16-1 winner in 1850) to such an extent with him that nearly £40,000 was paid over his list-counter alone about the lusty Richmond stallion,' recorded turf scribe The Druid in 1856, who pointed out that he was a prompt settler – 'He was also hit heavily in Teddington's year (1851), and the £15,000 cheque which he sent to Mr Greville the morning after the race stamped him at once as a very mine of Peru.'

In 1853, averred Blew, the Leviathan 'had no less a sum than £138,000 standing to his credit at the London and Westminster Bank when the racing season began'.

And Davis gives the lie to those who believe that 'betting in-running' is a modern phenomenon. The Druid explained: 'Although perhaps not abstractedly a great judge of a horse, he had a capital eye for finding out when they are in trouble, and keeps betting on till they are some twenty yards from the post; and if it is a very near thing, after they are past it.'

In 1853 West Australian took the Derby at 6-4 and the well-backed winner hit him extremely hard, costing him a reported £48,000 – of which £30,000 went to one punter, Mr Bowes. It was said that after this result 'he had only £200 in ready money to take to Ascot'.

Non-racing events intervened to interrupt his career when he fell through a dilapidated grandstand into the weighing room at the Rochester and Chatham meeting. 'With the idea of shaking off the effects of the fall, he ran twice round the racecourse,' wrote racing chronicler TH Bird in 1939.

This unorthodox remedy may or may not have cured him completely, but shortly after he was the victim of an attempted robbery in which he was knocked unconscious.

He began to wind his affairs and visits to the races down, and in 1857 made his final racecourse appearance at Newmarket.

499. DIVORCE DOSH

Bookies were stunned to discover that a huge gamble on Pactolus to win the 1986 Cesarewitch, which saw the horse's odds tumble from 20-1 to 8-1 favourite, was caused by a gambler out to win enough money to meet his wife's alimony payments following their divorce.

Robert de Lisser, a 29-year-old Jamaican businessman who owned Pactolus, revealed: 'I've had £40,000 on him. The best price I got was 20-1 and I averaged 13-1. I'm in England because my wife Nina and I are getting divorced. I will use the money to pay for Nina's alimony. In fact, that's the reason I've had such a huge bet. It's the biggest wager I've had in my life.'

But it didn't pay off – Pactolus finished well out of the money.

500. WELL DONE

Bookie Fred Done lost what he claimed to be the biggest bet ever struck, when his £1 million even-money bet with fellow layer Victor Chandler on whether Manchester

United or Chelsea would win the 2004-05 Premiership title ended in favour of the Londoners.

Huge United fan Done had no regrets: 'The man took me on and that's what gambling is all about.'

Done, the eponymous boss of the bookmaking chain, realised a double ambition by becoming co-sponsor of his favourite club and supplying all the betting outlets at the 'new' Wembley Stadium – although punters weren't overjoyed when they discovered they could not collect winnings on their way out of the ground.

He has always enjoyed being involved in his company's advertising material, but was not happy when the Gambling Commission put its oar in: 'They say it'll be encouraging children to gamble if I appear in our adverts dressed up as Spiderman. That really has annoyed me. They're making me feel like some sort of a bloody paedophile,' he complained in May 2007.

He was rated 253rd in the *Sunday Times* Rich List of 2007 with an estimated fortune of £290m, having built his 660-strong chain of shops from humble beginnings in the back-streets of Manchester.

666. DEVIL OF A BET

A 1714 book by Theophilus Lucas, Esq, celebrating *Comical Adventures of the most Famous Gamesters and Celebrated Sharpers*, recorded the fate of a gambler who took on the Devil.

'Near Bellizona in Switzerland, Three Men were playing at Dice on the Sabbath Day; and one of 'em, call'd Ulrick Schroetus, having lost his Money, and, at last, expecting a good Cast of the Dice, broke out into a most blasphemous Speech, threatening, That if Fortune deceiv'd him then, he would thrust his Dagger into the very body of God, as far as he could.

'The Cast miscarrying, the Villain drew his Dagger, and threw it against Heaven with all his Strength; when, behold, the Dagger vanish'd, and several Drops of Blood fell upon the table in the midst of them; and the Devil immediately came and carry'd away the blasphemous Wretch, with such a Noise and Stink that the whole City was amaz'd at it.'

BIBLIOGRAPHY

Anonymous. *Betting Book of the 2nd Battalion (78th) Seaforth Highlanders 1822-1908,*
St Catherine Press Ltd, 1909

Ashton, John. *History of Gambling in England*. Burt Franklin, 1899

Bartels, Jon. *Saratoga Stories*. Eclipse Press, 2007

Betts, Toney. *Across the Board*. Citadel, 1956

Bird, Alex. *The Life and Secrets of a Professional Punter*. Queen Anne Press, 1985

Blew W A C. *Racing*. Everett, 1900

Brogan, Barry. *The Barry Brogan Story*. Arthur Barker, 1981

Charlton, Peter. *Two Flies Up A Wall*. Methuen Haynes, 1987

Cottrell, John; Armytage, Marcus. *A-Z Of The Grand National*. Highdown, 2008

Curley, Barney. *Giving A Little Back*. 1998

Druid, The. *Post and Paddock*. Frederick Warne, 1856

Fairfax-Blakeborough, J. *Turf Who's Who 1932*. May Fair Press, 1932

Fairfax-Blakeborough, Noel. *J.F.B.* J A Allen, 1978

Gutman, Dan. *Baseball Babylon*. Penguin, 1992

Hickie, David. *Gentlemen Of The Australian Turf*. Angus, 1986

Hore, J.P. *History of Newmarket*. A H Baily, 1886

Kent, Graeme. *Olympic Follies*. JR Books, 2008

Lambton, Hon George. *Men and Horses I Have Known*. First published 1924, reprinted J A Allen, 1963

Linnane, Fergus. *London's Underworld*. Robson, 2003

Longstreet, Stephen. *Win Or Lose*. Bobbs-Merrill, 1977

Lord, Graham. *Just The One*. Sinclair-Stevenson, 1992

Lucas, Theophilus. *Comical Adventures of the Most Famous Gamesters and Celebrated Sharpers*. 1714

Marcus, Richard. *The World's Greatest Gambling Scams*. Undercover, 2007

Margetson, Stella. *Leisure & Pleasure in the Nineteenth Century*. Victorian Book Club, 1971

Mathieu, Paul. *Druid's Lodge Confederacy*. J A Allen, 1990

Nevill, R. *Light Come, Light Go*. Macmillan, 1909

Nevill, R. *The Sport of Kings*. Methuen, 1926

Nevison, Dave. *A Bloody Good Winner*. Highdown, 2007

Newman, David. *Esquire's Book of Gambling*. Muller, 1935

Onslow, Richard (Ed). *Great Racing Gambles & Frauds Vols 1, 2, 3 and 4*. Marlborough, 1991, 1992, 1993, 1994

Pollard, Jack. *Australian Horse Racing*. Angus & Robertson, 1988

Rickman, Eric. *On and Off the Racecourse*. T & A Constable, 1937

Sergeant, Philip W. *Gamblers All*. Hutchinson & Co, 1931

Sidney, Charles. *The Art of Legging*. Maxline, 1976

Stewart, Jackie. *Winning Is Not Enough*. Headline, 2007

Various. *Baseball As America*. National Geographic, 2002

Warner, Dave/Brasch, Nicolas. *Horseracing's Hall of Shame*. Harper Sports, 1999

Winants, Peter. *Steeplechasing*. Derrydale Press, 2000